Surefire Ways to Save Thousands of Dollars

CUT COLLEGE COSTS NOW!

Inside Tips from College Administrators, Financial Planners, and Tax Advisers

COREY SANDLER

Adams Media
Avon, Massachusetts

To William Sandler (Class of 2005) and Tessa Sandler (Class of 2007) . . .
without whom none of this would have been necessary.

Published by Adams Media, an F+W Publications Company
57 Littlefield Street
Avon, MA 02322
www.adamsmedia.com

ISBN: 1-59337-491-7
Printed in the United States of America

J I H G F E D C B A

Library of Congress Cataloging-in-Publication Data
Sandler, Corey
Cut college costs NOW! : surefire ways to save thousands of dollars / by Corey Sandler.
p. cm.
Includes index.
ISBN 1-59337-491-7
1. College costs—United States. 2. Education—United States—Finance. 3. Scholarships—United
States. 4. Student aid—United States. 5. Parents—United States—Finance, Personal. I. Title.

LB2342.S315 2006
378.3'8--dc22

2005026053

This publication is designed to provide accurate and authoritative information with regard to the subject
matter covered. It is sold with the understanding that the publisher is not engaged in rendering legal,
accounting, or other professional advice. If legal advice or other expert assistance is required, the services
of a competent professional person should be sought.

—From a *Declaration of Principles* jointly adopted by a Committee of the
American Bar Association and a Committee of Publishers and Associations

Many of the designations used by manufacturers and sellers to distinguish their products are claimed as
trademarks. Where those designations appear in this book and Adams Media was aware of a trademark
claim, the designations have been printed with initial capital letters.

This book is available at quantity discounts for bulk purchases.
For information, please call 1-800-872-5627.

CONTENTS

ACKNOWLEDGMENTS

This book would not have been possible without the guidance and support of dozens of people, including my dream team of academic advisers.

I'll start with thanks to Amy James, a longtime friend and former researcher in my office. Amy currently is an administrator at Hamilton College in Clinton, New York. Previously she worked in the admissions office for Mount Holyoke College in South Hadley, Massachusetts.

Thanks, too, to financial planner Patrick Curtin of Bank of America Investments; Monica Inzer, dean of admissions and financial aid at Hamilton College; Thom Hughart, director of guidance at Wellesley High School in Massachusetts; Kenneth Kogut, former director of financial aid at Hamilton College; Professor Richard Vedder, of Ohio University; and Robert Klein, who counts dollars, advises on tax issues, and cross-tabulates every sports statistic known to man and woman. You'll read their contributions in the roundtable section of this book.

On the publishing side, thanks to Gary Krebs and his team at Adams Media, including Jill Alexander, Larry Shea, Frank Rivera, and Holly Curtis.

Finally, thanks to you, the reader, for buying this book. In doing so you've taken an important step in a journey of a thousand miles and many thousands of dollars. I wish you luck and success.

INTRODUCTION

The grades are good, the SATs are high, and the high school guidance counselor has sent along a wish list of the best of all possible schools. Now, show us the money.

You're reading this book because you're smarter than the rest of the parents out there. The fact that you're preparing—calmly and thoughtfully, or in full-panic mode—is the first step in dealing with what has become an all-but-inevitable challenge for modern parents: paying for a college education.

Let's put this in perspective. In the lives of most people, the two largest single expenses are buying a home and paying for a college education. If you have two or three or more children, the total price tag for sending them to school may be more than the cost of putting a roof over your head.

About four decades ago, when most of the parents of today's college-bound students were born, the cost of a year's higher education at a private school was typically between one and two months of the family's annual income. Today, that same expense typically represents about six months' worth of income.

The purpose of this book is to present a *realistic* buyer's guide to help *every* student and his or her parents save thousands of dollars on a first-class education. There are way too many books on the market that tell one person's lucky story of how he attended college free by collecting 27 different scholarships and grants, or claim to show another person's foolproof scheme that helped her graduate from an Ivy League school for pennies on the dollar. Those sorts of wonders do happen from time to time. I don't know about you, but I long ago decided not to base my life on the one-in-a-hundred-million chance that I'll win the lottery. If it happens, you're all invited over for a heck of a party; in the meantime, I prefer to work as hard as I can to save and invest and make smart purchases.

In this book, we'll get *real* advice from experts: a financial adviser, a tax accountant, an economist, a director of admissions, and a director of financial aid. We'll talk about the nitty-gritty of putting aside money, making investments, and applying for financial aid. And you'll hear some important cautions against overspending, overborrowing, and neglecting your own retirement accounts.

MY BONA FIDES

So what gives this guy Corey Sandler the right to give advice about paying for college?

Here are a few reasons:

1. My wife and I (with help from our extended family) are nearly done with putting the second of our two children through a prestigious and expensive private college.

2. My son received good citizenship scholarships from our town and $32,000 in academic grant money from his college. He augmented that by earning most of his spending money from summer jobs and part-time work during his college years. And after graduation he enrolled in an AmeriCorps national service program for a year; in addition to the work experience he's gaining and the salary he's earning, he is due a scholarship for graduate school when he completes his service.

3. My daughter earned local scholarships and grants for academic and artistic excellence. Her grades and her personal story were so compelling to one small school that they offered her a full academic scholarship covering all tuition costs. (And as I'll explain, after much soul-searching we decided to decline that free gift.) And she contributed summer job savings for her walking-around money at school.

4. As an author I have written bestselling guides on how to save money on almost everything from food to clothing to travel, as well as books about how to pay for major purchases including homes and cars—the number one and number three largest single expenses in most people's lives. Number two, of course, is college.

5. Did I mention that we put two kids through private college . . . and that both of them will walk away without a penny of

personal debt? That was a personal decision of ours; we felt that the best gift we could give our children was to allow them to begin their independent lives without the pressure of owing tens of thousands of dollars. (The small amount of loans we did accept were strictly for strategic reasons, and they will be paid off by graduation day.)

I am also a very careful steward of our family finances. My wife and I have kept our spending in check, our debt within reason, and our investments in the black. We look forward with hope for a comfortable retirement, watching and helping where we can when our children begin to think about paying for college for their own kids.

FOUR BASIC SOLUTIONS

When it comes to paying for college, there are several basic solutions:

1. Be rich. Have enough money sitting around so that you can write a check for a hundred thousand dollars or so per child from petty cash.

2. Be poor. Feed yourself and your children and put a roof over your heads and hope that your meager savings (or dangerous debt) qualifies you and your child for a sufficient amount of need-based financial aid. You can also hope that your child somehow is talented enough and educationally able to qualify for additional merit-based scholarships. Between need-based and merit-based aid, you can hope to pay most or all of the costs of higher education. And then you can go into debt to pay for the rest of the cost.

3. Be panicked. The day your child is accepted to college, declare a four-alarm family emergency. Borrow tens of thousands of dollars without a plan for paying off the loan, sell your retirement funds, and switch from 120 channels of high-definition cable television to a black-and-white set with rabbit ears. And worry.

And then there's the fourth solution, for the vast middle class that makes up most of America and the readers of this book:

4. Be smart. Start planning for your child's college education as early as possible—the day he or she is born is a great time to begin—and learn how to be the smartest, most dedicated shopper for the second largest personal expense of your life.

In researching this book I consulted with dozens of experts and I also assembled a dream team of consultants. In the roundtable chapters of this book you can read the thoughts of a distinguished professor of economics, who educates us on the unusual operations of the business of higher education; a crackerjack financial planner, who shares his thoughts on how to get started on saving for college and where to put your investment over time; a dean of admissions, who lifts the veil to show how one prestigious school looks at its annual pile of applications; a high school guidance counselor, who tells us how an applicant can stand out from the crowd; a director of financial aid, who offers advice on maximizing the available assistance; and an experienced tax accountant, who offers help with making the most of available tax strategies.

It's not easy—not even close—to plan for and pay for four years of college of any type or location. But there are ways to be smarter and better prepared than the rest of the crowd. That's the goal of this book: to make you one of the well-prepared few.

chapter 1

COLLEGE COSTS 101

According to *Money* magazine, total expenses for the 2004–05 academic year averaged $27,516 at private colleges and universities, and about $11,354 at public schools of higher education. As you read these words, prices are climbing—in recent times, about 6 to 8 percent per year. In 2006, about 14 million undergraduates will attend American schools of higher education; 80 percent will enroll at a public college.

There are a few things to keep in mind while those numbers bounce around in your head:

1. They may be too low. The top end of college prices are north of $40,000 per year.

2. They may be too high. There are many great deals at state colleges and smaller private colleges. Like it or not, only some 2,000 or so undergraduates are admitted to Harvard University each year, which makes the odds of getting in rather slim. And it is also true that not every student is suited for the most competitive, most demanding colleges; a student can get a great education at a state college or at a small private institution.

3. The listed costs at private schools are the *sticker prices*. Some people walk into a car dealership and write out a check for the price listed on the sticker. Others do some comparison shopping among other dealers and other models and search out discounts and special programs. And some are willing or able to dig in their heels and bargain for a better deal.

   When it comes to college expenses, few if any schools are willing to haggle over the price of admission and room and board. However, there is usually quite a bit of latitude when it comes to the amount and type of grants, scholarships, loans, work-study jobs, and other assistance offered to parents and students. This is called the *discount rate*. In 2004–05 the average grant at private colleges was about $7,000; at public schools, it was about $6,200. Overall, about 76 percent of students at private colleges received some amount of financial aid (grants, scholarships, loans, and jobs); at public schools about 62 percent of those admitted received a financial package.

4. It is a fact that the vast middle class—with too much money to qualify for need-based grants and not enough money so that price does not matter—is hit hardest by college prices beyond the sticker price and the discount rate. However, there

are dozens of ways to reduce the cost or lessen its impact on your personal finances.

SHOW ME THE ESCAPE HATCH

Let's put aside mistaken assumptions and myths and talk about some realities of college expenses:

1. As noted, not every school costs $40,000 per year. In fact, about three out of four students go to schools that cost much less, including public colleges, where tuition may be as little as $5,000 for in-state residents, and smaller private colleges, where costs are half (or even less) of what they are at the high-priced schools.

2. You don't have to be poor to receive financial aid. There are tax credits that benefit middle-class families, and discounted loan programs that can be of value to people of any financial means.

3. It may seem impossible for a young and growing family to accomplish all of their financial goals: saving for college, building a nest egg for a down payment on a house, and setting aside money for retirement. Well, it's not easy, but it can be done. The members of the roundtable of experts you'll meet a bit deeper in this book will all give you a simple but critical piece of advice: do something. Do something small when you've got just a little bit of extra cash, and do something larger when there's more available. And look for ways to generate extra cash: take a part-time job dedicated to college and retirement funds, or make a decision to spread out car purchases so that they are a few years further apart.

4. Middle-class families are often warned that the more they save, the less financial aid their student will receive. Alas, that is mostly true, because financial aid formulas take into account assets and investments (and put a heavier weight on money held in the child's name). But it is also true that for most middle-class families, the largest portion of financial aid comes in the

form of loans rather than grants. Therefore, every penny saved is a penny that does not have to be borrowed.

5. If your student is smart and has good grades and a decent SAT or ACT score but she's not the valedictorian, she probably is not going to receive a free ride at Princeton. However, it does not take a straight-A 4.0 grade point average to earn an academic scholarship. Smart students and their parents make smart choices about where to apply. If a child has good grades and brings something else to the table—ethnic or racial diversity, a strong history of community service, or simply being the only New Hampshireite applying to a school in Iowa (or the only Iowan seeking admission in New Hampshire)—there may be a grant headed your way.

6. If you are eligible for need-based financial aid, don't limit your applications to relatively low-priced colleges. The bottom line of the federal financial aid formula is the calculation of an Expected Family Contribution (EFC). In theory, financial aid is supposed to scale up to bridge the gap between the EFC and the estimated cost of attendance.

Let's say a family's EFC is $8,000. College H costs $30,000 and College S charges half that much. Under federal methodology, this student is eligible for $22,000 in aid at the more expensive school and $7,000 at the other.

This formula, though, comes with a warning: aid in the form of a subsidized or unsubsidized loan is better than no aid at all, but either way, the debt has to be repaid by the student or parent. Compare apples to apples, loans to loans, and best of all, grants to grants.

BASIC FACTS ABOUT COLLEGE COSTS

The number of schools to choose from (more than 2,400 in the United States, plus hundreds if not thousands of international schools worthy of consideration) is daunting. The price can be frightening. And the process of taking tests, filling out applications, and writing essays can be overwhelming.

Here are some very important underlying principles to understand about college:

- The federal government and the colleges determine the amount of your financial need; you do not.

- Colleges are nearly immune from the ordinary rules of economics. They are able to set their prices at will without much regard to things like the rate of inflation, interest costs, or the ability of many families to pay the bills. They can continue to do so for as long as there are those wealthy enough to pay full freight or there is enough federal aid to pay the costs for others. Those of us in the middle have to scrimp, save, and borrow—or go elsewhere.

- There are plenty of "elsewheres."

- Don't give up hope. There are dozens of ways to cut costs, increase the amount of financial aid, and otherwise obtain a first-class education at a discount price.

DOES IT PAY TO GO TO COLLEGE?

Every few years some supposed expert comes along and says that four years of time and money spent on college is a waste: just look at George Washington and Abraham Lincoln as historical examples . . . and Bill Gates and Michael Dell in the modern era. If you've got a special skill—be it high technology or marketing know-how, or musical, acting, or sports talent—why give up four years of prime earning power?

And there are some jobs that pay quite well and are in great demand but do not require academic training; have you hired a $100-per-hour plumber recently? It is also a fact that even today many college graduates are the first in their family to receive higher education.

All of this is true, but for the vast majority of students, going to college is the key to higher earnings and better jobs. In 2005, a study by the U.S. Census Bureau reported that those with a college degree earn, on average, nearly double the amount of those without the diploma.

According to the census, workers eighteen and older with a bachelor's degree earned an average of $51,206 a year, while those with a high school diploma earned $27,915. Workers with an advanced degree made an average of $74,602, and those without a high school diploma averaged $18,734.

Let's assume that the average American works for about forty-two years between high school or college graduation and retirement; in fact, the number of people working for that long is increasing, as more of us are staying in the work force out of necessity or because we are in better shape. The gap starts out relatively small, but by retirement age is quite wide; some experts say that over the course of a lifetime of work, the typical college graduate will earn as much as $1 million more than will a person with only a high school diploma.

Other information in the Census Bureau's Educational Attainment report showed that the American educational level in 2004 reached record highs: 85 percent of those age twenty-five or older said they had completed at least high school, and 28 percent said they had attained at least a bachelor's degree.

Other highlights for the population twenty-five years and older in 2004:

- Minnesota, Montana, Wyoming, and Nebraska had the highest proportions of residents with at least a high school diploma, all at or near 91 percent.

- The District of Columbia's population had the highest proportion with a bachelor's degree or higher at 45.7 percent, followed by Massachusetts (36.7 percent), Colorado (35.5 percent), New Hampshire (35.4 percent), and Maryland (35.2 percent).

- The high school graduation rates for women was slightly ahead of that for men, 85.4 percent and 84.8 percent respectively. However, men had a higher proportion with a bachelor's degree or higher (29.4 percent compared to 26.1 percent).

- Non-Hispanic whites had the highest proportion with a high school diploma or higher (90.0 percent), followed by Asians (86.8 percent), African-Americans (80.6 percent), and Hispanics (58.4 percent).

- Americans of Asian descent had the highest proportion with a bachelor's degree or higher (49.4 percent), followed by non-Hispanic whites (30.6 percent), African-Americans (17.6 percent), and Hispanics (12.1 percent).

Other data in the survey showed that black and Asian women with bachelor's degrees earn slightly more than similarly educated white women, and white men with four-year degrees make more than anyone else. Analysts said that there could be several reasons for the income difference, including the fact that employers in some fields may be offering special financial incentives to attract a more diverse work force; it might also be related to the field of study chosen by the graduates.

Data for the survey was collected in the Annual Social and Economic Supplement to the Current Population Survey (CPS); as with any survey, the results are subject to sampling variability and other sources of error.

So if your high school student offers to skip college if you'll buy him a Porsche 911 Carrera coupe in seal gray with a cherry red interior, a 444-hp 3.6-liter engine, six-speed transmission, and a dashboard-mounted stopwatch for about $100,000 . . . suggest he hit the books and prepare for four years that should set him up to buy his own toys.

chapter 2

A DOZEN WAYS TO CUT COLLEGE COSTS NOW

College is expensive. That's a fact.

It is also true that there are many ways to reduce the bottom-line price by thousands of dollars, tens of thousands, and even more. There is, alas, no magic wand; it takes hard work and sacrifice—by the parents (and grandparents and extended family in some cases), and by the student.

In this chapter, I'm going to lay out a dozen strategies; we will return to each of them in much more detail later in the book. I pondered whether to organize these ideas by the order of the biggest potential payoff (starting with an all-expenses-paid no-strings-attached scholarship or grant), or whether to present them in a more realistic one-brick-atop-another structure. I chose realism, and I plan to maintain that sort of focus throughout the book.

Here, then, are the core strategies for a family with a college-bound student:

1. Save early, often, and intelligently.
2. Aim for a scholarship.
3. Seek financial aid.
4. Learn how to borrow wisely.
5. Grab a do-it-yourself discount.
6. Take advantage of special programs.
7. Make the most of regional price variations.
8. Consider state colleges and community colleges, and commuter enrollment or off-campus housing.
9. Consider foreign schools that offer substantially lower costs.
10. Choose a job that offers employee and legacy scholarships.
11. Put your child to work.
12. Spend less money after acceptance.

Save early, often, and intelligently.

The smartest thing you can do is to start putting aside money as soon as your child is born. Every dollar put aside on that first day is going to be worth about $4 eighteen years later; if it is invested in a plan in which interest accumulates tax free, or withdrawals can be made without paying tax—or both—the fund is going to be even more valuable.

Let's just say you or your parents or other family members have $25,000 available on a child's date of birth and can set it aside in a college fund; when the first college bill arrives there will be something close to $100,000 ready and waiting. (Where in the world will you get $25,000? Well . . . do you really need a new car right now, or could you make do with a well-maintained used machine for a few more years?)

However, I promised to be realistic: not everyone has that kind of money sitting around unallocated. Chances are good that you're a young couple, new to the workplace. There's a new baby, and there may be a down payment on a house in your future. And even at a young age, you should be making contributions to your retirement fund.

But you need to start putting money aside, even just $100 a month to start. Think of that as $3.33 per day; that might mean cutting down your intake of Grande Double Latte Half-and-Half from two to one a day.

Then keep on putting money aside on a regular basis, and look for ways to double and then triple that amount. If you can put away $250 per month—less than the equivalent of an extra car payment—for eighteen years in a tax-free investment that earns a fairly conservative 7 percent, you will have saved about $105,230 with relatively little pain.

The next part of the equation is to invest intelligently; it's not as simple as stashing money in a bank account. Later on, I'll show you how to set aside the most money with the least tax consequences, and I'll tell you why it's not always advisable to put your child's name on the account.

We'll explore 529 College Savings Plans, prepaid tuition plans, and other smart investments in Chapter 7.

Aim for a scholarship.

Encourage your child to do good, and be good.

Nearly every college and university offers substantial grants to incoming students with exceptional accomplishments in high school and in the community. Some extra effort in studying, or a bit of tutoring can help a student earn an academic scholarship.

You don't need to be at the top of your high school class to win a special scholarship based on your background, achievements, work experience, and skills. A student who can present a great story of community volunteer work and assistance to others can earn a citizenship award from a college.

In Chapter 6, you'll find out how to maximize your chances of receiving an award. I'll also explain when it makes sense to be a big fish in a small pond, or a small fry in a huge lake. And I'll show you how to be an unusual fish, taking advantage of college diversity programs.

Seek financial aid.

Need-based grants from federal, state, and private sources help low-income applicants pay for college. But you don't need to be at the poverty level to receive assistance; there are some programs that soften the bite of interest on student loans. If you've got special circumstances or an unusual financial story, contact the financial aid office and ask for reconsideration of the financial aid offer.

And if you are caught in the middle class—earning too much for most need-based programs and not quite rich enough not to care—there are some things you can do to improve the parents' or student's chances of receiving certain types of aid. I'll tell you everything you need to know about grants, work-study jobs, and subsidized loans in Chapter 5 and Chapters 12 through 14.

Learn how to borrow wisely.

If you need to take out a loan to pay for college, you'll find out in Chapter 9 how to get the best available deals, including interest-free subsidized loans and reduced-rate unsubsidized plans.

We'll also explore tapping into the equity in your home—an easy source of money in the proper circumstances, but not the best solution at every point in the changing economic cycle. And even if you don't need a loan, I'll show you how in certain situations it makes more sense to use someone else's money for a while.

Grab a do-it-yourself discount.

At most colleges, the standard tuition charge covers up to eighteen credits per semester; most students take only five courses for fifteen credits. If a student takes an extra course each semester, he or she will be eligible to graduate midway through the senior year, saving about 12 percent of the cost of a college degree—as much as $15,000 at a private school.

Another money-saving strategy: take Advanced Placement courses in high school. If the student receives a high enough score on an independent national test, colleges will grant credit; two AP course credits combined with three extra courses over the first three years of college will also allow graduation a semester early.

And don't overlook taking summer courses at a community college. Credits are almost always much less expensive there than at a four-year school, and room and board—well, you're paying for those already when the student is home for the summer. You can read about these strategies in Chapter 15 and in the chapters from our roundtable of experts.

Take advantage of special programs

At many schools around the nation, there is the list price and the sale price. In Chapter 15, you'll learn how a smart shopper can obtain discounts for prepayment or for in-state attendance, and also how to enroll in prepaid guaranteed tuition and other subsidized or special financing programs. In addition, I'll explain how many states offer grants or loan forgiveness to students who enroll in certain courses of study and then promise to work in that state for a period of time after graduation.

You'll learn about the financial advantages of monthly payment plans, and you'll see how you can get a free vacation along with a college education by earning frequent flyer miles on tuition payments.

Make the most of regional price variations.

You can shop for a college education at a high-priced school in the Northeast or California, or you can buy a first-class education at a lower-cost college in the South or Midwest. Our roundtable of experts will explain some of the advantages in considering colleges in different parts of the country.

Consider state colleges and community colleges, and commuter enrollment or off-campus housing.

The best of state colleges and community colleges offer a quality education without a name-brand price. One great strategy is to spend two years at a community college or a state college and the last two at a prestigious private school; your diploma will be from the private college or university.

We'll discuss which public college systems offer the best education and the best deals, and show where they may even make sense for out-of-state residents. Living at home can save thousands on room and board. Off-campus housing can offer a discount, too.

Consider foreign schools that offer substantially lower costs.

You may be able to save tens of thousands of dollars by enrolling at a quality school in Canada, Europe, and almost anywhere else in the world. We'll consider the international option in Chapter 15.

Choose a job that offers employee and legacy scholarships.

When a parent accepts a job, consider the value of all of the benefits offered by the employer. Is there a college scholarship program from the employer, a labor union, or an industry association? If your skills are of value to a university, consider the value of free tuition programs offered to the children of employees. We'll investigate job-related scholarships in Chapter 6.

Put your child to work.

Students can earn thousands of dollars at summer and part-time jobs in high school, and part-time and summer jobs after college begins. Before they spend every dime on video games, Manolo Blahnik sandals, or a celebratory trip to Europe, consider asking your child to put aside some money toward college expenses.

Here's one strategy: ask students to pay for their own walking-around expenses. Do the math this way: There are roughly forty weeks in a college academic year. If you and your child agree that $50 per week is enough, ask that he or she put aside $2,000 for each of four years in college. If the child would like an extra $20 per week, the response is: put away $800 more.

Put the money in a debit account and instruct the bank to dole out the agreed-upon funds once a week. Not only does this take some pressure off the parents, but it also helps the student understand that college is not free and that their sacrifices have a benefit.

Spend less money after acceptance.

Consider the full cost of college, including transportation, books, school supplies, and clothing. Then think about how to be a savvy shopper for each of these costs. There are discount programs for bus and train tickets, online sources for used books, discount Web sites for art and science supplies, and many other ways to pay less for just about anything.

The college dorm may be convenient, but it may not be as cost-effective as sharing an apartment. If you're an entrepreneurial type, how about buying an apartment or house near the college, collecting rent for four years, and fixing up the place to sell when graduation time arrives?

Students have to eat, but not all board plans make sense; don't pay for twenty-one meals a week if your child skips breakfast every day. These secrets, and more, are in Chapter 4.

chapter 3

A PLAN OF ACTION

One way or another, getting into and paying for college requires years of planning, lots of hard work in high school, decades of preparation by the entire family, assistance by appropriate outside experts, and often a bit of luck.

Let's deconstruct that last sentence:

Point # 1: Getting into college is different from paying for it. The first requires academic success, organization, and careful selection. The second requires a plan to come up with thousands or even tens of thousands of dollars to pay expenses—or a way to put aside money, borrow carefully, or latch on to grants or scholarships that whittle away or remove the burden.

Point # 2: The student has to put in the time preparing the way for college by establishing a strong high school record. Basically, all the things our mothers and fathers advised us to do to achieve success are true: Tend to our schoolwork, give back to society, and stay out of trouble.

Ten years of hard work on homework, tests, term papers, and classroom participation equals a strong grade point average, which is one of the criteria used by colleges in the admissions process. Along the way the student can build contacts who can write glowing recommendations about community service, which are also highly valued by admissions officers.

The student also has to prepare for the SAT or ACT test, still used by most private colleges and many public institutions as a component of their assessment. This is not something that should begin two weeks before the test near the end of the junior year of high school; practice can begin years before. Areas of weakness should be identified and dealt with early.

Finally, although it is possible to get into a good college with a heartfelt explanation for so-so grades and little evidence of community involvement, there are only a limited number of places available for someone with a horrific hard luck story. Colleges and universities are much more interested in success stories and people who will bring something special to the school.

Point # 3: The years of preparation by the entire family begins with a commitment by the parents or guardians to put aside savings for college—and do it wisely. We'll talk about strategies for saving in great detail in this book.

The preparation should also extend to helping the student succeed in high school and earn a high score on the SAT or ACT. A well-prepared family identifies strengths and weaknesses before a student enters high school. Time (and sometimes money) spent on tutoring and extra classes can help boost a student's verbal or math skills and open the door to an academic scholarship.

Likewise, choosing a college to apply to should not be a process that begins a few weeks before applications are due. Smart students and their parents think about institutions that are a good academic match and are more likely to be able to offer financial aid than are other schools. A worthy goal is to have the college want you at least as much as you want it. Be a big fish in a small pond, or an unusual fish in a place in search of diversity.

Point # 4: You may not, and perhaps should not, go through this preparation process all by yourself. On the academic side, students and parents should get involved with high school guidance counselors as early as possible. Meet with school advisers to choose classes that meet the student's strengths, and look for special tutoring and assistance in areas of weakness. The goal is to present a standout high school transcript and a strong SAT/ACT score.

Use the services of a financial adviser, beginning when your children are infants. Depending on your financial resources, it may make sense to hire a professional adviser who will charge an hourly or annual fee, or you may be able to find an adviser at a bank or brokerage who will assist you without charge. Be sure you fully understand the fees that may be built into any investment the adviser recommends.

As you'll learn from our panel of experts, you don't have to be a financial genius to build up a healthy nest egg over time as long as you begin saving for college eighteen years before you need to pay your first tuition bill. Money put in a conservative fund or bond should double in value every ten years.

Point # 5: And then there is luck. Before you dismiss luck as ephemeral, here's the definition that underlies this book: the harder you work, the luckier you get.

TAKING CARE OF YOURSELF FIRST

Harsh as it sounds to the parents of a newborn child or a youngster embarking on a kindergarten adventure, most financial advisers will tell you to think of yourself first: start funding your retirement as early as you can. Once that process is under way—and continuing—you can begin to set aside money for your child's college education.

Here are a few reasons why:

- There is financial aid available for college, but not for retirement. (In my opinion, one of the great shames of our society is the very low level of support for the aged poor.)

- You can always borrow against retirement savings, often at an advantageous rate, but it's not easy or cost-effective to transfer excess funds (you should be so lucky) from an education account to your retirement.

- Funds that are put into a retirement fund are not counted against the student's or parent's assets when the federal methodology is used to calculate financial aid.

- A trip of a thousand miles (or a few hundred thousand dollars) begins with a single step. The only way to start saving for retirement and for college is to go and do it, as soon and as often as possible.

As a father, I will be the first to agree with any reader of this book who reacts to the above arguments like this: "My children come first." But here's one more point to consider:

- If you reach retirement age without having a sufficient nest egg and a health-care plan, the chances are that you are going to be a burden on your children in your old age, just as they are launching their own families and thinking about college—and retirement plans.

Look at it this way: Have you ever paid close attention to the safety briefing from the flight attendant on an airplane? "In case of emergency, please place the oxygen mask on yourself first and then take care of your children." Why? Because you won't be capable of helping your children unless you are first able to help yourself.

In a 2003 survey by Charles Schwab, parents ranked saving for retirement as their second most important financial priority; at the top of the list was building up a down payment for a home. In third place was creating an emergency fund, and fourth spot was savings for college. Trailing behind was setting aside money for vacations and buying a car.

Underlying those survey results, according to Schwab, was this: Nearly half of the parents surveyed expected their children to receive scholarships or grants, and a slightly smaller proportion said they planned to rely on financial aid. Both numbers are unrealistically high, at least when it comes to paying the full cost of college.

Later in this book, you'll read advice that tells you to look for a way to save for both retirement and college. If that's not possible, some experts say to start with a retirement fund as early as possible. Then open the college fund and increase the proportion of savings that goes toward that goal as your children grow older.

You'll also read about how you can borrow against an IRA, Keogh, or 401(k) plan to help pay college bills. You may not like the idea of borrowing money, but in this case you are essentially borrowing from yourself and (with careful planning along the way) repaying yourself over time.

chapter 4

THE TRUE COST
OF COLLEGE—
AND 25 THINGS TO DO ABOUT IT

How much does it cost to go to college? Well, that depends: it's not as simple as calculating the cost of tuition, room, and board.

In this book we will talk about ways to seek grants and scholarships that come off the bottom line, but alas, there are some expenses—sometimes quite large— that are added back on.

Let's start with a basic formula for the cost of attending college:

	_____	Tuition
+	_____	Room
+	_____	Board
+	_____	Academic fees
=	_____	**List Price of Attendance**

We're not done yet, but let's stop and go over a few points. First of all, note that loans and work-study programs are not taken off our bottom line here: loans need to be paid back, and work-study jobs generally are paid to the student during the course of the year and are not deducted from college bills.

Academic fees are different from college to college, and among various courses of study. For example, science or art majors may be asked to pay laboratory fees not asked of literature majors. My daughter, an art student, was assessed nearly $1,000 per year in fees to pay for materials used in those classes.

Now let's move on to some variable costs:

	_____	Books
+	_____	Supplies
+	_____	Tools (including computers)
=	_____	**Additional Academic Expenses**

And then there are expenses that many parents initially overlook but can easily add up to thousands of dollars per year. Students have to get from home to school and back, and parents often like to come at least once a year to see where all their money has gone and to meet the roommate, significant other, and anyone else your child chooses to let you be in the presence of.

Most schools add a charge for student activities (sometimes ambiguously labeled as a "cocurricular fee") intended to pay for activities of the student union, parties, and events.

	_____	Student travel
+	_____	Parental visits to campus
+	_____	Dormitory furniture and equipment
+	_____	Telephone and Internet
+	_____	Entertainment
+	_____	Student activity fees
+	_____	Health insurance or medical fee
=	_____	**Campus Life Expenses**

So, the true bottom line is more like this:

	_____	**List Price of Attendance**
+	_____	**Additional Academic Expenses**
+	_____	**Campus Life Expenses**
=	_____	**THE TRUE COST OF COLLEGE**

The lesson here is simple. Sweat the details. The cost of tuition and room and board is the biggest expense, but for many students the bottom line is thousands of dollars higher.

Room and Board

The figure listed for "room and board" under a college's list of tuition and fees may seem like a fixed, unavoidable cost, but there are things you can do to lower this amount.

1. Compare dormitory options. Does your child sign up for a more costly single room or another type of premium housing, or a lower-priced double, triple, or quad room?

2. Consider off-campus housing. In some situations, the cost of sharing an apartment near the campus is less than the price of a dormitory. The student can share use of a kitchen, which may also save some money. Be sure to include the total cost of off-campus housing in your calculation: rent, utilities, and transportation to campus. At some schools, only

upperclassmen are permitted to move out of the dorms. And in all cases, make sure the housing arrangement is in a safe location and that the structure is properly maintained.

3. For students on campus, look carefully at available meal plans. Is a twenty-one-meal-per-week meal plan necessary, or is your child likely to sleep through a few breakfasts and skip a few lunches or dinners each week?

Books and Supplies

College-level textbooks can be outrageously expensive, with individual titles sometimes costing $100 or more. (Publishers justify the price by pointing to small print runs and short shelf life of some books. On the other hand, some critics have pointed to cozy relationships between publishers and professors, especially with teachers who are also authors.)

There are some things you can do to reduce the cost of books and supplies:

4. Buy used editions whenever possible. Used copies usually sell first; get to the college bookstore ahead of the crowd. This will typically reduce costs by 25 to 50 percent.

5. Consider sharing books with a roommate or close friend.

6. Make a private deal with former students from a class to buy their books at a price above the buyback price given by the bookstore but below the resale sticker.

7. Whenever possible, order textbooks from lower-priced online Web sites. Some books are available from major booksellers such as Amazon.com or Alibris.com. Specialized textbook Web sites include *www.cheapesttextbooks.com, www.campusbooks.com,* and *www.ecampus.com.*

8. Follow the same strategy in buying art and photography supplies and other necessary items. Look for places other than the college bookstore, including office warehouse stores and Web sites.

Computers

A personal computer has become a necessary tool for most college students. But there are $400 PCs and $3,000 PCs. For most students, the computer will be used for what are now very basic tasks such as research on the Internet and word processing; if you're lucky, your student will even send an occasional e-mail home. For these sorts of tasks, a well-built and well-supported lower-priced computer will work just fine.

9. Enlist the assistance of a knowledgeable computer user in shopping for a machine. Don't overlook the warranty and support desk offerings of the manufacturer as an element of your decision. Given a choice between a faster processor or more memory (RAM), go for the memory.

Make sure you meet the requirements of the college for Internet connection—this may include a built-in network interface or a wireless card. Call the college's computer support desk for advice.

10. Ask the college about special discount programs offered by some major computer manufacturers to incoming students.

11. Unless the student has a real need to use a laptop, try to stay with desktop machines. Laptops are more expensive, more likely to be damaged, and more likely to be stolen.

12. Microsoft, Adobe, and a number of other major software makers offer student discounts on many major programs including the Microsoft Office suite and the Adobe Creative Suite or their individual components such as Microsoft Word, Microsoft Excel, Microsoft PowerPoint, and Adobe Photoshop. You can find authorized resellers of software with educational discounts online or at college bookstores.

Travel Expenses

The cost of getting to and from school can be as little as a bus pass for a student commuting to a community college or as much as the cost of a car (and insurance, maintenance, and licensing). Most students head off to school in late August and return home in May, but don't overlook Christmas break, winter break, spring break, and, for some students, quick returns home for Thanksgiving and other holidays.

Obviously there's a big difference in the cost of transportation if the college is only a few hours from home by bus or train rather than several thousand miles away. And students who live a great distance from home will incur additional expenses in shipping their possessions back and forth.

13. Consider joining associations that offer discounts on bus, train, and airline tickets. The Student Advantage Card (*www.studentadvantage.com*) delivers discounts on Greyhound buses and Amtrak trains. Membership in AAA offers similar savings.

14. Try to find students or families who live near your home, and share the cost of renting a van for moving items to and from campus.

15. Compare the cost of renting a temporary storage space for the summer and leaving large objects near the school instead of taking them back and forth. Be sure items are properly packaged to avoid damage from water and mold.

16. If you plan to visit your student on Parents Weekend, make hotel reservations as far in advance as possible. In many small college towns, hotel rooms are very expensive (and scarce) for those who wait until the last minute. The same goes for graduation day.

Dormitory Furniture and Equipment

Allow me to sound like an old fogey for a moment: When I went off to college in the late 1960s, I traveled a few hundred miles from my home with two suitcases and a box containing my folk music record collection and turntable. Forty years later I drove my daughter to school in a gigantic U-Haul truck with a few thousand pounds of her dearest possessions.

Like it or not, the essentials of a modern college dorm room now seem to include (in addition to a bed, desk, and computer) a television set, VCR or DVD player, personal refrigerator and microwave, coffeemaker, and enough clothing to go weeks or months between trips to the laundromat.

17. Before the semester begins, roommates should get in touch with each other by phone or e-mail to discuss what they're planning to bring to school and look for ways to avoid expensive redundancy. Try to avoid having two microwaves, two refrigerators, and competing televisions.

At many colleges, students can rent refrigerators, microwaves, or a combination unit with both appliances from the bookstore or a private company. There are some advantages and disadvantages here; the principal advantage is that the unit is usually delivered at the start of the school year and picked up at its end, removing that headache from the moving process. And the rental company *may* offer a warranty or a replacement guarantee that extends through the school year.

SECRETS OF THE FRUGAL STUDENT

"Shop" for serviceable castoffs at the end of the academic year. You will be amazed—or dismayed—to see the barely used furniture, clothing, and appliances left by the curb or in garbage bins as students pack up to return home.

Take advantage of loyalty programs at supermarkets, other stores, and airlines.

Be on the lookout for ways to share: split the cost of renting a truck for moving, join a food co-op and buy large quantities of staples, and consider establishing a "kitchen commune" in which a group of students cooperate on shopping and cooking meals for the group.

On the down side, the rental units are often as expensive, or even more expensive than a new appliance purchased from a discount store. And then you'll have to do it again each year.

Compare the prices and look for ways to share purchases and storage places with other students.

18. If you do need to buy electronics or appliances, you can usually save a good deal of money and eliminate some of the hassle of shipping by ordering online and having the items sent directly to the student.

Telephone, Internet, and Entertainment

If you're lucky, your child will call you every once in a while—and not always to ask for more money. In today's world, though, there are many ways to communicate and many ways to save money.

Most colleges now offer high-speed Internet service in dorm rooms either as part of the room charge or as a separate (and usually non-negotiable) telecommunications fee that also brings basic telephone and cable television. At my daughter's expensive private university, the cost—non-negotiable—was $170 per semester or $340 per academic year, which works out to about $40 per month for the time she was at school. That's not a particularly great deal, especially when you consider that she was sharing the phone, cable television, and Internet connection with two roommates.

Here are some ways to make the most of what's offered:

19. Make use of free e-mail and instant messaging services for basic communication. E-mail's advantage is that it does not require the sender and receiver to be sitting at the computer at the same time, which works well when you consider the strange hours kept by many students. Instant messaging (including AOL's AIM and Microsoft's Messenger) is great for quick, short exchanges.

20. Cell phones have moved from novelty to necessity in many families. Kids love them to keep in near-constant touch with their friends, while parents recognize them as security tools. The trick here is to carefully research available plans to find one that fits best; college students often benefit from plans that offer unlimited nights and weekends. There are also family plans that allow unlimited calls within a single account, although that may not be as valuable as other benefits if your student is more interested in calling her roommate on the other side of the dorm room than calling home.

21. Some parents and students are beginning to adopt advanced technologies such as Voice over Internet Protocol (VoIP) phones that allow free or low-cost telephone calls. Providers here include Skype (*www.skype.com*), Vonage (*www.vonage. com*), and Lingo (*www.lingo.com*).

22. Although parents might imagine their child spending every waking moment in classes or deep in study, the truth is that there are many opportunities for students to spend money on entertainment. Keep a close eye on expenses such as pay-per-view cable television shows and DVD rentals. Joining a monthly rental club such as Netflix (*www.netflix.com)* or a similar program from Blockbuster *(www.blockbuster.com*) can save money here.

Health Insurance

Consult with your insurance company or agent to make certain your child is covered by your personal or business health policy. Most such plans cover dependent children while they are in college, up to the age of twenty-five; coverage extends for six months after graduation.

Some colleges insist that incoming students also pay an annual fee for use of an on-campus infirmary and emergency room.

23. Make sure your child understands the details of your health insurance plan, especially if the student is going to college in a different state than where you live or work. For instance, your

child may have to receive a referral from an HMO or preferred physician in order to be reimbursed for medical expenses, or may be able to save money on prescriptions by using certain pharmacies or mail-order sources.

DISCOUNTS FROM THE BOTTOM LINE

We've been talking about the True Cost of College. Now let's talk about the True Bottom Line.

What does it mean when a college offers $8,000 in financial aid? That may sound like a discount of that amount from the price tag for tuition, room, and board. But more than a few parents miss the fine print: $4,000 of the offer might be in the form of a college work-study program, and another $2,500 might be a subsidized or unsubsidized federal loan. When it comes time to pay the bill, it will be reduced—but only by $1,500.

The work-study program is a part-time job on or off campus, and the student is given a check to help defray the cost of living. The aid is not credited to the student's bursar account, and in any case the money arrives months after the semester's bills are due.

A loan becomes another source of income to pay the cost of attendance, but it is a debt that must be repaid after the student stops attending school. The benefit to the student and his or her parents is a reduction in the cost of interest but not the cost of college.

And more things to consider: a need-based grant, like one from the federal Pell program, is not guaranteed for all four years of college. It's kind of a good news–bad news situation: if one or both parents receives a raise or other income while a student is at school, the need-based grant may be reduced or go away the next year. Grants are almost always based on the previous year's federal tax filings.

And merit-based scholarships usually come with a gotcha: they usually require the student to maintain a minimum grade point average. (According to some studies, the typical college freshman's GPA drops between one-third of a point and a full point from the high school average.)

A school that has a high list price may end up a less expensive option if it makes a particularly generous offer of financial aid in the form of grants.

So here's one more equation. We'll start with The True Cost of College we calculated earlier in this chapter:

	_____	**THE TRUE COST OF COLLEGE**
-	_____	Scholarship for the current year
-	_____	Grants for the current year
=	_____	**THE TRUE BOTTOM LINE THIS YEAR**

Finally, from that number you can subtract temporary forbearances of payment. You might think of them as loans; I call them forbearances because when it comes down to it, they are merely delays before the bill is fully paid. As we've discussed, some loans do not need to be paid off until the student is out of school, while the repayment of others must begin immediately.

The last equation, then, we will call The Amount Due Now.

	_____	**THE TRUE BOTTOM LINE THIS YEAR**
-	_____	Education loans to be paid later
=	_____	**THE AMOUNT DUE NOW**

Now you have a way to compare actual costs between schools. (We'll go over this comparison in more detail in Chapter 6.)

Here are some of the things you may find:

24. A school that has a lower list price may be more expensive if it is so far away that parents and the student will have to spend thousands of dollars on travel to and from school.

25. Some schools may low-ball their published cost of tuition while they apply high fees—sometimes amounting to thousands of dollars—for labs, health services, student activities, or other ordinary elements of a year at college.

chapter 5

FINANCIAL AID:
A DEFINITION OF TERMS

Before we get much deeper into discussions of ways and means to pay for college, let's open the classroom for a definition of terms for types of financial aid offered to students by government, private sources, and schools. Federal programs are uniform across the nation, but state and private funding (including scholarships and aid offered by the colleges themselves) may differ slightly from place to place.

The first important point to understand is the differences among a **scholarship**, a **grant**, and a **loan**. The key difference? A loan has to be repaid, sooner or later. After that simple distinction, things get a bit more complex. Any of the three types of aid can be offered by governments, private individuals, companies, associations, or by colleges and universities.

The fourth category is work-study, which is a subsidized program that provides paid jobs to students to help with college expenses.

SCHOLARSHIPS

Some schools and programs define a scholarship as a sum of money—from a small portion of the bill to a completely free ride—given to recognize academic achievement, personal achievements, athletic ability, or in furtherance of certain goals of the college, such as diversity.

An academic scholarship may be awarded for all four years of an undergraduate career or may be offered one year at a time with an opportunity for renewal. A scholarship does not have to be paid back, but many colleges require that students maintain a particular grade point average and a good conduct record for renewal each year. Typically, scholarship programs demand a minimum GPA of 2.5; some insist on a more difficult 3.0 average, and a handful set an even higher academic bar.

At colleges, scholarships may be offered by academic departments during the review of applications for admission, or students may have to apply for a scholarship. Scholarships offered by government and private organizations usually involve a formal application.

Depending on the size of the school and its membership in national or regional athletic associations such as the NCAA, sports scholarships may have other strings. A scholarship cannot be taken away because a football player turns out to have two left feet; the student does, though, have to show up for practices and competitions and otherwise meet the reasonable requirements of the athletic department. In addition, student athletes are generally required to maintain an acceptable grade point average.

For information about NCAA scholarship rules, consult the organization's home page at *www.ncaa.org* or burrow a bit deeper by searching for a copy of the *Guide for the College-Bound Student-Athlete*.

GRANTS

A grant is a need-based scholarship. Colleges that offer grants to students usually do so on the basis of information gathered from the Free Application for Federal Student Aid (FAFSA) form, sometimes with additional information from CSS/Financial Aid Profile (see Chapter 14) and other data requested of the student or the family.

The student and parents generally have to file a current FAFSA each year, and need-based grants can be adjusted up or down based on changes in finances and the availability of funds at the school.

Need-based grants may also be offered by state and federal governments and from private sources. The best-known federal need-based scholarship is the Federal Pell Grant. Another is the Federal Supplemental Educational Opportunity Grant (FSEOG). These programs, which I discuss in Chapter 6, disburse funds based on federal criteria.

Many states have their own grant programs. Examples include the New York State Tuition Assistance Program (TAP), which provides need-based grants of as much as several thousand dollars per year.

LOANS

As I've noted, a loan has to be paid back. Though all loans have that fact in common, they can come in many different flavors. The three best-known national programs are Federal Perkins Loans, Federal Stafford Loans, and Federal PLUS Loans. We'll discuss these and other programs in more detail in Chapter 9.

A Perkins loan is a low-interest loan based on need; there's not a huge amount of money available under that program, but it can be combined with other offerings.

A Stafford loan can be subsidized (based on need; the interest rate is reduced and no interest is charged until after the student leaves school), or unsubsidized (not based on need; interest is charged as soon as funds are disbursed, although the loan can be written up so that payment of the principal and accrued interest does not begin until the student leaves school).

The Parent Loan for Undergraduate Students (PLUS) program is a straightforward loan that is not based on the student's or the parent's financial situation but is instead offered to anyone. Parents can borrow as much as they need, up to the full out-of-pocket cost of college (expenses minus any financial aid received). The interest rate on the loan is variable, but as of 2006 cannot exceed 9 percent; repayment begins sixty days after the loan is made. There is a built-in fee for the loan as well; a 4 percent fee is subtracted from the amount borrowed before it is disbursed to the college. (If you borrow $10,000, for example, the school will receive $9,600 but you will be responsible for repaying $10,000 plus interest on the outstanding balance.)

Many states offer subsidized or unsubsidized loans that can also be used to pay for a portion of the college bill. One example is the Massachusetts Educational Financing Authority (MEFA), which makes available student loans at reduced interest rates; borrowers may be able to claim some or all of the interest and fees paid on this sort of loan as an education tax deduction within federal income guidelines. And MEFA also has a program that allows borrowers to secure their education loan with the equity in the family home, allowing for deductibility of interest without any income restrictions.

Alternative loan programs from private sources can help bridge the gap between need-based financial aid and the bottom line. Loans vary on interest rates and fees, and students must have a creditworthy cosigner who guarantees repayment if the student is unable to pay off the note.

A personal or secured loan taken out by parents or the student may include a payback schedule that begins immediately, although some arrangements call for payments that only cover accrued interest while others require payment of a portion of the outstanding principal as well as interest. Examples of this sort of loan include an equity loan or line of credit that taps into the value of a home.

FEDERAL WORK-STUDY

This fourth category of "aid" is actually a need-based program that offers the student the opportunity for a paid job during the school year. The financial aid letter lists the amount of money that the student can earn under the program; the funds do not appear as a credit on the tuition bill.

The student receives a paycheck (with taxable income) during the school year; it is up to the family to determine how that money is applied—as partial repayment of college expenses, as repayment of student loans, or for week-to-week expenses such as books, food, and travel.

chapter 6

GRANTS
AND SCHOLARSHIPS

A grant is a gift; it's money that does not have to be repaid. The grant can be awarded because of financial need, academic excellence, good citizenship, or other special skills or attributes. (I'm leaving aside athletic scholarships, which are generally governed by rules of the various collegiate conferences, and organizations such as the NCAA.)

Grants can come from the accumulated endowment of the college, from a group or association, a union, a company, or some other benevolent donor. There are also grants from state and federal sources, generally given to those with financial need or with special circumstances such as veteran status or to recognize the children of deceased members of the military, police, or fire agencies.

The amount of the grant can vary from a few hundred or a few thousand dollars to the best deal of all: a complete free ride (tuition, room, board, books, and sometimes travel and other miscellaneous expenses) with no strings attached. About those strings: some are more binding than others.

Here are two examples of grants you may find:

- No strings attached. Some colleges say that their offer of a grant is guaranteed for four years; all the student has to do is follow the code of conduct and maintain the minimum GPA required for continued enrollment.

- High GPA required. Some colleges give a grant and then require that the student maintain a high GPA throughout a college career. Some schools insist on a reasonable 2.5 (equivalent to nearly a B-) or a difficult but not impossible 3.0 (equivalent to a B average).

A few set the bar even higher, raising the impolite question: Is the grant a bait-and-switch to lure a student who will end up having to pay full freight in later years?

Be sure you understand all of the fine print associated with an academic grant. If a minimum GPA level is required, find out if the school permits a one-term "grace period" to allow the student to bring the average back above the minimum. Does the entire grant go away if the student is unable to maintain the required GPA, or is there a lower level of aid that would be offered?

Looking a Gift Horse in the Mouth

Sometimes, painful though it may be, you've got to look a gift horse in the mouth and consider whether free is free and whether one college's apples compare in a meaningful way with another institution's oranges.

Let me explain with a story from our family's own quest for the best education. Our daughter, an above-average high school student, collected some unusual letters of recommendation and crafted a dynamite essay. Among the acceptances she received: a full four-year tuition scholarship to a small but prestigious (and expensive) liberal arts college in Boston.

That scholarship was worth at least $20,000 in the first year of school; our bottom line would be about $10,000 for room, board, and fees. Assuming that the tuition would go up about 5 percent per year, that full scholarship could have been worth $86,202 by the end of her senior year.

After a few weeks of agonizing analysis, we turned down the scholarship and instead accepted an offer of admission without any grant money from an even-more-expensive university.

Here's why:

1. First and foremost, we were not certain that this was the right school for our daughter. It was very small, and dedicated to liberal arts (although students could take one course per semester at one of a number of other small colleges nearby). There was no certainty that this would be a good fit for four years.

2. The full-tuition scholarship came with a significant bit of fine print. It required the student to maintain a 3.5 GPA (close to an A- average or better from the start and all through college) in order for the grant to be renewed at the end of each year. That's not an impossible task, but it clearly would have placed a huge burden on our daughter and left no room at all for errors.

Although we ended up walking away from the scholarship, there are some parents who would take a different strategy: enroll at the small school for a year or two, taking advantage of the discount, and then help the student transfer to a larger or better or more prestigious college for the final years leading to a degree. By concentrating on taking core courses at the first school with credits that can be transferred, you can create your own discount.

Remember that a college diploma bears the name of the school where you completed a degree, even if you only attended that school for one or two of the usual four years required.

PRIVATE SCHOLARSHIPS

There are millions upon millions of dollars in scholarship money sitting out there just waiting for the right match between the intent of the donor and the skills or attributes of the recipient. There are scholarships intended to boost particular skills; for example, an engineering association may sponsor scholarships for students who enroll in mechanical engineering programs. There are scholarships aimed at cultural or ethnic groups; within the bounds of civil rights laws, private groups can offer grants to minority groups or immigrant students who come from a particular part of the world.

Many unions and professional associations offer scholarships to the children of their members. Some companies help pay the college costs of the children of employees. (Don't overlook one of the greatest benefits of working for a college: most offer free tuition to children of employees, and there is a growing trend toward interchangeability of that benefit among groups of schools.)

Finally, don't overlook your own backyard. Your student's high school academic adviser should be able to provide a list of scholarships and work-study programs sponsored by area businesses, service groups, and individuals. As an example, my hometown has a large pool of money—a combination of private bequests and contributions by taxpayers who send an additional check along with the annual property tax payment (they really do)—that is offered through the high school and distributed at graduation.

Where to Find Private Scholarships

Let me start by saying that any book you might purchase that claims to list thousands of private scholarship programs you can apply to right now and *go to college for free!* is probably not worth the paper it is printed on. First of all, there is a nearly continuous stream of changes in these programs from month to month and year to year. Second, even if you expect that 50 percent of the scholarships listed in a book are no longer offered or have changed substantially, the publication is probably missing hundreds or thousands of new programs.

The best way to find private scholarships is to beat the bushes yourself: contact your student's guidance counselor, ask any association or group to which you belong, consult area service groups, and do a search on the Internet. *Beware of scholarship Web sites or consultants that offer to match you with a grant program after you pay a fee.* In most cases, you can find the same scholarships by searching on your own.

The best time to start looking for a local or association scholarship is a year or two before your student will actually be making application to college. Once you find a scholarship your student is eligible for, spend the time to carefully read all of the fine print. See if there is something in your child's background that can be highlighted to bring the application to the top of the pile. Find out whether your child would be a strong candidate for a particular scholarship if he or she were to perform a particular type of community service or commit to a highly specific major in high school or college. By checking early, you'll have a year or more to prepare.

Work your way down this list (adding any other sources that you know about) and make contact a year or more before you begin the college application process:

- **Unions.** Funds may be available to help young members, or the children of members.

- **Professional associations.** Special-interest groups may offer funds to the children of members, sometimes aimed at encouraging more graduates in a particular field.

- **Service clubs.** For example: Elks, Jaycees, Kiwanis, Lions, Rotary International, Sertoma, and Zonta, among others.

- **Employer programs.** Some companies offer financial aid to the children of their employees, or may offer to assist with night-school or part-time tuition for workers of any age.

- **Local governments.** Some towns, villages, and cities collect contributions from residents and use them to award scholarships to local students.

- **Local school districts.** In some areas, the schools themselves oversee endowments or one-time contributions from area businesses and groups aimed at assisting students in need or those who have demonstrated exceptional civic involvement.

- **Corporate scholarship programs.** Some of the country's best-known companies as well as hundreds of other lesser-known businesses disburse scholarships each year. Look for advertisements and promotions in stores and on the products you purchase.

- **Private foundations.** There are thousands of privately administered scholarships, worth millions of dollars. Many of these grants are aimed at special interests of the donors: minorities, persons with special needs, and immigrants, for example. Other programs may be aimed at encouraging students who promise to deliver needed services to remote areas; an example is medical scholarships that are based on the student's promise to work as a doctor or nurse in underserved areas.

FEDERAL AND STATE GRANT PROGRAMS

The federal government has several plans that offer funds—though nowhere near a free ride—to students with financial need. Some students are able to combine these grants with scholarships from the college, state funds, and private sources to put together a package.

Similarly, many states offer grants to students with financial need or special circumstances. Consult your state's higher education department for details. In some places, students are automatically eligible for grants on the basis of their FAFSA submission, while other states require that a separate application be filed.

Federal Pell Grant

Pell Grants are given to undergraduate students based on financial need; they are not required to be paid back. The funds are often the foundation of federal aid for the neediest students, with additional aid coming in the form of subsidized or unsubsidized loans, work-study programs, and other assistance.

In certain circumstances, Pell Grants can also be disbursed for students enrolled in a postgraduate teacher certification program.

Students do not directly apply for a Pell Grant; they are issued by colleges on the basis of the data extracted from the FAFSA and the Expected Family Contribution and funded from the pool of money they receive from the federal government. Each school is supposed to receive sufficient Pell Grant money for all students who qualify.

Colleges can credit Pell funds to a student's tuition and room-and-board bill, pay the student directly, or split the money between the outstanding bill and a check. For the 2005–06 academic year, the maximum Pell Grant amount was $4,050; the amount can be reduced by the college if it uses an institutional methodology that spreads available funding to a wider pool of financial aid applicants. Part-time students will receive a proportionally smaller payment.

The program is named after former U.S. Senator Claiborne Pell of Rhode Island, who championed its cause in Congress.

Federal Supplemental Educational Opportunity Grant (FSEOG)

This supplemental grant is aimed at students with exceptional financial need and is usually added to Federal Pell Grants. As a grant, it does not need to be paid back.

FSEOG funds range from as little as $100 to as much as $4,000 per academic year. Colleges are not guaranteed full funding for all eligible students, and applicants cannot count on receiving the maximum amount.

As with Pell Grants, FSEOGs are awarded on the basis of information provided on the FAFSA; there is no separate application. Funds can be credited by the school to student accounts, paid directly to the student, or split between direct payment and credit.

Federal Work-Study

This program provides jobs for undergraduate and graduate students with financial need. Funds are paid directly to the student in most cases, although some colleges will allow earnings to be directly credited to tuition and room-and-board bills.

Participants are guaranteed to be paid at least the current minimum wage. Jobs are usually on campus, although some may be at public agencies or private nonprofit organizations. The financial aid offer from the college will indicate the total amount of available funds per semester.

Students are offered work-study on the basis of information provided in the FAFSA; there is no requirement to accept the job or to work the full number of hours that are funded.

Bureau of Indian Affairs Higher ED Grants

Students who are members of an American Indian tribe or at least one-quarter blood descendants of a member of a tribe may be eligible for special grants administered by the Office of Indian Education Programs of the Bureau of Indian Affairs (BIA). The need-based grants can be used toward attendance at an accredited institution granting an associate's or bachelor's degree.

The agency's Higher ED grants supplement other federal financial aid programs. The grant application is available from the education office of many individual tribes; if the tribe is not administering the program, applicants can make direct contact with the BIA. Applicants must also file the FAFSA form, and they should make the financial aid office of the colleges they are applying to aware of their request for a supplemental Higher ED grant.

For more information, consult tribal offices, financial aid offices, or the Office of Indian Education Programs at (202) 208-6123 or *www.oiep.bia.edu*.

TAKING A CLOSE LOOK AT THE NUMBERS

When colleges offer a package that includes scholarships, you should figure out the real value of every offer. Start by figuring the true cost for each college. Use the formulas in Chapter 4 to calculate **The True Cost of College** and then subtract scholarships and grants for the current year to yield **The True Bottom Line This Year**.

Do not include loans, and also exclude work-study income unless your student is committed to apply that money to the cost of living and travel expenses.

Now comes the interesting part. Let's say we are comparing two schools that have greatly varying list prices but also offer significantly different amounts of financial aid and grants. Here are some of the things you may find:

- A school that has a high list price may end up a less expensive option if it makes a particularly generous offer of financial aid in the form of grants.

- A school that has a lower list price may be more expensive if it is so far away that parents and the student will have to spend thousands of dollars on travel to and from school.

Consider this hypothetical but realistic scenario:

SCHOOL A:

True Cost of College	$24,500
Federal financial aid	−$6,000
Discounted Bottom Line	= $18,500

SCHOOL B:

True Cost of College	$34,000
Federal financial aid	−$6,000
Academic grant in aid	−$10,000
Discounted Bottom Line	= $18,000

In this example, the school with the higher list price is offering a significant discount in the form of an academic grant, while the college that begins with a lower list price is staying with that price. Here's where you can shift your focus from cost and put your concentration where it should be: on the quality of the college education.

School B may be a superior school, and you may be getting a great deal with the discount. Or it may merely be a more expensive school.

chapter 7

COLLEGE SAVINGS PLANS

Ben Franklin did not have to pay the equivalent of half a year's income or so for college for his children, but he nevertheless had the right idea when he wrote in *Poor Richard's Almanack*: "A penny saved is a penny earned."

In today's more complicated world of very expensive higher education and a financial aid formula aimed mostly at lower-income (or lower-asset) families, we might want to modify old Ben's formula just a bit: "A penny saved is a penny earned, or a penny that doesn't have to be borrowed."

Here is the key to understanding how to save wisely: Keep college savings funds in your name rather than in your child's name, and encourage your children to invest in the Bank of Mom and Dad (an institution I'll explain in a moment).

The reason why you should avoid putting liquid assets in the name of your children is this: The bottom line for the federal methodology used to calculate the key number called the Expected Family Contribution (EFC) considers funds held by the student as a primary source of money for tuition. In 2005, the aid formula called for the student to spend as much as 35 percent of savings on college each year, while parents were expected to spend about 5.6 percent of their liquid assets.

That's what makes 529 Plans and Coverdell ESAs especially good vehicles for college savings; funds invested here are held in the parent's or (even better) the grandparent's or another person's name and do not impact the FAFSA financial aid calculations in the same way.

So what if junior has been saving for years to buy a car and has also been putting aside money for pizza and movie tickets in college? At some point before filing the FAFSA form, it may make sense for the child to make a gift of that money to the parents or make a major purchase on their behalf. Or the child can pay for SAT preparation courses, private touring, or other college-related expenses.

As a parent you can add these funds to your own investments, keeping track of the value on an informal basis in the Bank of Mom and Dad. You can use the funds to send weekly or monthly spending money or to buy junior that car someday, but along the way you may be able to decrease the expected family contribution.

I am in no way suggesting tax evasion here. I'd advise consulting with your tax preparer or financial adviser a year or so before the due date for the FAFSA to discuss appropriate—and legal—strategies to minimize the effects of money held in your child's name.

As you'll read in our roundtable of experts, financial adviser Patrick Curtin says there's one thing even more important than the exact type of savings account you establish. To borrow a phrase from a famous sneaker manufacturer: Just do it.

Once you make a commitment to setting aside money for college, consult a financial adviser or trusted banker to set up a program that best anticipates your needs and earning potential. Then do it for fifteen to twenty years.

In the following two tables, you can see a comparison of the key advantages and disadvantages of seven types of college savings plans. You do not have to choose just one; depending on your financial situation and the hopes and wishes of your children, you can invest in several plans. And if you're lucky, you can involve your extended family in contributing to one or another plan.

COMPARISON OF MAJOR COLLEGE SAVINGS PLANS

PART 1	State 529 Savings Plans	State 529 Prepaid Plan	Independent 529 Plan (3)
Federal Tax Benefits	Any funds withdrawn to pay for qualified educational expenses are not subject to federal income tax. (1) (2)	The owner of the account is not liable for federal income tax for withdrawals or refunds made for qualified educational expenses. (1) (2)	The owner of the account is not liable for federal income tax if a Tuition Certificate is used to pay tuition costs at a college that is a member of the plan. Refunds made for qualified educational expenses are also tax free. (1) (2)
State Tax Benefits	Some states offer tax credits or deductibility to residents.	Some states offer tax credits or deductibility to residents.	Some states offer tax credits or deductibility to residents.
Contribution Limit	No limit on annual contributions. Some states set a maximum total cash balance for each beneficiary.	Annual maximum contribution varies from state to state but most plans allow accumulation of five years of college costs.	No limit on annual contributions. The maximum account balance is set at the cost of five years attendance at the most expensive college participating in the program.
Income Restrictions	None.	None.	None.

PART 1	State 529 Savings Plans	State 529 Prepaid Plan	Independent 529 Plan (3)
Fees Charged	Fees vary by plan and are based on a percentage of assets invested. State-managed plans typically cost the least, while plans purchased through a broker or adviser may be charged several percentage points per year.	Fees vary from state to state.	No fees are assessed to account owners, with 100 percent of contributions allocated to the tuition plan.
Flexibility	Funds can be used for tuition, room, board, books, fees, equipment, and other qualified educational expenses at the undergraduate or graduate level.	Varies by state, but withdrawals from most plans are limited to tuition and fees at in-state colleges. Some plans also can be used for room and board.	Funds can be used for undergraduate tuition and fees at any member college to which the beneficiary student is admitted.
Impact on Federal Financial Aid	Treated as an asset of the parent. The federal methodology generally counts no more than 5.6 percent of the plan's value against the Expected Family Contribution each year.	Treated as an asset of the student. Federal methodology mandates that withdrawals from the plan reduce aid eligibility dollar for dollar.	Treated as an asset of the student. Federal methodology mandates that withdrawals from the plan reduce aid eligibility dollar for dollar.
Gift Tax Status	Each donor to the plan is allowed to make an annual gift of $11,000 without the beneficiary incurring a tax liability. Donors can also give as much as $55,000 in a single year with the funds prorated over a five-year period and treated as a gift in each of those years.	Each donor to the plan is allowed to make an annual gift of $11,000 without the beneficiary incurring a tax liability. Donors can also give as much as $55,000 in a single year with the funds prorated over a five-year period and treated as a gift in each of those years.	Each donor to the plan is allowed to make an annual gift of $11,000 without the beneficiary incurring a tax liability. Donors can also give as much as $55,000 in a single year with the funds prorated over a five-year period and treated as a gift in each of those years.

PART 1	State 529 Savings Plans	State 529 Prepaid Plan	Independent 529 Plan (3)
Level of Risk	Investments are subject to market fluctuations and can decline.	In most states, higher education funding agencies guarantee a specific or minimum level of return. (4)	Assets are held in a qualified trust, and participating colleges assume the risk of market fluctuations and guarantee tuition levels.

(1) Any funds withdrawn for purposes other than educational expenses are subject to taxation as income, and may be assessed an additional 10 percent penalty tax.

(2) Federal regulations that make qualified withdrawals tax free are scheduled to expire on December 31, 2010, unless Congress extends the law.

(3) Investment in the Independent 529 Plan does not guarantee that a student will be accepted at a particular college—or any college—that is a member of the group. Students who own a Tuition Certificate do not receive preferential treatment in the admissions process.

(4) After several years of a declining or stagnant stock market in the early 2000s, a number of states have closed plans to new entrants or have eliminated or placed limits on guaranteed returns.

COMPARISON OF MAJOR COLLEGE SAVINGS PLANS

PART 2	Coverdell Education Savings Account	Custodial Accounts	Savings Bonds	Taxable Savings
Federal Tax Benefits	Any funds withdrawn to pay for qualified educational expenses are not subject to federal income tax. (5)	Minors under fourteen receive an exemption from taxation on the first $800 of earnings with income above that amount taxed at the parent's tax rate. Minors over fourteen pay tax on earnings at the child's rate.	Interest is exempt from federal tax to the extent that withdrawals are used for qualified educational expenses.	Earnings are fully taxable at the rate paid by the owner of the account.
State Tax Benefits	Interest may be subject to state taxation.	Interest generally subject to state taxation at the child's rate.	Interest is exempt from state tax to the extent that withdrawals are used for qualified educational expenses.	Earnings are fully taxable at the rate paid by the owner of the account.
Contribution Limit	A total contribution of $2,000 per year until the beneficiary reaches the age of eighteen.	Unlimited.	Annual limit of $30,000 per owner of bonds.	Unlimited.
Gift Tax Status	Each donor is allowed to make an annual gift of $11,000 without the beneficiary incurring a tax liability.	Each donor is allowed to make an annual gift of $11,000 without the beneficiary incurring a tax liability.	Each donor is allowed to make an annual gift of $11,000 without the beneficiary incurring a tax liability.	None.

PART 2	Coverdell Education Savings Account	Custodial Accounts	Savings Bonds	Taxable Savings
Flexibility	Any legitimate educational expense, from kindergarten through postsecondary schools.	Can be expended by custodian for any purpose that benefits the minor. At the age of majority (eighteen or twenty-one) the account becomes the property of the child and can be spent for any purpose.	To maintain tax benefit, can be used for tuition and fees.	Can be used for any purpose.
Fees Charged	Varies by type of investment.	Varies by type of investment.	None.	Varies by type of investment.
Income Restrictions	Single filers: $95,000 to $110,000 of modified adjusted gross income. Joint filers: $87,750 to $117,750 of modified AGI.	None.	In 2005, the full interest exclusion was offered to single filers with modified adjusted gross incomes of up to $61,200 and joint filers with modified AGIs up to $91,850. Above those levels the income exclusion is reduced in steps to zero at $76,200 or $121,850 for single or joint filers respectively.	None.

PART 2	Coverdell Education Savings Account	Custodial Accounts	Savings Bonds	Taxable Savings
Impact on Federal Financial Aid	Treated as an asset of the parent. The federal methodology generally counts no more than 5.6 percent of the plan's value against the Expected Family Contribution each year.	Treated as an asset of the student. The federal methodology generally assesses 35 percent of the plan's value against the Expected Family Contribution each year.	Treated as an asset of the parent. The federal methodology generally counts no more than 5.6 percent of the plan's value against the Expected Family Contribution each year.	If it is an asset of the parent, federal methodology generally counts no more than 5.6 percent of the plan's value against the Expected Family Contribution each year. If it is an asset of the student, federal methodology generally assesses 35 percent of the plan's value against the Expected Family Contribution each year.
Level of Risk	Investments are subject to market fluctuations and can decline.	Investments are subject to market fluctuations and can decline.	Fixed rate.	Investments are subject to market fluctuations and can decline.

(5) Federal regulations that make qualified withdrawals tax free are scheduled to expire on December 31, 2010, unless Congress extends the law.

Note: The language that enables the Coverdell program allows administrators special discretion in dealing with students with special needs, including an extended contribution period. Contact your college admissions or financial aid office for assistance.

COVERDELL EDUCATION SAVINGS ACCOUNTS

Coverdell ESAs, originally known as Education IRAs, are worth consideration for families in higher tax brackets. They are set up as a trust or custodial account and funds within must be used solely for the purpose of paying for higher education tuition or other related expenses.

Contributions to an ESA are not tax-deductible, but the earnings on the account are not taxed. The funds can be invested in any sort of recognized financial vehicle.

Withdrawals can be made for any qualified educational expense, including college tuition as well as tuition at elementary or secondary schools and even associated expenses such as the purchase of a computer.

Here are the essential details:

- The maximum ESA contribution is $2,000 per child per year. More than one person can open and contribute to an ESA for a particular child, but the total amount put into ESAs in a calendar year must not exceed the annual limit or additional taxes will be due.

- Qualified expenses include tuition, fees, books, and supplies. For students enrolled at least half-time at an eligible school, certain room and board expenses are also permitted to be paid from an ESA.

- The account must be opened before the student reaches age eighteen, and must be fully distributed no later than thirty days after the student reaches the age of thirty. An exception is given for students with special needs.

- The maximum contribution is available for married couples with a modified adjusted gross income of as much as $190,000 per year; the limit is gradually reduced to zero for those with modified AGIs between $190,000 and $220,000.

- You can contribute to both an ESA and a 529 Plan in the same year for the same beneficiary. And in certain circumstances, the beneficiary can be changed.

The biggest disadvantage of an ESA is that money held in these accounts is considered to be an asset of the student. Because of that, the federal methodology for the Expected Family Contribution goes right after that investment. Students are expected to spend 35 percent of their assets per year toward their college bills, as compared to no more than 5.6 percent per year for the assets of the parents of a dependent child.

If you have an ESA, one strategy is to spend down some or all of its funds for qualified expenses before the FAFSA is filed. For example, use some of the money to pay for an SAT preparation course or tutoring.

Coverdell accounts were named after former U.S. Senator Paul Coverdell of Georgia.

STATE 529 PLANS

Until the next great thing, 529 Plans are the best college savings vehicle for most families. Money invested in a 529 grows without taxation, and withdrawals used for qualified educational expenses are also free of taxes.

Another important advantage is that a 529 Plan set up by a grandparent, another family member, or an unrelated person is not considered an asset of the student or the parent of a dependent student when it comes to calculating federal financial aid. (If set up by the parents, though, it is an asset.)

All fifty states have also set up plans that offer tax exemptions, credits, or other benefits for residents. In most cases, you should invest in a plan certified in your home state; otherwise you may lose the state tax benefits. This doesn't mean you have to use the funds in a college in that state, although some plans boost the incentives to do exactly that.

(There's a big "if" here, though; the provisions of the Economic Growth and Tax Relief Reconciliation Act of 2001 that allowed withdrawals to be sheltered from taxation are due to expire on December 31, 2010. Unless the U.S. Congress extends the law or makes other changes that continue the exemption, after that date withdrawals will once again be taxable. Will that happen? There's no way to be sure, but I'm willing to predict that most politicians are smart enough to realize that a sudden change to this plan—to the disadvantage of millions of voters—would be highly unpopular. In a worst-case scenario some or all of the gains—not the amount invested—would be taxable when withdrawn after the start of the year 2011.)

If the grass seems greener on the other side of the border, nearly every existing state plan allows participation by residents of other states. A handful add some relatively small fees, though, and you may not receive the same state tax breaks as do residents. Be sure to study the fine print yourself and enlist the assistance of an accountant or tax adviser if you can.

And then you also must deal with the number of options for types of investments; short-term or long-term bias; and even, in some states, a selection among more than one management company. Choice is good, but sometimes too large of a selection can be overwhelming.

Your goals in investing in a 529 Plan are threefold:

- To take advantage of tax-advantaged savings
- To earn a reasonable rate of return on your investment
- To begin—and continue—a regimen of regular savings over time.

Remember that we live in a profit-driven society. What does that mean? Well, the investment manager and the investment company will take a cut of the proceeds. And in most localities, the long arm of the state reaches in to extract an annual fee.

In theory, your hope is that the increase in the value of your investment over time, whether through a rise in the value of the securities held or through reinvestment of interest or both, will be much more than the cost of any fees. You may want to investigate whether you can set up and fund your plan directly through a state higher education agency rather than through an investment company; in most cases this will reduce the annual fee overhead.

In some states, a government agency manages investments. Elsewhere major companies including Fidelity Investments, T. Rowe Price, Merrill Lynch, and TIAA-CREF handle the funds. Most do a decent job, but there are some exceptions; when you're starting out your plan, ask to see the returns for the previous few years and the account fees and broker (or load) fees. You can find comparisons of state plans in financially oriented magazines such as *Money* and *BusinessWeek*.

But the bottom line, as investment adviser Patrick Curtin says in our roundtable, is that the most important thing to do is to get a plan started and keep contributing. Over time—ten to twenty years is best—you are almost certain to see a substantial increase in the value of your investment.

Here are the essentials of a 529 Plan as they currently exist:

- Anyone can contribute to a plan, regardless of their income.

- Contributors can be parents, extended family, or even friends of the family.

- The lifetime contribution level for each student is based on a calculation of the average total expenses of five years of higher education. In 2005 that limit was $235,000.

- An individual can contribute as much as $11,000 per student per year, or $55,000 for an individual or $110,000 for a husband and wife as an advance payment for a five-year period, without making the student subject to paying a gift tax.

- Some states encourage participation in their 529 Plan by making a portion of contributions to the plan deductible from state taxes. The amount of this benefit may be limited based on family income levels.

- Gifts made to a 529 Plan are generally considered removed from the donor's taxable estate even though the donor retains control over the account.

- The principal contributed to a 529 Plan is not insured like a bank account, and there is no guarantee that the investment will earn interest or dividends at a particular rate. And in economic downturns, an investment could even lose value.

- Under certain circumstances, the beneficiary of the plan can be changed. For example, if there are excess funds in the account it could be reallocated to a different family member or other student.

- You can contribute to a 529 Plan and an ESA in the same year for the same beneficiary.

- A 529 Plan set up and owned by the dependent parent is counted as an asset of the parent in calculating federal financial aid.

- However, a 529 account owned by someone other than the parent of a dependent child is not considered an asset of the parent or the student and therefore does not affect the Expected Family Contribution (EFC) calculation under federal financial aid rules.

There are usually fees and charges imposed on the holdings in a state 529 account, and some investment managers may deliver a higher rate of return than others. You should work with your investment adviser to choose a plan that is in concert with your tolerance of risk. In general, you might be willing to invest in a more volatile selection of funds, stocks, or other financial instruments if you are setting up a plan for a young child but should be much more conservative with investments for a student who is within a few years of entering college.

Depending on the state and the plan, you can expect to be offered several options for the type of equities held in the account. Most common include a guaranteed option (which promises a specific rate of return based on a long-term investment in annuities or bonds), an aggressive equity-based account, or an age-based option that starts out with more volatile investments when your child is very young and becomes more conservative as the time for payout approaches.

Plans allow you to make changes to the type of investments held within the account once per year, or any time there is a change to the beneficiary. Similarly, the holdings in one 529 Plan can be rolled over to another only once a year.

You also need to understand that if a family decides to end a 529 Plan for reasons other than paying for qualified educational expenses—including changing investment strategies before a child enters college—most plans impose a 10 percent penalty on gain on the investment; in addition, the money that is withdrawn is taxed at the owner's tax rate.

If you make a large gift to a 529 Plan, you should work closely with your tax preparer or accountant to assure that it is properly reported to the

IRS. You'll have to file IRS Form 709 to treat a gift larger than $11,000 given as an individual or $22,000 given as a couple as if it were spread out over five years.

When a withdrawal is made from a 529 Plan, the owner of the account or the student will receive IRS Form 1099-Q, which reports information about the disbursement to the tax agency.

STATE 529 PREPAID TUITION PLANS

A specialized type of 529 Plan, prepaid tuition accounts are set up by individual states or sometimes groups of states. These accounts are contracts intended to allow residents to lock in the current tuition fees at public colleges within the state or states. A group of more than 200 private schools of higher education, including some of the nation's most prestigious institutions, have set up independent prepaid tuition plans with most of the same benefits.

Prepaid plans offer the same benefits as a regular 529 Plan, with earnings exempt from federal income tax (at least through the end of 2010). In addition, they offer many state benefits.

Here are a few of the special wrinkles of this sort of college savings plan:

- In most plans, funds invested are used to prepay for a particular number of semesters or units of education as defined by the state. Money in the plan does not earn interest or dividends or otherwise appreciate.

- Most plans offer some sort of an escape hatch if, despite your years of planning, your student decides to attend college out of the state or region where you have set up prepaid tuition. Some offer full refunds, and some pay a small amount of interest on funds that have been left with the state but will not be used.

- Withdrawals from a prepaid tuition plan for educational purposes reduces federal financial aid dollar-for-dollar.

Be sure you understand all of the ramifications of a prepaid tuition plan before you enroll in one. You are, in essence, making these assumptions:

1. Your child will choose to attend a public college in the state where the plan has been set up, or in a state with which your state has a reciprocal or regional agreement.

2. The cost of public college will continue to rise at a rate higher than you would receive from investing the same amount of money in a standard 529 Plan.

INDEPENDENT 529 PLAN

State-run prepaid tuition plans have their place, especially if you live in a state that offers high-quality public colleges and if your student is willing to cooperate and attend one of the eligible colleges. (He or she also has to be accepted.) In some programs, residents of one state are permitted to attend a public college in another.

You should be sure you understand any restrictions on the use of a prepaid plan before you become involved. Some plans require out-of-state students to pay a higher tuition rate than do residents. And there may be a penalty for withdrawal of accumulated funds if the student chooses to attend a college that is not a participant in the plan.

One possible solution is the Independent 529 Plan, developed by a consortium of colleges around the country. It has many of the same benefits as a state-run 529 plan, with one major exception: The value of the plan is considered an asset of the student, and withdrawals made for educational purposes reduce eligibility for federal aid dollar-for-dollar.

Here are some things to consider about the Independent 529 Plan:

- If you don't expect to receive financial aid, the fact that it is treated as an asset of the student is not an issue.

- The participating colleges bear all of the risk of advance payment of tuition.

- Earnings on your investment will grow free of taxes at least through the end of 2010, when Congress must decide whether to extend this benefit of all 529 Plans.

- There are no setup fees, annual fees, or investment loads. Every dollar invested goes toward tuition costs.

- Just as with a state-run 529 prepaid tuition plan, you stand the chance of losing some of the financial advantage if your student chooses to attend a college that is not a participant in the plan (or is unable to receive acceptance at one of the schools).

In 2005, there were more than 240 colleges participating in the plan. They run the gamut from small lesser-known schools to several of the nation's best-known private universities; from Agnes Scott College in Georgia to York College of Pennsylvania. Some of the brand-name schools include the Berklee College of Music, Boston University, Carnegie Mellon University, Massachusetts Institute of Technology, University of Notre Dame, and Princeton University. For information on the plan, consult *www. independent529plan.org.*

The plans allows participants to lock in tuition costs at a price that is less than today's cost (generally offered at a discount of 1 percent), with the college bearing the risk of inflation and the possibility of decline in the value of investments. Your investment, made all at once or over a period of time, buys you a Tuition Certificate of a certain value.

If the owner of the account takes a refund instead of using the value of the account at one of the participating colleges, the refund will be adjusted based on the net performance of the Program Trust, subject to a maximum return of 2 percent per year and a maximum loss of 2 percent per year. Either way, you will be disappointed in the check you receive.

On the other hand, if you consider that college tuition costs have been increasing at just under 6 percent annually in recent years, the value of this plan is at least that amount (plus the initial discount and the tax benefit).

At the time you open an Independent 529 Plan, you have the opportunity to select as many as five "sample" colleges from the list of participating institutions. Each quarter, owners of accounts receive a statement that shows the total value of the account as well as the amount of tuition (expressed as a portion of an academic year) at each of the sample schools.

Choosing a set of sample schools does not lock you into applying to those colleges, and the selection can be changed at any time. The Web site also includes a calculator that helps you estimate the future value of an investment over time.

Just as an example, I considered a $50,000 lump sum investment made on July 1, 2005, for a student who would be going to college in ten years. If no further investments were made in the account, that amount of money would be worth the following on the bursar's office due date in 2015:

- 1.648 years of tuition and fees at Boston University in Massachusetts

- 1.765 years of tuition and fees at Princeton University in New Jersey

- 3.083 years of tuition and fees at Greensboro College in North Carolina

U.S. SAVINGS BONDS

The trusty old U.S. Savings Bond offers a very secure and modestly profitable route to funding at least some of the costs of education. The deal becomes a bit more attractive if you can take advantage of provisions that make the interest paid by certain bonds free from federal tax.

Lower- and middle-class families can exclude from their taxes all or some of the interest earned on Series EE (also called Patriot Bonds) and Series I bonds if the investments are used for qualified higher educational expenses.

Series EE bonds issued January 1990 and later, as well as all Series I bonds, can be used in this way. There's nothing special to be done at the time of purchase; when you file your taxes in the year following redemption, you'll need to include Form 8815 with your federal taxes. It may also be necessary to document your payment of tuition and other qualified expenses by providing a copy of Form 1099-T, which is sent by the school to the taxpayer.

Here are some of the details:

- The tax exemption is available to parents of dependent children, or to the taxpayer if that person uses the proceeds of a bond for higher education for himself or herself, or for any other dependents listed on the owner's tax return.

- Buyers of the bonds must be at least twenty-four years of age on the first day of issuance of the securities, and the bonds must be registered in the buyer's name and/or a spouse's name. A minor child can be listed as a beneficiary on the bond, but not as a co-owner.

- Interest can be excluded from federal tax when the bond holder pays qualified education expenses at an eligible institution (or a state tuition plan) in the same year that the bonds are redeemed.

- The interest exclusion phases out above specified income levels. In 2005, the full exclusion was offered to single filers with modified adjusted gross incomes (AGIs) of up to $61,200 and joint filers with modified AGIs up to $91,850; after that income level, the exclusion is reduced in steps to zero at $76,200 or $121,850 for single or joint filers respectively.

- Funds redeemed from savings bonds can be rolled over into a 529 Plan without penalty as long as the owner meets the same income limits for exclusion of taxes on interest.

- If the amount of eligible bonds cashed in during a particular year exceeds the amount of qualified expenses in that year, the amount of excludable interest is reduced proportionately. (If your qualified educational expenses represent 50 percent of the value of the redeemed bond, you can exclude from income 50 percent of interest earned.)

- Interest from savings bonds used for education is exempt from state and local taxes without regard to your income.

You can learn more about the IRS's view on tax benefits for higher education by obtaining a copy of the agency's Publication 970 through one of its offices or over the Internet at *www.irs.gov*.

You can purchase savings bonds through most financial institutions, and many employers offer payroll deduction plans for bonds. You can also buy bonds over the Internet at *www.treasurydirect.gov*. If you purchase bonds through Treasury Direct, you can manage and redeem them directly from your Web browser.

Series EE Savings Bonds

Beginning in mid-2005, newly issued Series EE bonds earned a fixed interest rate for the thirty-year term of the bond (twenty years to maturity plus a ten-year extended maturity period; in that period, at the government's option, the rate paid by the bond can continue at the same rate or be adjusted up or down, while owners can hold on to the bond at the same interest rate or sell it at any time).

The interest rate in the summer of 2005 was 3.5 percent. Interest on Series EE bonds accrues monthly and is compounded semiannually. Bonds must be held a minimum of one year, and owners must pay a three-month interest penalty for any bonds cashed in less than five years after the date of issue.

The U.S. Treasury guarantees that a bond's value will double by its maturity date twenty years after purchase; if a bond is not worth twice its original value based on earnings from the fixed rate, the Treasury will make a one-time adjustment on the original twenty-year maturity date to make up the difference.

Series I Savings Bonds

The other federal savings bond eligible for exempt earnings when used for educational purposes are Series I bonds. These bonds are accrual-type instruments, meaning that purchasers pay the full price—$50 for a $50 bond, for example—and earned interest is added to the value of the investment.

Interest rates are adjustable, based on a formula that includes a fixed rate for the life of the bond plus an inflation rate that changes twice a year. In the summer of 2005, Series I bonds were earning 4.8 percent.

These bonds must be held at least one year, and redemptions made before five years after purchase are penalized by an amount equal to the three most recent months of interest. After five years the bonds can be redeemed without penalty; the interest-earning period ends after thirty years.

CUSTODIAL, UGMA, AND UTMA ACCOUNTS

Custodial accounts (also called UGMA, as an acronym for their origin in the Uniform Gifts to Minors Act, or UTMA, under the Uniform Transfers to Minors Act) are simple to set up, but they are limited in their tax advantages and, depending on circumstances, may not turn out the way the parents or other family members intended.

Any accounts set up in this way are essentially joint accounts held by an adult and a minor under the age of eighteen. (In some states the age of majority—at least for custodial accounts—is twenty-one.) The adult custodian is not supposed to make any withdrawals that are not for the benefit of the minor; the money can be used for any purpose.

Funds put into a UGMA/UTMA account are post-tax dollars, and interest and dividends that accrue in the accounts are taxable. The advantage is that as an asset of the child, those gains are taxable at the minor's federal and state tax rates, which usually are lower than those of the parent or other adult guardian.

The account can be funded with cash or with securities. One tax strategy is to move some of a parent's stocks or other securities that have gone up in value into a custodial account so that when the financial holdings are sold they are taxed at the child's rate.

Here are the details, and a warning:

- There are no limits on the amount of money that can be put in a custodial fund, although gifts of more than $11,000 per person or $22,000 per set of parents may be subject to gift taxes; consult your accountant or tax preparer for advice.

- The existence of a custodial account does not prevent parents from qualifying for the Hope and Lifetime Learning tax credits. (See Chapter 8 for information about these credits.)

- Once a child reaches the age of eighteen (or twenty-one in some states), he or she can control disbursement of the funds. That means the money could be spent on a motorcycle, body piercing, or whatever your particular worst-case parental scenario is.

If your child is a willing participant in building up savings for college, that last sort of situation is not going to happen, right?

I am in no way suggesting that you break any laws, but some parents deal with the custodial account problem by not discussing the details of the investment with their minor children. They simply spend the funds on college or other educational expenses as soon as those bills come due. The child will still be liable for taxes for as long as the funds are in this sort of account.

In general, custodial accounts—once thought of as a great way for parents and grandparents to set aside money for college at a tax-advantaged rate—have been mostly supplanted by 529 Plans. Consult a tax accountant or a financial adviser if you still have funds earmarked in this way.

TAPPING INTO YOUR RETIREMENT FUNDS

Earlier in this book I introduced the sometimes difficult notion that parents should be sure to fund their own retirement along with setting aside money for college plans for their children. That said, in some cases it may make sense to borrow against retirement assets to pay for college. However, you must do so very carefully and make a strong commitment to repay yourself for any money taken out of your old-age fund.

Spending Your IRA Funds

The idea of an Individual Retirement Account is to allow taxpaying workers to set aside money to accumulate tax free until they are ready to tap those funds for their own retirement. In general, withdrawals from an IRA taken before the age of fifty-nine years and six months are subject to a 10 percent penalty and may also be taxable. The regulations for IRAs do allow for unexpected needs for the money, and there are some pathways to use the money for education.

That said, there are a few loopholes:

- Withdrawals for qualified higher educational expenses for yourself, your spouse, your children, your grandchildren, or great-grandchildren are not subject to the penalty.

- Qualified expenses include tuition, fees, books, and supplies for all students. If the student attends school at least half-time, allowable expenses expand to include room and board.

- The amount of qualified expenses is reduced by the amount of most other tax-free income, including tax-free scholarships and grants, tax-free educational aid given by employers, and withdrawals from Coverdell ESAs and redemption of Series EE and Series I savings bonds for educational purposes.

- Earnings taken from a traditional IRA are subject to taxation as income. And if the original contributions to the IRA were tax-deductible, the principal will also be subject to taxes as ordinary income.

- Withdrawal from a Roth IRA (based on post-tax dollars) for educational uses can be made without taxation up to the amount of contributed principal. In other words, you can draw down a Roth IRA to the point at which the account includes only earned interest. At that point the funds in the account can be left there until you reach the age of fifty-nine years and six months, or you can withdraw the earnings and pay taxes on them.

- Using funds from an IRA adds a complication to federal financial aid applications because the federal methodology used to calculate the Expected Family Contribution counts distributions from an IRA—even if they are nontaxable for educational purposes—as income for the parents. For that reason it may make sense to hold off on tapping into IRAs for as long as possible in a child's college career; if the distribution does not occur until after the student is in the second term of the junior year, the federal methodology will not include that money in the calculation for EFC for the senior year of college.

In any case, educational expenses are not the intended use of IRAs and I cannot recommend this as a strategy for members of the great middle class. The very wealthy may find some tax advantages to using sheltered retirement funds to pay a portion of college expenses, while those who earn the least income can hope for a greater share of financial aid. Taxpayers in the middle need to put away as much as possible for their eventual retirement as well as look for ways to pay for college for their children. It's not an either/or choice.

Getting Funds from a 401(k) Account

A 401(k) account is a fund set up by an employer for the benefit of workers when they retire. Contributions from the employee are taken from their salary before tax is calculated; in most cases, the employer makes a full or partial match of contributions. (The company's match can be made in the form of cash or company stock; stock is great if it appreciates in value, while an all-cash 401(k) can be invested in mutual funds or other securities and ride that long-term wave of appreciation.) The earnings on the account accrue tax free until they are withdrawn.

This is a great deal for many employees, especially if they can stay with a company for many years, or can transfer assets from one 401(k) to another company's similar plan.

As with an IRA, the federal tax code regulations that define the 401(k) include ways to access the money in the account for college expenses as a loan or as a hardship withdrawal. (Whether these options are included in a particular plan is up to the employer; most do permit loans and withdrawals.)

If you take the money out as a withdrawal before the age of fifty-nine and six months, you'll have to pay a penalty and the money will be treated as ordinary income for tax purposes. That's not a great deal for taxpayers; to make it worse, there's a third hit when the income shows up in the EFC calculations and reduces financial aid. And the fourth hit: you're taking away from your eventual retirement funds.

A better option—for some—is to take a loan against the assets in the account. The cost of the loan is paid back into your retirement fund.

The biggest problem with taking out a loan against your 401(k) account is the risk that you will quit or be laid off from your job. If that happens, in most cases the loan becomes immediately due. You'll either have to repay all of the money you took out or you'll have to convert the loan into an early distribution from the retirement plan and pay a penalty plus report the money as taxable ordinary income.

That's a big risk, and as I said about taking money out of an IRA, this is not a great idea for people in the middle class who are going to have to find a way to get along in expensive retirement years.

REBATE PROGRAMS

One way to pick up a bit of cash for college is to participate in a rebate program. In this case—for the careful shopper—a penny spent is a fraction of a penny earned.

The leading college rebate program is Upromise; others include Babymint and Edexpress.

Upromise is the largest program and probably the simplest to use; membership is free. For information and to join, visit *www.upromise.com*. You register your credit card and certain frequent buyer's cards from participating stores with Upromise and then go forth and shop. Upromise is able to track your purchases on the registered cards, looking for purchases made at merchants who are in the program. When it finds one, a rebate is calculated and held for you by Upromise.

Other ways to earn money in a Upromise account is to make purchases through the group's Web site or to accept and use its branded credit card.

The amount of the rebate can be as little as a few percent per purchase or as much as 10 percent at some restaurants and under special promotions. Accumulated rebates, once they reach certain levels, are invested in mutual funds. Members of Upromise are encouraged—but not required—to open a 529 Plan through the group; this may or may not make economic sense, because most such plans level annual service charges that might all but wipe out savings. (As a registered broker, Upromise also manages New York State's College Savings Plan, which is a 529 Plan, and works with managers of state plans elsewhere in the country.) Instead of opening a 529 Plan, you can hold the money in taxable funds or ask Upromise to send you a check from time to time.

Babymint works in a similar manner; you can learn about the program at *www.babymint.com*. This plan involves some 500 merchants as well as a credit card that earns rebates that are deposited into an existing 529 Plan. There are no charges to join, although managers of savings accounts associated with the program may charge fees or require minimum contributions or both.

Edexpress claims that its plan, which works much like the other rebate programs, delivers a higher rebate to its members because it does not extract a fee from the stream of revenues. Instead there is an annual fee to members; in 2005 it cost $24.95 each year for an account. For information visit *http://ifap.ed.gov/edexpress*.

There is no downside to participating in any of the programs unless they cause you to spend money you would not otherwise spend. There is no point to buying a new GM car just to get the $150 rebate that company was offering Upromise members in 2005. And if gas at a different station is ten cents cheaper per gallon, there is no reason to fill up your tank at Exxon for a penny-per-gallon rebate. There are a few big-ticket rebates in the program, including paybacks by a national real estate brokerage company and a mortgage company that could add a few hundred or even a few thousand dollars to your account—assuming they represent the best deal in the first place.

The best way to use these sorts of programs is to get grandparents, relatives, and willing friends to register their cards and list your student as the beneficiary of the rebates. Then continue to be a very careful shopper. When the best price for breakfast cereal also results in a rebate of a few dimes to your account, it's free money. And over time those dimes should add up to make a small contribution to the cost of college.

Before you join any of these three plans, check to see which one has affiliations with merchants or service providers you are likely to use.

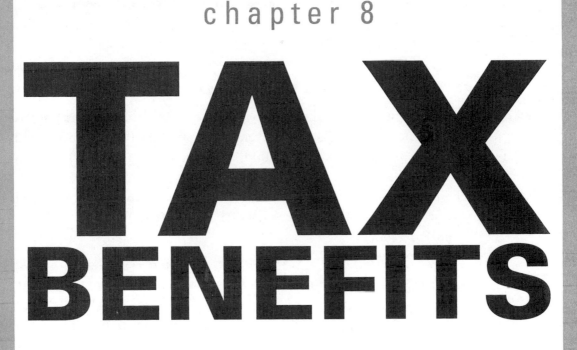

chapter 8

TAX BENEFITS

Don't ever let a politician stand on a soapbox or address you on television and tell you about the tremendous tax benefits your federal government offers for parents and students facing huge tax bills. There are some credits worth a few thousand dollars here and there, within a window that shuts somewhere in the range of income of the middle class.

I'm not being ungrateful here: take advantage of tax credits if you can. I'm just hoping that someday Congress and the president—any Congress, any president—will make a serious effort at helping all of us pay for a quality education for our children.

HOPE EDUCATION TAX CREDIT

The HOPE benefit is a federal tax credit, not a scholarship, and it is limited in its scope. The tax credit is 100 percent of the first $1,000 of tuition and fees and 50 percent of the second $1,000, for a maximum of $1,500 for each eligible dependent.

The credit is subtracted from the amount of taxes you owe the federal government, not from the amount you owe the college.

In order to collect:

1. You have to pay tuition and fees for a dependent student. All grants, scholarships, and other tax-free educational assistance are subtracted from the bottom line. Of course, if you're lucky enough to get a completely free ride, you don't need a tax break; otherwise, almost every college student spends at least $2,000 and is thus eligible.

2. You have to file a federal income tax return.

3. You have to owe taxes in order to have a balance against which to apply the credit. If taxes have already been withheld, you may receive the credit as a tax refund. If you have no tax liability, the credit is not available.

And there are a few more limits:

4. The credit is only available for two tax years, the freshman and sophomore years in college.

5. The maximum benefit is only available for single taxpayers with an adjusted gross income (AGI) of up to $40,000 or married taxpayers with an AGI up to $80,000. The credit is phased out

for single taxpayers with an AGI of $41,000 to $51,000, and for married taxpayers with an AGI of $83,000 to $103,000.

6. The HOPE credit cannot be used in the same year as a Lifetime Learning Tax Credit.

LIFETIME LEARNING TAX CREDIT

This is another federal tax credit, worth up to $2,000 per tax year per family for the taxpayer, the taxpayer's spouse, and any eligible dependents. The credit is a percentage of a larger expenditure: 20 percent of the first $10,000 of qualified tuition and expense.

Among the pieces of good news:

1. The credit can be used for an unlimited number of years.
2. The credit can be applied to educational expenses for anyone in the family, including the parents or guardians.

As with the HOPE credit, you have to file a federal tax return and you have to owe taxes; the credit is applied against the amount due. And the full tax credit is only available to taxpayers with incomes of no more than $41,000 for single filers and $83,000 for joint returns. The credit phases out for single taxpayers with an AGI of $41,000 to $51,000 or joint taxpayers with an AGI of $83,000 to $103,000.

And finally, the Lifetime Learning Tax Credit cannot be used in the same years as a HOPE Education Tax Credit. (But remember that the HOPE is only good for two years of college, and only for dependents.)

Applying for a HOPE Education Tax Credit or Lifetime Learning Tax Credit

In order to apply for either of the federal tax credits, your tax return must reflect the amount of tuitions and fees paid as well as any scholarships, grants, and other untaxed income used to offset the cost of college. Colleges are required to send this information on an IRS 1098-T form that is sent to the student and to the IRS; the form is supposed to be mailed to the student by January 31. The credit is based on payments made for any academic period beginning in the previous year and for the first three months of the following year. For freshmen this may cover only the first term, while the next year it may cover the second term of the freshman year and the first term of the sophomore year.

The figure below shows the 2005 version of the Form 1098-T Tuition Statement that was due to be sent to students at the end of that year for use in figuring federal taxes. Note that this form is generated by the college and sent to the IRS; do not photocopy the form from this book or download it from the Internet for submission.

If you have any questions about the information included on the 1098-T form, contact the college at the phone number it is required to list on the document.

IRS FORM 1098-T ▼

Tuition Statement,
generated by the college or other educational institution.

☐ CORRECTED			
FILER'S name, street address, city, state, ZIP code, and telephone number	1 Payments received for qualified tuition and related expenses $	OMB No. 1545-1574 20**05** Form **1098-T**	**Tuition Statement**
	2 Amounts billed for qualified tuition and related expenses $		
FILER'S Federal identification no. STUDENT'S social security number	3 Adjustments made for a prior year $	4 Scholarships or grants $	**Copy B** **For Student**
STUDENT'S name	5 Adjustments to scholarships or grants for a prior year $		This is important tax information and is being furnished to the Internal Revenue Service.
Street address (including apt. no.) City, state, and ZIP code	6 The amount in box 1 or 2 includes amounts for an academic period beginning January- March 2006 (if checked) ☐	7 Reimbursements or refunds of qualified tuition and related expenses from an insurance contract $	
Service Provider/Acct. No. (see instructions)	8 Check if at least half-time student ☐	9 Check if a graduate student . . . ☐	

Form **1098-T**   (keep for your records)   Department of the Treasury - Internal Revenue Service

When it comes time to file taxes, the actual claim for the credit is made on an IRS 8863 form. The bottom line, the calculated education credit is also entered as an itemized deduction on Form 1040 or 1040A.

The next figure shows the 2004 version of Form 8863 Education Credits (Hope and Lifetime Learning Credits).

IRS FORM 8863 ▼

Education Credits,

used to figure and claim particular education credits.

Form **8863** Department of the Treasury Internal Revenue Service (99)	**Education Credits** **(Hope and Lifetime Learning Credits)** ▶ See instructions. ▶ Attach to Form 1040 or Form 1040A.	OMB No. 1545-1618 20**04** Attachment Sequence No. **50**
Name(s) shown on return		Your social security number

Caution: You **cannot** take both an education credit and the tuition and fees deduction (Form 1040, line 27, or Form 1040A, line 19) for the **same student** in the same year.

Part I   Hope Credit. Caution: You **cannot** take the Hope credit for more than **2** tax years for the **same student.**

1

(a) Student's name (as shown on page 1 of your tax return) First name Last name	**(b)** Student's social security number (as shown on page 1 of your tax return)	**(c)** Qualified expenses (see instructions). **Do** **not** enter more than $2,000 for each student.	**(d)** Enter the **smaller** of the amount in column (c) or $1,000	**(e)** Subtract column (d) from column (c)	**(f)** Enter one-half of the amount in column (e)

2	Add the amounts in columns (d) and (f)	**2**		
3	Tentative Hope credit. Add the amounts on line 2, columns (d) and (f). If you are taking the lifetime learning credit for another student, go to Part II; otherwise, go to Part III ▶		**3**	

Part II   **Lifetime Learning Credit**

4

Caution: You **cannot** take the Hope credit and the lifetime learning credit for the **same** **student** in the same year.	**(a)** Student's name (as shown on page 1 of your tax return) First name Last name	**(b)** Student's social security number (as shown on page 1 of your tax return)	**(c)** Qualified expenses (see instructions)

5	Add the amounts on line 4, column (c), and enter the total	**5**	
6	Enter the **smaller** of line 5 or $10,000 . . . . ▶	**6**	
7	Tentative lifetime learning credit. Multiply line 6 by 20% (.20) and go to Part III . . ▶	**7**	

Part III   **Allowable Education Credits**

8	Tentative education credits. Add lines 3 and 7		**8**
9	Enter: $105,000 if married filing jointly; $52,000 if single, head of household, or qualifying widow(er)	**9**	
10	Enter the amount from Form 1040, line 37*, or Form 1040A, line 22	**10**	
11	Subtract line 10 from line 9. If zero or less, **stop;** you cannot take any education credits	**11**	
12	Enter: $20,000 if married filing jointly; $10,000 if single, head of household, or qualifying widow(er)	**12**	
13	If line 11 is equal to or more than line 12, enter the amount from line 8 on line 14 and go to line 15. If line 11 is less than line 12, divide line 11 by line 12. Enter the result as a decimal (rounded to at least three places)	**13**	× .
14	Multiply line 8 by line 13 . . . . ▶	**14**	
15	Enter the amount from Form 1040, line 45, or Form 1040A, line 28	**15**	
16	Enter the total, if any, of your credits from Form 1040, lines 46 through 48, or Form 1040A, lines 29 and 30	**16**	
17	Subtract line 16 from line 15. If zero or less, **stop;** you cannot take any education credits . . . . ▶	**17**	
18	**Education credits.** Enter the **smaller** of line 14 or line 17 here and on Form 1040, line 49, or Form 1040A, line 31 . . . . ▶	**18**	

* If you are filing Form 2555, 2555-EZ, or 4563 or you are excluding income from Puerto Rico, see Pub. 970 for the amount to enter.

For Paperwork Reduction Act Notice, see page 3.	Cat. No. 25379M	Form **8863** (2004)

TUITION AND FEES DEDUCTION

Yet another way to deduct as much as $4,000 per year for the costs of college is to claim qualified tuition and fees as an adjustment to income. You cannot, though, apply for this adjustment and take a HOPE or Lifetime Learning credit based on the same expenses; you're allowed only one of the three in a particular tax year.

The deduction comes on expenses after they have been reduced by any tax-free scholarship, fellowship, grant, or education savings account including a Coverdell plan, tax-free savings bond interest, or employee-provided education assistance.

You also cannot use this deduction without accounting for expenses paid from a tax-exempt distribution from a qualified tuition plan such as a 529 plan, except for payments that are a return of your own contribution to the plan. And you cannot deduct education expenses that are also deducted elsewhere on your return, such as those listed as a business expense.

Finally, the deduction for tuition and fees is limited by single or family income. In 2004 the maximum deduction of $4,000 per year was only available if a single filer's modified AGI was not more than $65,000 or a married filing jointly form's modified AGI was not more than $130,000. If the modified AGI was greater than $65,000 for a single filer or $130,000 for married filing jointly, but not more than $80,000 ($160,000 for a joint filing), the maximum deduction for tuition and fees dropped to $2,000. For modified AGIs above those levels, no deduction is allowed.

Applying for a Tuition and Fees Deduction

To receive the deduction, the amount of qualified tuition and fees is entered in the Adjusted Gross Income section on the first page of Form 1040 or 1040A. The information generally must not conflict with data provided to the student (and the IRS) on Form 1098-T, which is sent to each student by January 31 of each year following payment of tuition and fees in the previous year.

STUDENT LOAN INTEREST DEDUCTION

Another adjustment to your gross income is a deduction of as much as $2,500 per return for interest on a qualified student loan.

The deduction, entered in the Adjusted Gross Income section on page one of Form 1040 or 1040A, is limited by income. The maximum amount is available only for modified AGIs of $100,000 or less for married filing jointly forms; the amount is reduced on a sliding scale for joint modified AGIs between $100,000 and $130,000. Above that level, the deduction is not available.

For those filing a single tax form, the full deduction is available for modified AGIs up to $50,000; the deduction phases downward to zero for modified AGIs between $50,000 and $65,000.

The deduction is not available for married couples who file separately, for students who are claimed as a dependent, or for interest paid on a loan from a relative or from a qualified employer education plan.

TAKE NOTE

The author is not a tax accountant, and this section is not intended as tax advice; please consult a qualified tax preparer or the IRS for specific questions about filing your federal taxes. You can also request a copy of Publication 970, "Tax Benefits for Education," from an IRS office or download it from the *www.irs.gov* Web site.

Note that the definition of qualified college costs differs from one program to another. Some are limited only to tuition, while others may also allow consideration of room and board, books, fees, and other expenses.

It is also important to note that 1) Congress or the IRS can make changes to tax laws or the regulations issued to implement them, and 2) many of the provisions of the current tax code expire in the year 2010 and may or may not be extended, or may be altered at that time. (I'm betting on an extension, but there is no certainty.)

MORE TAX CODE MINUTIAE

Be sure to consult with a qualified tax preparer or accountant to find out whether you are eligible for some of these other deductions and exclusions:

- Grants and scholarships given are generally excluded when calculating the student's adjusted gross income.

- In qualified programs, if a student loan debt is forgiven, those funds are generally not reportable as income.

- Free or reduced tuition given to a family member of an employee of a college or university does not count as income.

chapter 9

COLLEGE LOAN PROGRAMS

A loan is a debt. You borrow money you don't have in order to protect assets you don't want to cash in or to pay an immediate bill. And sooner or later you're going to have to pay back the money you borrowed.

The idea of borrowing money is an emotional issue for many people, while others are quite used to living in a situation of indebtedness. Nearly everyone who owns a home has a mortgage, and we learn to make payments on that debt as if it were a monthly rent payment. Most car purchases involve a secured loan from a bank, a dealer, or a lending company; a leased car is technically not a loan, although lessees do sign a contract that requires regular payments to reimburse the actual owner of the vehicle for the cost of borrowing money as well as the decline in the value of the car.

These are "secured" loans, meaning that they are tied to a tangible piece of property—a home or a car, for instance—that technically is owned by the lender until the loan is paid off. If you default on a secured loan, the bank can foreclose on your home or repossess your car and sell either to pay the outstanding balance.

When you borrow for a college education, though, the loan is an unsecured debt in most cases. (Is a lender going to come after the student and take away an education for resale to another?) Ordinarily, an unsecured loan is more difficult to obtain and carries a higher interest rate than does a secured loan. This is where the federal government and some state higher education agencies have stepped in to offer assistance. Depending on your financial need, you may be offered a subsidized loan (with a reduced interest rate and a delayed repayment schedule), an unsubsidized loan (which may require repayment to begin immediately), or other types of loan programs aimed specifically at college financing.

Finally, there is the issue of whether the loan is made to the parents (or guardians) or to the student. In some cases, the best rates and plans are offered to students, especially if they can demonstrate financial need.

More important is the question of whether college loans are used as a short-term solution by parents or whether the student will graduate under the burden of tens of thousands of dollars in debt before he or she takes the first step into the workplace. According to a Roper Survey conducted in 2002, one in five twenty-one- to thirty-four-year-olds said that after graduation they had to take a job other than the one they wanted in order to earn enough to pay off their student loans.

For many families the best solution is to put together a package of loans from various sources. Just because a loan is made to the student does not preclude the parent from paying off the note or reimbursing the student over time.

As CPA Robert Klein put it, "The greatest gift one can give their child is to allow them to graduate debt-free from college."

PARENT LOAN FOR UNDERGRADUATE STUDENT (PLUS) PROGRAM

Any parent is eligible to apply for a PLUS loan without regard to financial need. There is no minimum, and the amount borrowed can be up to the total cost of attendance minus any other financial aid received. These loans come in two types: a Federal PLUS Loan (Direct PLUS Loan), and a FFEL (Federal Family Education Loan Program) PLUS Loan.

Description: A federally insured loan program available from state agencies, banks, lending companies, and directly from some colleges.

Availability: A Direct PLUS Loan is available from the U.S. Department of Education.

Applications for a FFEL (Federal Family Education Loan Program) PLUS Loan are submitted by a college financial aid office to banks and other lenders.

Eligibility: Parents or legal guardians of a dependent student enrolled in an undergraduate program. Loans are not need-based.

Borrowers must not have a history of credit problems; parents cannot be turned down if they have no credit history at all. If parents or guardians do not pass the credit check they may still be able to receive a PLUS loan if a creditworthy family member or friend endorses the loan—promising to repay the note in case of failure to repay.

Loan amounts: No minimum; maximum amount is up to the cost of attendance (including tuition, room, board, fees, supplies, and travel) minus any other financial aid received.

Disbursement: In most situations the funds are sent directly to the college in at least two installments based on the school's billing cycle. If the amount borrowed is greater than the outstanding balance owed the school, the parents (or the student, if authorized) will receive the extra funds as a check from the school. Any such excess funds must be used for education expenses.

Tax issues: Limited federal tax deductibility, depending on family income, under the HOPE Education Tax Credit.

Interest formula: Variable rate based on the most recent sale of ninety-one-day Treasury Bills held prior to June 1 of each year, plus a margin. Rates become effective on July 1 of each year. In 2006, the margin above the index was 3.1 percent and the variable interest rate was guaranteed not to exceed 9 percent. Rates in 2006 worked out to 6.1 percent.

Fees: The guarantee and origination fees cannot exceed 4 percent, and some lenders will offer lower fees. Fees are deducted from loan proceeds at the time of disbursement. In other words, if you are borrowing $10,000 and the fees are 4 percent, you (or rather, the college) will receive $9,600, but you will start out owing the full amount.

Repayment: Repayment period of as much as ten years with no penalty for prepayment. Billing for principal and interest begins within sixty days of final disbursement to the college. Under certain circumstances, including unemployment and illness, the borrower may request a temporary deferral (or forbearance) of principal and interest payments, although interest continues to accrue.

There are several repayment plans:

- A ten-year plan with a minimum monthly payment of $50, with the amount based on a prorated portion of the total amount due

- A graduated monthly payment plan that starts out low and increases gradually during the repayment period

- An extended plan that spreads out repayment of the principal over a longer period

Certain FFEL PLUS lenders will also offer another option:

- A plan that adjusts the monthly payment based on family income

Special programs: Some state agencies, state colleges, and other lenders may offer interest rates discounted below the official index plus margin. Some lenders may offer additional interest rate deductions for automatic payment from a checking or savings account.

How to apply: For a Direct PLUS Loan, a combined application and promissory note is available through college financial aid offices.

For a FFEL PLUS Loan, parents must fill out an application available through the college financial aid office; after the school certifies the application, it is made available to lenders for evaluation.

FEDERAL PERKINS LOAN

Administered by the U.S. Department of Education, Perkins Loans are offered to the student at below-market interest rates. No interest is charged while the student is enrolled at least half-time in college.

Although in theory any student is eligible to take out a Perkins Loan, colleges are required to give priority to students with exceptional financial need. In practice, this means that the pool of money available for Perkins Loans is usually emptied well before students with some personal or family assets are reached.

Description: A federal program awarded by colleges, subject to government funding levels and limitations. The school is the lender.

Availability: Offered to students with exceptional financial need, based on information provided on the FAFSA form.

Eligibility: Students must be enrolled at least half-time at an eligible college; parents and student must complete and submit the FAFSA form before the deadline date.

Loan amounts: In 2005, the program allowed for a maximum of $4,000 per year, not to exceed $20,000 for an undergraduate program. The amount offered is determined by the college's financial aid office and may be less than the maximum. Congress may increase or decrease overall funding for the program each year, and maximums may change.

Disbursement: Borrowed money is paid directly to the school.

Tax issues: Interest may be tax-deductible based on income level.

Interest formula: Fixed rate set by the U.S. Department of Education. In 2005, Perkins Loans bore a 5 percent interest rate.

Fees: No application fee.

Repayment: Repayment is scheduled to begin nine months after the student graduates, withdraws from college, or drops below a minimum of half-time status. The repayment period extends for ten years.

Under certain circumstances, including unemployment and illness, the borrower may request a temporary deferral (or forbearance) of principal and interest payments, although interest continues to accrue.

How to apply: File the FAFSA. Contact the college's financial aid office for additional information.

FEDERAL STAFFORD LOAN (SUBSIDIZED OR UNSUBSIDIZED)

Loans are available to students; those with financial need are eligible for a subsidized loan, while those who do not meet financial aid requirements are eligible for an unsubsidized loan.

Description: Federally insured loans available directly from some colleges, banks, other lenders, or state agencies.

Availability: Families must complete the FAFSA to apply.

Eligibility: Students who demonstrate financial need may be offered a subsidized loan; students who do not meet the criteria for financial aid may be offered an unsubsidized loan.

Loan amounts: In 2005, annual maximums were:

- $2,625 freshmen
- $3,500 sophomores
- $5,500 juniors and seniors

Students who are not dependent on a parent or guardian, or students who have been denied a Federal PLUS Loan, may be eligible for additional amounts of as much as $4,000 for freshmen and sophomores and as much as $5,000 for junior and seniors.

Disbursement: Direct Stafford Loans come from the U.S. Department of Education and are delivered to the student through the college; repayment is made to the federal government.

Federal Family Education Loan (FFEL) Stafford Loans come from banks or other lending institutions; repayment is made to the lender or to a servicing agent it appoints.

Tax issues: Interest may be tax-deductible based on income level.

Interest formula: Variable interest rate based on the most recent sale of ninety-one-day Treasury Bills held prior to June 1 of each year, plus a margin. Rates become effective on July 1 of each year. In 2006, the margin above the index was 1.7 percent while the student is enrolled, in a grace period, or in a deferment period; the margin above the index was 2.3 percent while the loan was being repaid. The variable interest rate was guaranteed not to exceed 8.25 percent.

In 2006 actual interest rates were 4.7 percent for students still in school or still in a grace period, and 5.3 percent for students in the repayment period.

Fees: The guarantee and origination fees cannot exceed 4 percent, and some lenders will offer lower fees. Fees are deducted from loan proceeds at the time of disbursement. In other words, if you are borrowing $10,000 and the fees are 4 percent you (or rather, the college) will receive $9,600, but you will start out owing the full amount.

Repayment: Differs for the two types of Stafford loans.

- **Subsidized Stafford Loans.** Repayment of the principal is deferred and interest is subsidized by the government for as long as the student is enrolled at least half-time in school and during deferment periods.

- **Unsubsidized Stafford Loans.** Repayment of the principal is deferred and interest payments can be deferred as long as the student is enrolled at least half-time and during deferment periods. Any unpaid interest is added to the principal and is the responsibility of the borrower once repayment begins.

For all Stafford loans, repayment is scheduled to begin six months after the student graduates, withdraws from college, or drops below a minimum of half-time status. The repayment period extends for ten years. There is no prepayment penalty.

Under certain circumstances, including unemployment and illness, a borrower may request a temporary deferral (or forbearance) of principal and interest payments, although interest continues to accrue.

Special programs: Some state programs (such as MEFA in Massachusetts) offer discounts for state residents. In the MEFA program, students receive a .5 percent reduction during repayment of the loan, an additional .5 percent reduction if payments are made as automatic withdrawals from a checking or savings account, and a 2 percent additional interest rate reduction after forty-eight consecutive on-time payments have been made.

How to apply: Students are automatically eligible for Stafford Loans if they file a FAFSA. Contact the college's office of financial aid and your state's educational financing agency for additional information about special programs.

Service-Cancelable Stafford Loans

One way to reduce the cost of college—at least the portion of expense that is paid by a Federal Stafford Loan—is to enroll in a degree program that is considered a "critical field of study" and then take a job in that field. A number of states offer a Service-Cancelable Stafford Loan to encourage trained professionals to meet regional needs.

The loan may be a need-based subsidized loan or an unsubsidized loan made available to any applicant. For the service-cancelable program, though, states add residency requirements, a minimum grade point average, and a commitment to one of the listed fields of study.

Check with your state's higher education funding authority or the financial aid office of your school for details.

In many states, the greatest need is for people in the health field. Acceptable programs of study include those for dental hygienists, laboratory technicians, nurses in almost any specialty or degree level, occupational or physical therapists, and physician assistants. Graduate health fields include dentistry, optometry, pharmacy, and veterinary medicine.

As an example of this sort of program, the Georgia Student Finance Authority requires participants to be a legal resident of the state under its definition of that status, be accepted for admission or enrolled at least half-time in an approved school, maintain at least a "C" average in most programs, and not be in default on any Federal education loan or owe a refund on any Federal Pell Grant, Federal Supplemental Educational Opportunity Grant (FSEOG) or Student Incentive Grant (SIG).

After graduation, students can repay their loan by working in their field of study in the state where the program is based. In the Georgia plan, the trade is one-for-one: for each calendar year of full-time qualifying service, the state will cancel one academic year of assistance in most programs. (If the original Service-Cancelable Stafford Loan was unsubsidized, the student or the parents are still responsible for all accrued interest.)

CONSOLIDATING STUDENT LOANS

Federally subsidized education loans have their variable interest rates reset every July 1. That's an important date for borrowers because it presents an opportunity to refinance outstanding debt at lower rates if interest costs are headed down, or a deadline to watch if rates are going up.

Keep in mind that most students or parents who borrow using Stafford or PLUS loans end up with a portfolio of loans—one for each year of college. The lender may be the same institution, or for various reasons there may be four different sources for the funds for each academic year. And because the interest rate is variable, rates may be different on each note.

The regulations for federal loans allow borrowers to "consolidate" several or all outstanding educational notes into a single fixed-rate loan; you are refinancing the outstanding balance and locking in at a fixed rate. The new interest rate is set at a weighted average of the rates on the existing loans, rounded up to the nearest $1/8$ of a percent.

Consolidating does not always make sense. Consider these points:

- You should find out the numbers and consult your financial adviser to make sure that the resulting new loan will not be more costly than what you have now. You only get to consolidate existing loans once; although it is impossible to precisely predict interest rates, you may be able to make an educated guess about the general direction of rates and choose to hold off rewriting the loan for a year.

- It may not make sense to consolidate if you have just a few years remaining on a loan if that causes you to spread out the repayment term and pay more interest (unless you want to reduce your monthly payments even though the total cost will be higher).

- If you are in the six-month grace period after the end of college before loan payments begin (under certain types of loan) you don't have to make a decision on consolidation until just before those payments begin. In most cases that extends your decision period six months past July 1 to January 1 of the following calendar year.

Most federal student loans can be consolidated, including Stafford, PLUS, Perkins, Federal Nursing, and Health Education Assistance loans.

As with most other federal loan programs, there are both direct and FFEL sources for consolidation loans. Direct Consolidation Loans are made by the U.S. Department of Education, and repayment is made to the federal government. FFEL consolidation loans come from banks and other lending institutions, and repayment is made to the lender or to a servicing agency it appoints.

The maximum term for a consolidation loan is thirty years, and there is no prepayment penalty.

STUDENT LOAN TRACKING WEB SITES

You can visit the National Student Loan Data System (NSLDS) Web site at *www.nslds.ed.gov* to see a listing of loans and other federal student aid you or your student has received. Personal information is protected by your Social Security number and the PIN issued to the student as part of the FAFSA process.

If you have received a Direct Loan, you can visit the Direct Loan Servicing Web site at *www.dl.ed.gov* for information about your account.

To track the processing of an online application for a Consolidation Loan, visit the Web site *www.loanconsolidation.ed.gov*.

chapter 10

BORROWING AGAINST THE EQUITY IN YOUR HOME

In the best of situations and for the most disciplined of borrowers, the equity in your own home can provide an inexpensive and easy-to-access source of funding for college. Rates for a secured loan are usually lower than they are for ordinary consumer credit, and the interest you pay may be tax-deductible: most borrowers can deduct the interest on up to $100,000 borrowed in an equity loan or line of credit.

But—and consider this one of the biggest red flags in this book—in the worst of situations and for borrowers who are not in the best financial shape, borrowing against the value of your home can be a very dangerous and ill-advised strategy.

In the starkest of terms: If you default on the loan you could end up losing your home. Or if the value of your home declines, you could find yourself "upside-down" on the loan: the sale price of the home would not be enough to cover the outstanding balance on the primary mortgage plus the equity loan. If you were to sell the house, you might have to write a check at the closing instead of receiving one.

Equity is the portion of the value of your home that is above the amount that is mortgaged or otherwise owned by others or owed to others. For example, if your home is worth $300,000 and you owe the bank $200,000, your equity in the home is $100,000. (Put another way, if you were to sell the home for its full value in that situation, you would walk away with $100,000 minus the cost of selling.)

We'll discuss the pluses and minuses in a moment, but first let's define the two types of equity borrowing.

HOME EQUITY LINE OF CREDIT

This is a revolving credit line, much like you receive with an ordinary credit card. You can choose the amount of money you want to take out and there are various schedules for repayment of interest and principal.

Homeowners may receive a checkbook or a debit card that draws on the equity. Some lenders tack on a transaction charge each time you draw on the line; that may not matter much if you are only using the line for a twice-yearly tuition payment, but you should be aware of all costs involved.

The process begins with an appraisal of your home. Most lenders then set a credit limit calculated from a percentage of the appraised value minus the amount owed on the principal mortgage.

Here's the way it might work if the lender sets a credit limit percentage of 80 percent:

Appraised value of the home	$300,000
Credit limit percentage	x .80
Credit limit	**$240,000**
Balance owed on mortgage	−$200,000
Available equity credit	**$40,000**

In a hot real estate market, where home values are on the rise and homes are easily sold, lenders may be more lenient about the percentage of the value of the home they are willing to give you. In a cool market, the percentage may shrink.

How an Equity Line of Credit Works

Because this is a secured loan—the lender is somewhat protected because it can always sell your house out from under you or collect from your insurance company in the case of fire or other damage—there is less emphasis on investigating your ability to repay the loan. Depending on the lender, though, you may be asked to provide proof of income, and the credit limit percentage may be adjusted up or down based on your credit history.

Depending on the economic climate, banks and other lenders may be chasing after homeowners with cash in their hands, or they may be more conservative. In times when lenders are eager to loan they may waive most or all of the up-front fees. In 2005, a combination of a steady rise in the value of homes and historically low mortgage interest rates saw many institutions offering equity loans without any charge to the borrower.

At other times you may be asked to pay fees, including:

- A charge for a professional appraisal of the value of your home. (If you bought your home not long ago or otherwise have a recent appraisal, you may be able to have the lender accept that evaluation.)

- An application fee, which is merely added profit for the lender for performing the work it is set up to do anyway.

- Points, which is a way for the lender to collect interest up-front; one point is equal to 1 percent of the amount borrowed or the credit limit. If you are comparing a loan that requires payment of points to one that does not, you should see a lower interest rate if you are prepaying interest.

- Closing costs, including attorney fees, title searches, title insurance, recording fees at local government offices, and special mortgage taxes.

The lender will record its interest in the home on deeds or other records held in your locality to prevent you from selling the home to someone else before the loan is paid off. You will also have to add the lender as a beneficiary to your homeowners' insurance so that they are protected. (Issuers of equity loans and second mortgages are generally second-in-line behind the primary mortgage company when it comes to collecting from the insurance company; the homeowner is last in line behind creditors.)

There may even be some terms of the loan that require you to maintain the value of the property through scheduled maintenance and repair (which you should be doing anyway). And some lenders may insist that the home remain as your principal dwelling; if you move elsewhere and rent out the property to someone else, the loan may become immediately due.

Some plans are open-ended, meaning that as long as you own the home and keep current on interest payments, the account is active.

Other equity lines have a fixed "draw period"; at the end of this period— a typical term is ten years—you will not be able to borrow more money and must begin paying off the principal as well as the interest.

Another form of equity line of credit calls for the outstanding balance to be paid off in full at the end of the draw period, while others give the borrower the right to "renew" the loan at the end of the draw period, although interest rates and other terms might change.

If the loan requires full repayment at the end of a specific period of time, you will have to come up with a "balloon payment" from one source or another. You may be able to take out a new equity loan for the balance; you may have to take money from other investments you have; or you may be forced to sell the home to pay the creditor.

Interest Rates on Equity Lines of Credit

Most equity lines use variable interest rates; the agreement between lender and borrower ties the rate to a published index such as the prime rate or the U.S. Treasury Bill rate. The rate can be set to exactly mirror the index, or might be something like "prime minus 1 percent" or "LIBOR plus 2 percent." (LIBOR is an international index, the London InterBank Offered Rate, used by some lenders.)

When the interest rate charged is above or below the index rate, the difference is called the margin.

Some lenders will offer a discounted introductory interest rate for the first few months or even for a year or more before the rate becomes set by an index. Variable rate equity lines of credit are required by federal regulations to have a cap (a ceiling on how high the rate can rise).

And some agreements permit you to change the terms of the loan so that the interest becomes fixed at a certain rate, usually a point or so higher than the current variable rate. If you see that interest rates have begun an upward climb, you should consider locking in a fixed rate if you can.

However the interest rate is structured, be sure you fully understand the process. If it is variable, find out which index it is tied to. How often can it be adjusted? What is the cap? Can the loan be converted to a fixed rate?

HOME EQUITY LOAN

Also called a second mortgage, this is a loan of a fixed amount of money for a fixed period of time. Just as with a first mortgage, you will be given a schedule of payments that includes principal and interest; by the end of the loan period of the loan the full amount due will be paid.

Qualifying for a home equity loan involves a process very similar to that of a line of credit. However, because there will be a schedule of payments that includes principal, the lender may demand proof that you have a stream of income that will allow you to make payments and that you have a good credit history.

As with a line of credit, the lender will determine what portion of the estimated equity it will issue a loan against. There may be fees charged or they may be waived, and the lender will be listed on deeds and insurance records as having a lien on a portion of the value of the home.

Interest Rates on Equity Loans

Interest rates on an equity loan may be variable or fixed, and the lender may require prepayment of points (or offer a lower interest rate if you choose that option).

When you compare the APR (annual percentage rate) for an equity loan to an equity line of credit, be careful to take into account that the number is calculated differently on the two types of loans:

- The APR for an equity loan (second mortgage) is based on the interest rate plus points and other charges.
- The APR for an equity line of credit is based on only the interest rate.

This is a distinction without a difference if the two loans you are comparing do not require payment of points and other charges. Be sure to compare apples to apples, though.

UNDERSTANDING THE RISKS

Although you are tapping into what most people would consider unearned income—the appreciation in value of a home over time—you will have to pay back the money you borrow in one way or another.

If you plan on paying off the equity line of credit or equity loan and keeping your house, you will have to pay principal and interest from money you earn or from the proceeds from other investments. If you plan on paying off an equity loan when you sell your home, you not only have to pay interest and possibly a portion of the principal during the time the loan is on the books; you also will have to pay off the outstanding balance from the proceeds of the sale. You will have that much less money for the purchase of a new home or for your retirement.

Don't pay large up-front fees for a small amount of borrowing or for a loan that will have a short life. And don't assume that just because your home went up 10 percent in value last year that it will do so again this year and next; just as with most other legitimate investments, real estate values tend to rise over time but are subject to cycles that may include slowed growth and even declines.

Some experts predict that the real estate price "bubble" will burst in coming years, resulting in a significant—though not permanent—reduction in home values. Economists call this a "correction" in prices; you might call it a disaster if you ended up owing more than your home is worth or losing all of the equity you thought you had for future purposes like retirement.

COMPARING EQUITY LINES OF CREDIT AND EQUITY LOANS

Be sure to take the time to read all of the fine print in any offer for an equity line of credit or an equity loan. The most straightforward situation is an offer in which you are not asked to pay any up-front costs.

On page 100 you'll find a checklist you can use to compare two or more equity loan offerings. If the information is not readily available to you, ask the lender to help you fill out the form. In the process, the lender may see that you have a better offer from someone else and may adjust some of the elements to become more attractive to you.

	Offer A	Offer B	Offer C
INTEREST			
Fixed APR	%	%	%
Variable APR	%	%	%
* Index used			
* Margin			
* How often are rates adjusted?			
* Is there a discount from the index, and if so, when is it removed from rate?			
* Interest rate cap			
* Interest rate floor			
TIME PERIODS			
* Draw period			
* Repayment period			
INITIAL FEES			
* Application fee			
* Appraisal fee			
* Points			
* Closing costs			
REPAYMENT DURING DRAW PERIOD			
* Interest and principal payments			
* Interest-only payments			
* Fully amortizing payments			
REPAYMENT WHEN DRAW PERIOD ENDS			
* Balloon payment			
* Renewal of loan offered?			
* Refinancing of balance by lender?			

chapter 11

TRADING MILITARY SERVICE FOR COLLEGE TUITION

One way to go to college free, or for nearly nothing, is to take advantage of one of several plans offered by the U.S. military and the National Guard. You can receive benefits prior to enrollment in college and earn an income or forgiveness of loans, or both, by agreeing to serve in the armed forces.

That's the good news. The more difficult part of the offer is the fact that in the current state of the world, members of the National Guard may be called up for service in the Middle East or elsewhere at almost any time, and graduates of Army, Navy, Marine Corps, and Air Force programs may be dispatched to war zones or other unfriendly places once their diploma is in hand.

The theory is a good one: You will be rewarded for your volunteer commitment to serving your country, and the armed services will receive a steady stream of well-educated, mature recruits. Whether this deal is right for you is a matter that should be decided only after some careful research and reflection.

Consult with high school guidance counselors and take the time to study any contract you are offered by military recruiters. It is the job of the recruiter to supply a certain number of candidates per month; at best, their advice is colored by their desire to reach their quota, and at worst they may not give full information about obligations and requirements.

For the right sort of person, the tradeoff of a period of eligibility for active duty (and the chances of being mobilized for overseas duty for periods up to a year or more) may well be worth the tens of thousands of dollars in educational aid offered to members of the National Guard. For others, it may be a bad or uncomfortable fit.

NATIONAL GUARD COLLEGE PLANS

The Army National Guard College Plan is aimed at high school students who are about to apply for college. Those accepted as recruits apply for admission at colleges in their home state. The traditional training obligation is one weekend per month and two full weeks in the summer, although some units may place greater demands on those who have signed up for the program.

Benefits include pay for drill time, expense allowances, and a set of education benefits that include monthly payments to the student under the Montgomery GI Bill, a supplementary monthly payment called a GI Bill Kicker, eligibility for Federal Tuition Assistance Programs, a student loan repayment program, and more.

Students who sign up in high school receive free SAT, CLEP, or GRE testing and Reserve Officers' Training Corps (ROTC) scholarships. Once enrolled, they are eligible not only for college credit for military training and job experience but also for leadership training and officer commissioning opportunities as well as state tuition programs and state-funded education incentives where available.

Although the programs generally guarantee availability of funds for all four years of college (and sometimes graduate school), it is also possible that members of the National Guard will be called to active service and be required to take a leave of absence from college to fulfill military duties. That is, in fact, what has happened in recent years to many members of the Guard during the conflicts in Iraq and Afghanistan.

For information about the GI Bill, state educational incentives, and other National Guard Education benefits, consult *www.virtualarmory.com* or call the ARNG Education Support Center at (866) 628-5999.

RESERVE OFFICER TRAINING CORPS

Enlistment in ROTC represents a formal commitment by incoming college students to become officers in the U.S. Army, Marine Corps, Navy, and the Air Force upon graduation. There are ROTC programs at more than 1,000 colleges and universities across the country.

Students take a full course load in their chosen field of study, plus a number of military science courses that provide special training for officers. Students are also required to attend military drills, labs, and other training, and wear their uniforms on campus once a week. There is additional training during summer breaks (including midshipmen cruises for members of the Naval ROTC).

Each of the four branches of the military that offer ROTC offer four-year scholarships that include full tuition, books, fees, and a monthly tax-free stipend. Some shorter scholarships are also offered for students who join while already in college. There are also some specialty scholarships for students enrolled in health-related courses of studies.

Students who receive an Army ROTC scholarship or enter the Army ROTC Advanced Course must agree to serve full-time in the Army for three years; scholarship winners must serve for four years. Depending on the needs of the Army and other criteria, some cadets are allowed to serve part-time in the U.S. Army Reserve or Army National Guard while pursuing a civilian career after graduation.

Naval ROTC college graduates typically enter into the service as midshipmen with military service obligations of eight years. Scholarship midshipmen must serve at least four of those years in active duty status while those who enroll as college program midshipmen must serve at least three years of active duty service if they accept a commission. Marine Corps college program midshipmen are obligated to three and a half years of active duty if they accept a commission.

Upon graduation, Air Force ROTC cadets under contract must accept a commission as a second lieutenant in the Air Force. Most cadets are obligated to four years of active duty. Pilots are required to serve ten years on active duty, and navigators must serve for six.

ROTC includes nearly 150 "host" institutions where a military detachment is physically located and conducting classes, and more than 1,000 "crosstown" schools are affiliated. Students who enroll at a crosstown school will have to travel to the other school for their military training.

For a chart outlining the details of different ROTC programs, and links to more information, go to *www.todaysmilitary.com/app/tm/get/collegehelp/rotc/rotcglance*. Other sites include:

- U.S. Army—*www.armyrotc.com* or (800) 872-7682

- U.S. Navy/Marine Corps—*https://www.nrotc.naval.mil* or (800) 628-7682

- U.S. Air Force—*www.afrotc.com* or (334) 953-2091

Scholarships for Family of Members of the Military

Many states offer special educational assistance to children of members of the armed services on active duty. Other programs assist the surviving children of members of the armed forces killed in action. Consult college financial aid officers for details. The federal methodology for EFC, as calculated from the FAFSA, also gives some preference on aid to military dependents.

Private sources of aid include the Scholarships for Military Children Program, which offers assistance through the operations of the Defense Commissary Agency worldwide. For information, consult *www.militaryscholar.org*.

chapter 12

FINANCIAL AID METHODOLOGY

I've pointed out several times already how those of us in the vast middle class are literally caught in between. We're not so rich that we can write out a $30,000 check each year for tuition, room, and board without giving it a second thought. And we're not so poor that the federal government and private sources of funding will open their generous—but nevertheless limited—vaults to pay some or all of the cost of college for our children.

If you choose to pay your own college bills in one way or another, you should concentrate on ways to reduce the cost and build up your savings and tax credits.

On the other hand, if you are counting on receiving grants and scholarships, the bottom line for all of the hard work outlined in this book should be to reduce one number to the lowest amount possible. That number is the Expected Family Contribution (EFC), which is calculated by the U.S. Department of Education based on the information provided in the FAFSA.

Whatever your situation, you will still be eligible for unsubsidized loans, scholarships based on academics and good citizenship, and various tax credits and allowances.

But simply put: If your EFC is high, the amount of financial aid you will be offered will be low.

THE FEDERAL METHODOLOGY

A computer under the direction of the U.S. Department of Education crunches the numbers on the FAFSA, assigning different values to various assets, liabilities, and the family situation to calculate the Expected Family Contribution. The Federal Need Analysis Methodology—commonly referred to as the federal methodology—is set by law.

In theory, there are two propositions that underlie the calculation of the EFC:

1. When it comes to paying for college, parents are expected to pay as much as they can afford.

2. The student is expected to contribute an even higher proportion of any assets held in his or her own name.

And then there is a third piece of the pie, something that exists outside of the computer's ability to assign a number: special circumstances. The EFC is based on a family's current finances, not on its financial history over time, and not on expected increases or decreases in coming years. And though the FAFSA asks questions about marital status and touches on medical expenses, it cannot take into account all of life's events: divorce, illness, death, loss of job, loss of income, or other happenings.

And so, here's a third important point:

3. If your life situation does not translate easily to a sheaf of papers or a computer form, get in touch with the financial aid office of all schools where your student has applied or has been accepted. Send a letter, with documentation, that augments the information on the FAFSA as filed. And specifically ask the college to adjust its financial aid offer.

The EFC is based on a combination of factors:

- The family income, as reflected in the modified adjusted gross income
- The assets of the family, excluding the home
- Investments held by the parents
- Investments held in the name of the student

Before the EFC is calculated, adjustments are made to take into account certain tax credits and benefits taken by the parents or students, certain untaxed income, and the number of other children in the family who will be in college at the same time.

How the Student's Assets Are Allocated

If your child has managed to put aside $100,000 in earnings from his lemonade stand or from her personal investments in Chicago Mercantile Exchange frozen pork belly futures, the federal methodology is going to say—in an electronic sort of way—"aha!" and ask the student to start writing checks to the college bursar's office.

The same goes for children whose well-meaning parents, grandparents, other relatives, and friends of the family have given money that is listed in the student's own name: UGMA and UTMA accounts, savings accounts, and piggybanks. The standard formula calls for students to contribute 35 percent of their assets each year.

If a child started out with $100,000, and leaving aside any interest or dividends earned on the investment, the contribution would be something like this:

- Freshman year: as much as $35,000 of the $100,000

- Sophomore year: as much as $22,750 of the remaining $65,000

- Junior year: as much as $14,787 of the remaining $42,250

- Senior year: as much as $9,612 of the remaining $27,463

The bottom line is that the student would be expected to pay nearly $82,000 from savings, which essentially is full freight for four years of college at most institutions of higher education.

Are you thinking that perhaps your student would be better off making a gift of that money to you a few years before college, and then receiving a gift from you after graduation? Or perhaps the student might want to fund a retirement account at age sixteen. Done properly, either is a good idea. Consult a tax preparer or accountant for specific advice.

How the Parents' Assets Are Allocated

In the government's infinite wisdom, recognition is given to the fact that parents have expenses other than those of their college-bound student. You know, things like a mortgage or rent, utilities, health care, and food for the table.

The basic formula calls for parents to contribute 5.6 percent of their assets (not including the value of the family home, retirement funds, and some other exclusions) to college for one child. The percentage goes down a bit if there is more than one child in college at the same time and goes up a bit if parents have certain types of investments or deductions from income. The percentage is also effectively reduced based on the age of the parents; the older they are, the larger the portion of assets protected from allocation to college. The thinking here is that older parents will have greater need for their savings when they retire.

Let's assume that a pair of relatively young parents have that same $100,000 nest egg (not set aside as an IRA or other retirement fund). Under the basic federal methodology, the annual contribution (without taking into account interest or dividends earned on that money) would be:

- Freshman year: as much as $5,600 of the $100,000

- Sophomore year: as much as $5,286 of the remaining $94,400

- Junior year: as much as $4,990 of the remaining $89,114

- Senior year: as much as $4,711 of the remaining $79,412

The bottom line is that parents with $100,000 in savings would be expected to contribute about $20,588 for four years of college at most institutions of higher education.

So What Have We Learned?

Saving for your child's education is a good thing. Putting the money in your child's name is probably not.

Consult a financial adviser or a tax accountant as early in your child's life as you can to set up 529 Plans (which are not considered the child's assets) and other investments that are to your best advantage. And if as you read this page you have a significant amount of money listed in your child's name, you may want to consult with your accountant about legal ways to transfer the funds to shelter them from the EFC.

INDEPENDENT STUDENTS

It's not easy for a student to be able to claim to be totally independent of his or her parents. Colleges will assume that a child is dependent upon his or her parents, and will use the family's financial information in determining financial aid, unless the student meets certain criteria. A child cannot simply make a declaration of nondependency, nor is a parent's refusal to provide support enough to give the student independence when it comes to applying for aid.

There are, though, some specific exceptions to this rule that the federal government (and thus the college aid office that is using federal aid money) uses. A student is deemed independent of parents if he or she meets one of these conditions:

- is orphaned
- is a ward of the court
- is at least twenty-four years of age
- is married
- has a dependent child
- is enrolled in graduate or professional school
- is a veteran of the U.S. Armed Forces

There are also some unusual circumstances that may earn an exception but will probably require an appeal to the financial aid office:

- a student whose parents live in another country and are unable to provide financial support
- a student who has been granted refugee status by the U.S. Immigration Service and whose parents live in another country
- a student whose parents are incarcerated, or a student whose parents have been served with a restraining order barring contact

THE INSTITUTIONAL METHODOLOGY

Colleges can use an alternate methodology, called the institutional methodology, to calculate the expected contribution from families, or to come up with a factor to adjust the federal methodology. The institutional methodology is actually tougher on family assets than is the federal formula.

Many colleges will ask parents and their student to file a CSS/Profile form in addition to the FAFSA; some will also ask for additional documentation. The tougher calculation places different weights on certain assets and expenses including medical costs, and also takes into account the value of the family home (the value minus outstanding mortgages and loans).

That doesn't mean that a school that uses an institutional methodology will offer less in aid than one that sticks to the federal methodology. It does mean that the same family may receive different offers from different schools even if the cost of attendance is the same.

A BIG ENDOWMENT MAY NOT MEAN A LARGER OFFER

The size of a college's endowment (its available pool of money raised from alumni and its own investments) obviously has an impact on the amount of money available for scholarships and grants. But that does not automatically translate into a boost to financial aid for all applicants.

Some of the endowment money may be used for construction of buildings and other facilities, and some schools choose to offer a larger number of all-expenses-paid scholarships to needy and academically exceptional students.

TAKING THE FM AND IM OUT FOR A SPIN

You can estimate your EFC using both the federal methodology (FM) and the institutional methodology (IM) *before* you go through all of the trouble of filling out a FAFSA by visiting *www.collegeboard.com* and searching for "federal methodology."

I plugged in some average numbers—an *adjusted* gross income of about $70,000, one child in college, just a few thousand dollars in savings held by the parents and the student—and then used two different answers to the key institutional methodology question, which asks for the home equity value (value of the home minus any outstanding mortgages and debts).

With a modest $100,000 in home equity, the two numbers were:

Federal Methodology:

Parents' Contribution for Student	$10,348
Student's Contribution	$2,830
Total Estimated FM Contribution	**$13,178**

Institutional Methodology:

Parents' Contribution for Student	$5,085
Student's Contribution	$3,869
Total Estimated IM Contribution	**$8,954**

Now let's look at the results if this family had two children in college at the same time, using the same numbers. Here are the results for one child, based on his or her modest income and savings; the parental contribution for the second child would be about the same while the student's contribution might be slightly higher or lower depending on how much the child had socked away in savings:

Federal Methodology:

Parents' Contribution for Student	$5,734
Student's Contribution	$2,830
Total Estimated FM Contribution	**$8,564**

Institutional Methodology:

Parents' Contribution for Student	$3,043
Student's Contribution	$ 3,869
Total Estimated IM Contribution	**$6,912**

As you can see, the estimated contributions of the parents are reduced if there is more than one student in college at the same time. However, each student's contribution remains unchanged.

Here is one more set of numbers. In this case I have boosted the family's home equity from a modest $100,000 to a more substantial $500,000; many people who have owned their homes for ten years or more have seen the value of their residence rise sharply. The trap here is that this is a profit on paper only, unless you are willing to sell your home. The adjusted numbers, for a family with one child in college and all other entries the same as listed earlier, are:

Federal Methodology:

Parents' Contribution for Student	$10,348
Student's Contribution	$2,830
Total Estimated FM Contribution	**$13,178**

Institutional Methodology:

Parents' Contribution for Student	$25,085
Student's Contribution	$ 3,869
Total Estimated IM Contribution	**$28,954**

The results here show how much effect home equity has on the institutional methodology. A family with a modest income and a home that has risen in value with the real estate market is essentially priced out of the market for most financial aid.

As we have already learned, it does not help for the child to have much money under his or her name. Both formulas go right after the student's savings and income—and, as mentioned earlier, the institutional methodology is even more aggressive here.

It is also obvious that having a large home equity value will also have a major impact on the institutional methodology (it is not considered in the federal methodology). You may want to consult with a financial adviser and your tax accountant to investigate ways to tap into your home equity in ways that increase your debt-to-value ratio. And you may also want to apply to colleges that rely only on the federal methodology.

Colleges have a bit of leeway in adjusting the EFC from the federal methodology and more flexibility in dealing with unusual situations when basing financial aid decisions on the institutional methodology. And in any case, private colleges have complete control over special grants and scholarships from their own resources.

Princeton University began a trend in 2001 by eliminating all need-based loans, replacing them with grants. Harvard University, blessed with a huge endowment, has announced it would not ask for any contribution from parents making less than $40,000 per year, and sharply decreased the amount expected from those earning less than $60,000.

If your EFC prices you out of financial aid because of an unusual situation, such as a high home equity, an unusually large one-time salary bonus or capital gain, or just about anything that does not fit neatly into a multiple-choice form, it may be worthwhile to send a letter to the financial aid office.

Explain any unusual real estate situations in your area; for example, some regions have seen extremely high run-ups in value of all homes. An appeal that says, "Although our home has gone up in value, we have no option to borrow against that equity and pay off the loan from our present income, or to sell the home and move to a less-expensive neighborhood."

Or give the details of unusual financial situations: your company recently bought out fifteen years of accumulated but unused vacation time, for example.

And finally, as we'll explain later, keep in mind that the EFC is a fixed number, while the cost of attendance at college varies greatly from college to college. If your EFC is $15,000 and you are looking at College A, which costs $15,001, and College B, which costs $28,000, you are not likely to receive any financial aid for the first school, but are eligible for as much as $13,000 at the second school.

SCAM ALERT

One of the downsides of our information age is that it gives new avenues to an old art: the scammer, the grifter, the electronic thief. In a nutshell, never respond to a phone call or an e-mail asking for financial information or soliciting money unless you are absolutely certain that the caller is legitimate.

In most cases, applications for federal and state grants and loan programs are made through the FAFSA. Anyone calling you and claiming to be representing a federal agency or a private lender should not be asking you for information contained on that form; they should have that data in front of them. In some cases you may be contacted and asked to verify or confirm information from the form, but you should not be asked on the phone or over the Internet to provide details of your banking accounts or investments.

If you have the slightest doubt about the legitimacy of a caller, ask for the person's name, the name of the agency or company he or she claims to represent, and the company's telephone number. Tell the caller you will return the call at another time, and then call the college's financial aid office or your bank or the U.S. Department of Education to confirm whether the call is for real. If you have caller ID on your telephone line, make a note of the phone number from the incoming call.

In 2005, one particular scam involved someone calling students or parents and claiming to be a representative of the U.S. Department of Education. The caller was delivering what seemed to be a heck of a deal: replacement of outstanding federal student loans with an $8,000 grant. Along the way, though, the scammer also asked for bank account numbers so a processing fee could be charged.

The federal agency advises that it has no such program to replace loans with grants, and in any case, there is no processing fee charged to apply for or obtain federal educational grants.

If you do end up giving information to a caller or e-mailer and fear that you have been improperly approached, here are some steps to take:

- Immediately contact your bank. Explain the situation and ask that the account be monitored for unauthorized withdrawals, or that the account be closed and proceeds transferred to a new account.

- Report any fraud to the U.S. Department of Education's Office of Inspector General hotline at (800) 647-8733 or by e-mail at *oig.hotline@ed.gov.*

- Report fraud to the Federal Trade Commission (FTC) through its hotline at (877) 382-4357 or file an online report at *www.ftc. gov/scholarshipscams.*

- Notify your local police about the incident. Impersonating a federal officer is a crime, as is identity theft.

For information about preventing financial aid scams, visit *www. studentaid.ed.gov/lsa.* For further advice about how to avoid identity theft, consult *www.ed.gov/misused.*

chapter 13

FIGURING OUT THE FAFSA

The doorway to nearly all federal grant and loan programs and most state and institutional (direct from the college or university) funding is through the Free Application for Federal Student Aid, universally referred to as the FAFSA form.

Some programs are even more demanding of information, requiring an additional privately managed document, the CSS/Profile. And depending on your particular circumstances, you may also be asked to provide specific additional information about your investments and sources of income. We'll discuss the CSS/Profile in Chapter 14.

THE KEY TO THE VAULT

For most students, the quest for financial aid begins with the FAFSA. Throughout this chapter I will be speaking primarily to the parent or guardian; be aware, though, that the student is also responsible for filling out the portion of the form that relates to his or her assets and earnings. In most families it probably works like this: the parents and student work together to answer the student-only questions, and then the parents work on the rest of the form. As a parent you have no obligation to disclose all of your finances to your child, but you do have to do so to the U.S. Department of Education, at least if you want to be considered for financial aid.

You can obtain a printed copy of the form through high school guidance counselors, from many colleges and universities, and directly from the U.S. Department of Education. It's a good idea to hold one in your hands and read it to get an idea of the sort of information it demands. But when it comes time to fill out the form, the easiest and fastest way to do so is through the government's online Web sites: *www.fafsa.ed.gov* and the more general *www. studentaid.ed.gov* site, which explains many available federal programs and offers entrance to the FAFSA site.

WARNING!

There are some for-profit companies that will offer to assist you in filling out the FAFSA, and a few have Web sites that are very similar to the government's site. For example, *www.fafsa.com* takes you to a private company's operation, which offers to help you submit a FAFSA for a not insignificant fee. Remember the name of the form: it's the *Free Application for Federal Student Aid*. If you truly need assistance with the form, you should be able to obtain it through high school guidance counselors, the U.S. Department of Education's free Federal Student Aid Information Center at (800) 433-3243 or (319) 337-5665, and from some college financial aid offices.

Applicants for financial aid can file a FAFSA by hand, filling in the form and mailing it to the processing center. Filling in the form by hand may require more than an hour.

But if you have access to a computer, you will save time and possibly avoid rejection of the form due to errors by filling in the form over the Internet through the official government portal (*www.fafsa.ed.gov*) and submitting it electronically.

Using the Internet has several advantages:

1. There is built-in help for every page of the form; click on the Help icon for further explanation of questions.

2. You can fill out the form a section at a time, saving your work in progress and returning later. Information saved in progress is kept in storage for retrieval and editing for forty-five days. If you do not file the form within that period, you will have to start a new application.

3. Worksheets that are linked to the form can be used to calculate the answers to some of the financial questions, and the resulting numbers are automatically inserted into the FAFSA you are working on.

4. Based on some of the answers you give to questions, the computer will skip over areas that are not relevant to your personal situation or your finances.

5. Before the form is completed, the computer at the other end of the connection will proofread your form and check the math, alerting you to omissions, errors, and contradictory answers.

6. Filing the form electronically will shorten the processing time by as much as two weeks as well as avoid delays caused by the postal service.

7. Once you have filed electronically, you can easily re-enter the site to correct, change, or update information.

8. In subsequent years you can begin the process with much of the background information automatically filled in from the original filing.

If you don't have a computer with an Internet connection, you should be able to arrange for use of a machine at a friend or acquaintance's home, at the student's high school, or at a public library. Be aware that if you use a public machine, there may be a risk that some of your private information may be observed or recorded by others. One step you can take to protect data is to shut down the Internet browser after you have completed your work in order to clear the "cache" (pronounced "cash") of recent work.

Deadlines and Details

The FAFSA for the coming academic year can be filed between January 1 and June 30 of the overlapping calendar year. That means, for example, that the 2006–2007 FAFSA (which covers the academic year from July 1, 2006, through June 30, 2007) can be mailed or electronically filed no earlier than January 1, 2006, and no later than midnight (Central Daylight Time) on June 30 of that same year.

Corrections to forms filed on the Web must be submitted by midnight Central Daylight Time in the middle of September; for 2006, the date was September 18.

It's probably not a good idea to wait until the last possible date and minute to file a FAFSA anyway, because if there is a problem with any critical piece of information, the form may be rejected after the deadline.

Warning: Some schools may ask for all of your financial information on a date before the final FAFSA deadline. Or the college may require that the form be submitted *and* processed by a certain date, in which case you will need to include sufficient time in advance of the submission deadline. Be sure to read all application requirements and call financial aid offices if you have any questions.

If you file online, the computer will display a confirmation page after you have electronically signed the form using your PIN. The confirmation includes a code number; you should print out the page or record the number for your records in case there is any doubt about the date of submission. The code number is twenty-two characters long for the initial submission and includes within it the date and time the form was received. If you file a correction, the number expands to thirty characters in length.

There's another number associated with a successfully submitted FAFSA. A Data Release Number (DRN) is included on the bottom left corner of the

Student Aid Report (SAR), which you will receive several weeks after you file the FAFSA. The DRN is necessary if you contact the Federal Student Aid Information Center to make corrections to your mailing address or your school list, and it is necessary in order to release FAFSA data to schools you did not select on your original form.

If you fill out the FAFSA online but do not have a PIN or choose not to sign the form electronically, the final step in the online process is to print out a signature page, which will be prefilled with a student ID made up of a code for the type and year of the application, your Social Security number, and the first two letters of your last name. The form must be signed by the student and at least one parent if the student is a dependent; for a renewal or a correction of a previously filed FAFSA, the parent needs to sign the page only if information about the parent has been changed.

However you sign and submit the form, you are agreeing to the following:

- Federal student financial aid will be used only to pay the cost of attending a school of higher education.

- The student will not receive a Federal Pell Grant for more than one school during the same academic year.

- The student or parent are not in default on a federal student loan and do not owe a refund of a federal student grant.

- The financial aid office of the college you or the student attends will be notified if a borrower goes into default on a federal student loan after the FAFSA is submitted.

- You and your student give permission to the U.S. Department of Education to verify income and other data reported on the FAFSA with the Internal Revenue Service and other federal agencies.

And just for the record, intentionally providing false or misleading information could be punished by a fine of as much as $20,000 or a prison sentence or both.

Planning Ahead

The FAFSA requests information from students applying for college and from their parents if the students are dependent upon them, as defined by the U.S. Department of Education.

Get yourself organized before you begin the worksheet or the FAFSA itself. Most applicants—students and their parents—need the following information at hand:

- **Social Security number.** Both you and your student need to have a Social Security number. This is a requirement for all U.S. citizens and all legal residents of the U.S. You can obtain information about applying for an SSN at *www.ssa.gov.*

- **State driver's license number.** It's not a requirement, but the FAFSA does ask the question. Some states track student applicants using this number.

- **Current federal income tax return or underlying documents.** If you or your student has already filed the tax return for the previous calendar year, you will be able to quickly retrieve the precise answers to tax-related questions. If the return has not yet been filed, you will have to make estimates based on W-2s, 1099s, and other documents received from employers, banks, investment companies, and other sources. In most cases, these financial institutions are required to get tax information to taxpayers by the last day of January following the end of the tax year. If you do file a FAFSA based on estimates, you are required to update the form once you and your student have the actual returns; you may also be asked to submit copies of the return to college financial aid offices once they are available.

- **Personal Identification Number (PIN).** If you plan to file the FAFSA online, the easiest way to "sign" the form is to use a previously issued PIN. Even if you send in a hand-filled FAFSA, having a PIN allows you to look at your processed FAFSA data online and make corrections.

The parent filling out the form and the student each need to have their own PIN. To obtain a PIN, visit *www.pin.ed.gov* and request it be sent by mail or e-mail. Remember that your PIN is the equivalent of an electronic signature; don't give it out to others.

Begin with the Worksheet

However you choose to fill out the form—on paper or online—the easiest way to get through the more than 100 questions on that form is to fill out the Pre-Application Worksheet. The worksheet helps you gather all of the necessary information and put it in an order that allows quick input into the form itself. You can see a copy of a worksheet on pages 124 to 129. You can print out a copy of the worksheet from the FAFSA Web site, and you also can obtain a copy from guidance counselors and financial aid offices.

In this chapter we will go through the 2005–2006 FAFSA on the Web Pre-Application Worksheet. Note that the worksheet (and the FAFSA itself) sometimes changes slightly from year to year based on alterations to the IRS Code or other federal programs. Some of the questions are very straightforward for most people: last name, date of birth, and the like. Some may be a bit trickier: legal residency, for example. And a few—depending on the complexity of your family finances—may require the assistance of a professional tax preparer.

STEP-BY-STEP:
THE FAFSA PRE-APPLICATION WORKSHEET

As we go through the worksheet, we'll pause at questions where the answer— for some applicants—may not be simple.

We'll begin with questions posed of the student; some of the same questions are also asked of parents or guardians.

Questions for Student Applicants

What is the student's state of legal residence?

If the student has lived in a particular state full-time for more than a year, and still lives there, that's generally sufficient to establish that state as a legal residence. It does not matter if the student earns income in another state; for example, a student living in New York with a part-time job across the border in Connecticut is still a New York resident.

2005-2006 FAFSA on the Web
Pre-Application Worksheet

Please **DO NOT** mail in this worksheet.

Before filing your *FAFSA on the Web* application we recommend that you (and one of your parents) apply for a PIN at www.pin.ed.gov. There are advantages to applying for a PIN prior to filing your application. With a PIN you are able to:

- Electronically sign your application
- Make corrections to your submitted application
- Review your processed application data on the Web

Instructions:

1. Complete this worksheet only if you plan to use *FAFSA on the Web* to apply for financial aid. You can use the completed worksheet to fill in the online FAFSA at www.fafsa.ed.gov.
2. Use this worksheet to collect your (and your parents') information before beginning your 2005-2006 online *Free Application for Federal Student Aid* (FAFSA). The worksheet does not include all questions asked on the online FAFSA, just the ones that you might not readily know.
3. Questions on this worksheet are in the same order as they appear on the online FAFSA; however, because the online FAFSA allows you to skip some questions based on your answers to earlier questions, you may not have to answer all of the questions on this worksheet.
4. In addition to completing the Pre-Application worksheet, also complete the student (and parent) Worksheets A, B, and C on page 6 before beginning your online FAFSA.

We recommend that you supply student and parent e-mail addresses when filing your *FAFSA on the Web* application. E-mail notifications are the fastest way to receive information regarding the student's application. The e-mail addresses are optional and can be left blank. All notifications will then be mailed to the student's mailing address.

All of the gray shaded questions refer to parent's information. Please read "Who is Considered a Parent" in the middle of page 3 to determine if the shaded questions should be completed.

Question	Answer
Student's Last Name	
What is the student's state of legal residence?	
Student's Social Security Number	
Are you, the student, a U.S. Citizen?	☐ Yes, I am a U.S. Citizen ☐ No, but I am an eligible noncitizen ☐ No, I am not a citizen or eligible noncitizen

Generally you are an eligible noncitizen if you are: (1) a U.S. permanent resident and you have an Alien Registration Receipt card (I-551); (2) a conditional permanent resident (I-551C); or (3) an other eligible noncitizen with an Arrival-Departure Record (I-94) from Department of Homeland Security showing any of the following designations: "Refugee", "Asylum Granted", "Parolee" (I-94 confirms paroled for a minimum of one year and status has not expired), or "Cuban-Haitian Entrant". If you are in the U.S. on an F1 or F2 student visa, or a J1 or J2 exchange visitor visa, or a G series visa (pertaining to international organizations), you must answer "No, I am not a citizen or eligible noncitizen." If you are neither a citizen nor an eligible noncitizen, you are not eligible for federal student aid. However, you may be eligible for state or college aid. If you're not sure how to answer, *FAFSA on the Web* (www.fafsa.ed.gov/help.htm) provides additional information to help you answer these questions.

Student's Alien Registration Number If you are an eligible noncitizen, enter your eight or nine digit Alien Registration Number.	A _ _ _ _ _ _ _ _
Student's marital status as of today	☐ Single, Divorced, or Widowed ☐ Married/Remarried ☐ Separated
Month and year you, the student, were married, separated, divorced or widowed	(Month and Year; e.g., 05/1995)
Did you, the student, become a legal resident of this state before January 1, 2000?	☐ Yes ☐ No
If no, what date did you, the student, become a legal resident of your state?	(Month and Year; e.g., 05/1995)
If you are male between the ages of 18 and 25 and NOT already registered with Selective Service, answer "Yes" and Selective Service will register you. All other applicants should skip to the next question.	☐ Yes ☐ No
What degree or certificate will you, the student, be working on during 2005-2006?	☐ 1st Bachelor's degree ☐ 2nd Bachelor's degree ☐ Associate degree - occupational/technical program ☐ Associate degree - general education or transfer program ☐ Certificate or diploma for completing an occupational, technical, or educational program of less than two years ☐ Certificate or diploma for completing an occupational, technical, or educational program of at least two years ☐ Teaching credential - nondegree program ☐ Graduate or professional degree ☐ Other/Undecided

Question		Answer	
What will be your, the student's, grade level when you begin the 2005-2006 school year?	❑ Never attended college and 1st year undergraduate ❑ Attended college before and 1st year undergraduate ❑ 2nd year undergraduate/sophomore ❑ 3rd year undergraduate/junior	❑ 4th year undergraduate/senior ❑ 5th year/other undergraduate ❑ 1st year graduate/professional ❑ Continuing graduate/professional or beyond	
Will you, the student, have a high school diploma or GED before you begin the 2005-2006 school year?		❑ Yes	❑ No
Will you, the student, have your first bachelor's degree by July 1, 2005?		❑ Yes	❑ No
In addition to grants, would you, the student, like to be considered for student loans (which you must pay back)?		❑ Yes	❑ No
Are you, the student, interested in work-study (employment arranged or sponsored by the institution for which you are enrolled or plan to be enrolled)?		❑ Yes	❑ No
Student's Father's Highest Educational Level Completed	❑ Middle school/Jr. High ❑ High school	❑ College or beyond	❑ Other/unknown
Student's Mother's Highest Educational Level Completed	❑ Middle school/Jr. High ❑ High school	❑ College or beyond	❑ Other/unknown
Do you, the student, have a drug conviction that will affect eligibility for aid? If you have a conviction for possessing or selling illegal drugs go to *FAFSA on the Web* (www.fafsa.ed.gov/q31wksht56.pdf). You can print a PDF version of the Drug Worksheet that walks you through a series of questions to help you determine if a drug conviction will affect your eligibility for federal aid in 2005-2006.		❑ No	❑ Yes
Were you, the student, born before January 1, 1982?		❑ **Yes**	❑ **No**
At the beginning of the 2005-2006 school year, will you, the student, be working on a master's or doctorate program?		❑ **Yes**	❑ **No**
As of today, are you, the student, married? (Answer Yes if you are separated but not divorced.)		❑ **Yes**	❑ **No**
Do you, the student, have children who receive more than half of their support from you?		❑ **Yes**	❑ **No**
Do you, the student, have dependents other than your children/spouse who live with you and receive more than half of their support from you?		❑ **Yes**	❑ **No**
Are both of your parents deceased, or are you or were you (until age 18) a ward/dependent of the court?		❑ **Yes**	❑ **No**
Are you, the student, a veteran of the U.S. Armed Forces? **Answer "No" (you are not a veteran) if you (1) have never engaged in active duty in the U.S. Armed Forces, (2) are currently an ROTC student or cadet or midshipman at a service academy, or (3) are a National Guard or Reserves enlistee activated only for training. Also answer "No" if you are currently serving in the U.S. Armed Forces and will continue to serve through June 30, 2006.** **Answer "Yes" (you are a veteran) if you (1) have engaged in active duty in the U.S. Armed Forces (Army, Navy, Air Force, Marines, or Coast Guard) or are a National Guard or Reserves enlistee who was called to active duty for purposes other than training, or were a cadet or midshipman at one of the service academies, and (2) were released under a condition other than dishonorable. Also answer "Yes" if you are not a veteran now but will be one by June 30, 2006.**		❑ **Yes**	❑ **No**
Have you, the student, completed a 2004 IRS income tax return or other income tax return?		❑ Have already completed my return ❑ Will file, but have not yet completed my return ❑ Not going to file	
What income tax return did you, the student, file or will you file for 2004?	❑ IRS 1040 ❑ IRS 1040A, 1040EZ, or 1040 TeleFile ❑ A foreign tax return	❑ A tax return for Puerto Rico, Guam, American Samoa, the U.S. Virgin Islands, the Marshall Islands, the Federated States of Micronesia, or Palau	
If you, the student, filed a 1040, were you eligible to file a 1040A or 1040EZ? In general, a person is eligible to file a 1040A or 1040EZ if he or she makes less than $100,000, does not itemize deductions, doesn't receive income from his or her business or farm, and does not receive alimony. A person is not eligible if he or she itemizes deductions, receives self-employment income or alimony, or is required to file Schedule D for capital gains. If you filed a 1040 only to claim Hope or Lifetime Learning credits, and you would have otherwise been eligible for a 1040A or 1040EZ, you should answer "Yes."		❑ Yes ❑ No ❑ Don't Know	
Please Note: Adjusted Gross Income and Taxes Paid should not be the same dollar amount. Please refer to the IRS Form line numbers referenced in each question.			
What was your, the student's (and spouse's), adjusted gross income for 2004? Adjusted Gross Income is on IRS Form 1040-line 36; 1040A-line 21; 1040EZ-line 4; or TeleFile-line I.		$	

Question	Answer
What was your, the student's (and spouse's), income tax for 2004? Income tax amount is on IRS Form 1040-line 56; 1040A-line 36; 1040EZ-line 10; or TeleFile-line K(2).	$
Enter your, the student's (and spouse's), exemptions for 2004. Exemptions are on IRS Form 1040-line 6d or 1040A-line 6d. For Form 1040EZ, if a person answered "Yes" on line 5, use EZ worksheet line F to determine the number of exemptions ($3,100 equals one exemption). If a person answered "No" on line 5, enter 01 if he or she is single, or 02 if he or she is married. For Form TeleFile, use line J(2) to determine the number of exemptions ($3,100 equals one exemption).	
How much did you, the student (and spouse), earn from working (wages, salaries, tips, etc.) in 2004? Answer these questions whether or not you, the student, filed a tax return. This information may be on your W-2 forms, or on IRS Form 1040-lines 7+12+18; 1040A-line 7; or 1040EZ-line 1. TeleFilers should use their W-2 forms.	Student $ Spouse $
What is the student's household size? Include in your (and your spouse's) household: (1) yourself (and your spouse, if you have one), and (2) your children, if you will provide more than half of their support from July 1, 2005 through June 30, 2006, and (3) other people if they now live with you, and you provide more than half of their support, and you will continue to provide more than half of their support from July 1, 2005 through June 30, 2006.	
What is the student's number in college? Always count yourself as a college student. **Do not include your parents.** Include others only if they will attend at least half time in 2005-2006 in a program that leads to a college degree or certificate.	

Who is Considered a Parent?

> If your parents are both living and married to each other, answer the questions about them.

> If your parent is widowed or single, answer the questions about that parent. If your widowed parent is remarried as of today, answer the questions about that parent **and** the person to whom your parent is married (your stepparent).

> If your parents are divorced or separated, answer the questions about the parent you lived with more during the past 12 months. If you did not live with one parent more than the other, give answers about the parent who provided more financial support during the past 12 months, or during the most recent year that you actually received support from a parent. If this parent is remarried as of today, answer the questions on the rest of this form about that parent **and** the person to whom your parent is married (your stepparent).

You **must** answer questions about your parents if you answered "No" to all dependency questions (the 7 bolded questions) listed on page 2 of this worksheet, even if you did not live with your parents. Please note: all questions related to your parents are shaded. (Note that grandparents and legal guardians are not parents.)

What is your parents' marital status as of today?	❑ Married/Remarried ❑ Single ❑ Divorced/Separated ❑ Widowed
Month and year your parents were married, separated, divorced, or widowed	(Month and Year; e.g., 05/1995)
Have your parents completed a 2004 IRS income tax return or other income tax return?	❑ Have already completed their return ❑ Will file, but have not yet completed their return ❑ Not going to file

What type of tax return did your parents file, or will they file in 2004?	❑ IRS 1040 ❑ IRS 1040A, 1040EZ, or 1040 TeleFile ❑ A foreign tax return	❑ A tax return for Puerto Rico, Guam, American Samoa, the U.S. Virgin Islands, the Marshall Islands, the Federated States of Micronesia, or Palau

If your parents have or will file a 1040, were they eligible to file a 1040A or 1040EZ? In general, a person is eligible to file a 1040A or 1040EZ if he or she makes less than $100,000, does not itemize deductions, doesn't receive income from his or her business or farm, and does not receive alimony. A person is not eligible if he or she itemizes deductions, receives self-employment income or alimony, or is required to file Schedule D for capital gains. If you filed a 1040 only to claim Hope or Lifetime Learning credits, and you would have otherwise been eligible for a 1040A or 1040EZ, you should answer "Yes."	❑ Yes ❑ No ❑ Don't Know
What was your parents' adjusted gross income for 2004? Adjusted Gross Income is on IRS form 1040-line 36; 1040A-line 21; 1040EZ-line 4; or TeleFile-line I.	$
How much did your parents earn from working (wages, salaries, tips, etc.) in 2004? Answer these questions whether or not your parents filed a tax return. This information may be on their W-2 forms, or on IRS Form 1040-lines 7+12+18; 1040A-line 7; or 1040EZ-line 1. TeleFilers should use their W-2 forms.	Father $ Mother $

Student's FAFSA Worksheet A, B and C answers

For help with answering the questions below, complete the Worksheets on **page 6**.

Student's amount from FAFSA Worksheet A	$
Student's amount from FAFSA Worksheet B	$

Question	Answer	
Student's amount from FAFSA Worksheet C	$	

The questions below ask you, the student, about your (and your parents') asset net worth.

Net worth means current value minus debt. If net worth is one million or more, report $999,999. If net worth is negative, report 0.

Investments include real estate (do not include the home you live in), trust funds, money market funds, mutual funds, certificates of deposit, stocks, stock options, bonds, other securities, Coverdell savings accounts, college savings plans, installment and land sale contracts (including mortgages held), commodities, etc. Investment value includes the market value of these investments as of today. Investment debt means only those debts that are related to the investments.

Investments do not include the home you live in, the value of life insurance, retirement plans (pension funds, annuities, noneducation IRAs, Keogh plans, etc.), and prepaid tuition plans, or cash, savings, and checking accounts.

Business and/or investment farm value includes the market value of land, buildings, machinery, equipment, inventory, etc. Business and/or investment farm debt means only those debts for which the business or investment farm was used as collateral.

Question	Answer	
As of today, what is the student's (and spouse's) total current balance of cash, savings, and checking accounts?	$	
As of today, what is the net worth of the student's (and spouse's) current investments, including real estate (not your home)?	$	Net Worth means current value minus debt
As of today, what is the net worth of the student's (and spouse's) current business and/or investment farms? Do not include a farm that a student lives on and operates.	$	Net Worth means current value minus debt
If you, the student, receive veterans' education benefits, for how many months from July 1, 2005 through June 30, 2006 will you receive these benefits?		Use 01 to 12
What VA benefits amount will you, the student, receive monthly?	$	
What is the student's father's (or stepfather's) Social Security Number?		
What is the student's father's (or stepfather's) last name?		
What is the student's father's (or stepfather's) first name initial?		
What is the student's father's (or stepfather's) date of birth?		(Month, Day, and Year; e.g., 05/15/58)
What is the student's mother's (or stepmother's) Social Security Number?		
What is the student's mother's (or stepmother's) last name?		
What is the student's mother's (or stepmother's) first name initial?		
What is the student's mother's (or stepmother's) date of birth?		(Month, Day, and Year; e.g., 05/15/58)
What is the student's parents' e-mail address? (optional)		
What is the student's parents' household size? Include in your parents' household; (1) your parents and yourself, even if you don't live with your parents, and (2) your parents' other children if (a) your parents will provide more than half of their support from July 1, 2005 through June 30, 2006, or (b) the children could answer "No" to all of the dependency questions (the 7 bolded questions) listed on page 2 of this worksheet, and (3) other people if they live with your parents, your parents provide more than half of their support, and your parents will continue to provide more than half of their support from July 1, 2005 through June 30, 2006.		
What is the student's parents' number in college? Always count yourself as a college student. **Do not include your parents.** Include others only if they will attend at least half time in 2005-2006 in a program that leads to a college degree or certificate.		
What is the student's parents' state of legal residence?		
Did the student's parents become legal residents of the state before January 1, 2000	☐ Yes	☐ No
If "No," give month and year legal residency began for the parent who has lived in the state the longest.		(Month and Year; e.g., 05/1995)
What was the amount the student's parents paid in income tax for 2004? Income tax amount is on IRS Form 1040-line 56; 1040A-line 36; 1040EZ-line 10; or TeleFile-line K(2).	$	
Enter the student's parents' exemptions for 2004 Exemptions are on IRS Form 1040-line 6d or 1040A-line 6d. For Form 1040EZ, if a person answered "Yes" on line 5, use EZ worksheet line F to determine the number of exemptions ($3,100 equals one exemption). If a person answered "No" on line 5 enter 01 if he or she is single, or 02 if he or she is married. For Form TeleFile, use line J(2) to determine the number of exemptions ($3,100 equals one exemption).		

Student's parents' FAFSA Worksheet A, B and C answers					
For help with answering the questions below, complete the Worksheets on **page 6**.					
Student's parents' amount from FAFSA Worksheet A				$	
Student's parents' amount from FAFSA Worksheet B				$	
Student's parents' amount from FAFSA Worksheet C				$	
As of today, what is the student's parents' total current balance in cash, savings, and checking accounts ?				$	
As of today, what is the net worth of the student's parents' investments, including real estate (not their home)?				$	Net Worth means current value minus debt
As of today, what is the net worth of the student's parents' current business and/or investment farms? Do not include a farm that your parents live on and operate.				$	Net Worth means current value minus debt

Federal School Codes	1st school code	2nd school code	3rd school code	4th school code	5th school code	6th school code
If you do not know the code for the school, use www.fafsa.ed.gov/fotw0405/fslookup.htm to look up the code. If you access this link prior to January 01, 2005 you will be using the 2004-2005 school code listing, which should be the same in 2005-2006. If you access this link on or after January 01, 2005 you will be using the 2005-2006 school codes.						

For each school code indicate the corresponding housing plan	1st housing	2nd housing	3rd housing	4th housing	5th housing	6th housing
	❑ on campus ❑ off campus ❑ with parent	❑ on campus ❑ off campus ❑ with parent	❑ on campus ❑ off campus ❑ with parent	❑ on campus ❑ off campus ❑ with parent	❑ on campus ❑ off campus ❑ with parent	❑ on campus ❑ off campus ❑ with parent

For the 2005-2006 academic year, please report your, the student's, enrollment status	❑ Full time ❑ 3/4 Time ❑ Half time ❑ Less than half time ❑ Not sure

If someone other than you, your spouse, or your parents completes the online FAFSA for you, that person must complete the preparer's section of the online FAFSA.

Worksheets

Calendar Year 2004

These worksheets are **solely** for the purpose of completing the Pre-Application Worksheet questions, **on page 3**, for the student and, **on page 5**, for the student's parents.

Worksheet A
Report Annual Amounts

Student/Spouse For Page 3		Parent(s) For Page 5
$	Earned income credit from IRS Form 1040—line 65a; 1040A—line 41a; 1040EZ—line 8a; or TeleFile—line L	$
$	Additional child tax credit from IRS Form 1040—line 67 or 1040A—line 42	$
$	Welfare benefits, including Temporary Assistance for Needy Families (TANF). Don't include food stamps or subsidized housing.	$
$	Social Security benefits received, for all household members as reported in student's household size (or parents' household size), that were not taxed (such as SSI). Report benefits paid to parents in the parents' column, and benefits paid directly to student in the student's column.	$

$ [ ] **Enter in Worksheet A question -- on Page 3** **Enter in Worksheet A question on Page 5--** $ [ ]

Worksheet B
Report Annual Amounts

Student/Spouse For Page 3		Parent(s) For Page 5
$	Payments to tax-deferred pension and savings plans (paid directly or withheld from earnings), including, but not limited to, amounts reported on the W-2 Form in Boxes 12a through 12d, codes D, E, F, G, H, and S.	$
$	IRA deductions and payments to self-employed SEP, SIMPLE, and Keogh and other qualified plans from IRS Form 1040—total of lines 25 + 32 or 1040A—line 17	$
$	Child support you received for all children. Don't include foster care or adoption payments.	$
$	Tax exempt interest income from IRS Form 1040—line 8b or 1040A—line 8b	$
$	Foreign income exclusion from IRS Form 2555—line 43 or 2555EZ—line 18	$
$	Untaxed portions of IRA distributions from IRS Form 1040—lines (15a minus 15b) or 1040A—lines (11a minus 11b). Exclude rollovers. If negative, enter a zero here.	$
$	Untaxed portions of pensions from IRS Form 1040—lines (16a minus 16b) or 1040A—lines (12a minus 12b). Exclude rollovers. If negative, enter a zero here.	$
$	Credit for federal tax on special fuels from IRS Form 4136—line 10—nonfarmers only	$
$	Housing, food, and other living allowances paid to members of the military, clergy, and others (including cash payments and cash value of benefits)	$
$	Veterans' noneducation benefits such as Disability, Death Pension, or Dependency & Indemnity Compensation (DIC), and/or VA Educational Work-Study allowances	$
$	Any other untaxed income or benefits not reported elsewhere on Worksheets A and B, such as workers' compensation, untaxed portions of railroad retirement benefits, Black Lung Benefits, disability, etc. Don't include student aid, Workforce Investment Act educational benefits, or benefits from flexible spending arrangements, e.g., cafeteria plans	$
$	Money received, or paid on your behalf (e.g., bills), not reported elsewhere on this form	XXXXXXXXXXXXX

$ [ ] **Enter in Worksheet B question -- on Page 3** **Enter in Worksheet B question on Page 5--** $ [ ]

Worksheet C
Report Annual Amounts

Student/Spouse For Page 3		Parent(s) For Page 5
$	Education credits (Hope and Lifetime Learning tax credits) from IRS Form 1040—line 49 or 1040A—line 31	$
$	Child support you paid because of divorce or separation or as a result of a legal requirement. Don't include support for children in your (or your parents') household.	$
$	Taxable earnings from need-based employment programs, such as Federal Work-Study and need-based employment portions of fellowships and assistantships.	$
$	Student grant and scholarship aid reported to the IRS in your (or your parents') adjusted gross income. Includes AmeriCorps benefits (awards, living allowances, and interest accrual payments), as well as grant or scholarship portions of fellowships and assistantships.	$

$ [ ] **Enter in Worksheet C question -- on Page 3** **Enter in Worksheet C question on Page 5--** $ [ ]

For financial aid purposes, the U.S. Department of Education defines residency as your "true, fixed, and permanent home." If the student has recently moved to a state for the sole purpose of attending a school, that is not considered the student's legal residence.

If there is any doubt about legal residence, contact the college's financial aid office for assistance on legalities. Some states have forms that must be filed and verified to establish a student's residency.

If the student is a foreign national, Question 18 on the FAFSA will allow entry of Canadian provinces or "Foreign Country" instead of a state.

Are you, the student, a U.S. Citizen?

The allowable answers, other than "Yes," are that the student is either an "eligible noncitizen" or "not a citizen or eligible noncitizen."

An eligible noncitizen is someone who is a permanent resident, including those with an Alien Registration Receipt (informally referred to as a "green card" and issued as Form I-151, I-551, or I-551C) or someone in possession of an Arrival-Departure Record (I-94) from the Department of Homeland Security designated as one of the following: "refugee," "asylum granted," "parolee" (with a current status and permission to reside in the United States for a minimum of one year), or "Cuban-Haitian entrant."

Applicants who are in the country on an F1 or F2 student visa, a J1 or J2 exchange visitor visa, or a G series visa related to international organizations must answer "No, I am not a citizen or eligible noncitizen."

Students who are neither a citizen nor an eligible noncitizen are not eligible for federal student aid. However, the student or family may be eligible for state or college aid.

If a student's status changes from noncitizen to citizen after a FAFSA is filed or once a student is enrolled, he or she should contact the Social Security Administration to update records and become eligible for federal financial aid. For more information on Social Security issues, contact the agency at (800) 772-1213 or visit *www.ssa.gov.*

Student's marital status as of today.

In governmentese, the key word "today" does not really mean today; it means as of the day the student will submit the FAFSA. So if a student is getting married in a week and will file the form in eight days, the correct marital status is "married." If marital status changes after a FAFSA is filed or once a student is enrolled, notify the college's financial aid office for assistance.

Married/remarried does not include people who are living together without a marriage license, unless the student's state of legal residence recognizes this as a common-law marriage. (There are about a dozen states—mostly in the south and west—that recognize common-law marriages in one way or another, although it may take a court hearing or finding to certify co-residency as equivalent to marriage.)

The question cannot be left blank.

Did you, the student, become a legal resident of this state before January 1, 20XX?

The FAFSA looks back five years for the answer to this question; the 2005–2006 form used the date of January 1, 2005. If the student moved to the state where he or she now claims legal residency more recently than five years ago, the form requires entry of the month and year residency was established.

The whole point of this particular exercise is to assist states in determining whether an applicant meets criteria for state financial aid. You cannot assume that any two states have the same definition of legal residency; contact college financial aid offices for information if necessary.

If you are male between the ages of 18 and 25 and NOT already registered with Selective Service, answer "Yes" and Selective Service will register you. All other applicants should skip to the next question.

Although the military draft was ended in 1973, the federal Selective Service System still exists. Since 1980, males over the age of eighteen have been required to register with that agency. Failure to register can result in denial of financial aid, most federal jobs, and federal job training.

Registration can be accomplished through many high schools, by calling the agency at (847) 688-6888, or over the Internet at *www.sss.gov.*

The registration requirement also applies to immigrant males (documented or undocumented). Nonimmigrant males living in the United States and in possession of a valid visa are not required to sign up. Females are not required or permitted to register.

What will be your, the student's, grade level when you begin the 20XX–20XX school year?

This awkwardly phrased question would be easier to understand if it was posed in two parts, like this:

A) When your upcoming college school year begins, will you be enrolling for the first time as an undergraduate, never having attended college anywhere else?

B) If you are returning to school, which college school year will you be in? (Not all students are enrolled full-time, and not all students complete a full college year within a calendar year. If you are going back to school for your second year of attendance but are still at the freshman or first-year undergraduate level, that is the proper grade level to select on the form.)

Will you, the student, have your first bachelor's degree by July 1, 20XX?

Answer "Yes" if you have already received your first bachelor's (undergraduate) degree or will receive it before July 1 of the current year.

In addition to grants, would you, the student, like to be considered for student loans (which you must pay back)?

Unless you are absolutely certain you will not want to take out any loans, you might as well answer "Yes" here. There is no obligation to accept any financial aid, including loans, that is offered to the student or parents.

Information supplied on the FAFSA will be released to colleges and other education institutions—that is, of course, the reason for the form's existence. Private lenders, though, will not receive all of the details of your finances unless and until you formally apply for a loan.

Are you, the student, interested in work-study (employment arranged or sponsored by the institution for which you are enrolled or plan to be enrolled)?

The Federal Work-Study Program underwrites jobs for undergraduate and graduate students with financial need; most jobs are on campus, and colleges are encouraged to offer work that is related to the student's course of study. (In truth, though, many work-study jobs are in places like the dining hall, library, or dormitory services.)

Recipients of this form of financial aid receive a paycheck from the college or university based on hours worked, up to the maximum dollar amount underwritten by the federal government for each term of a school year. The money can be used for any purpose and is *not* deducted from the tuition or room-and-board bill that must be paid before a student is enrolled.

Unless the student is certain he or she does not want to accept a work-study job, there is no harm in saying "Yes" to this question. There is no guarantee that work-study will be offered, and in any case a student can always decline any part of the financial aid package that is offered.

Student's Father's Highest Educational Level Completed/Student's Mother's Highest Educational Level Completed.

Some state scholarship programs consider the family's educational history, seeking to encourage a break in the cycle of poverty. The answer given here does not affect eligibility for federal student aid.

For this question only, "father" and "mother" refer to the student's birth parents, adoptive parents, or legal guardians. It does not apply to foster parents or stepparents.

Do you, the student, have a drug conviction that will affect eligibility for aid?

This question cannot be left blank.

If a student has never been convicted for possessing or selling illegal drugs, the answer is "No."

Otherwise, welcome to a somewhat complex world of shades of gray. A student with a conviction that remains on his or her legal record is not eligible for most aid. The best way to properly answer this question is to visit FAFSA on the Web at *www.fafsa.ed.gov* and locate and print out the Drug Worksheet, which gives guidelines on whether you can answer "Yes" or "No" to this question.

If a student is convicted of possessing or selling drugs after the FAFSA is submitted, he or she must notify the financial aid office at the college or university immediately. The student will lose eligibility and must pay back all aid received after the conviction.

In filling out the Drug Worksheet, include only federal or state convictions. Do not count any convictions that have been removed or expunged from records. Do not include any convictions that occurred before the student was age eighteen unless he or she was tried as an adult.

If the student has a conviction on the record but has successfully completed a drug rehabilitation program since the last conviction, the student can answer

"No" to the question and will be eligible for federal aid. (The federal government considers a drug rehabilitation program to be acceptable if it includes at least two unannounced drug tests and is qualified to receive funds from a federal, state, or local government or federally or state-licensed insurance company, or if it is administered by a federal, state, or local government agency or court or a federally or state-licensed hospital or clinic.)

If a student has more than two convictions for possessing drugs, or more than one conviction for selling drugs, the student is not eligible for federal student aid for the upcoming school year unless he or she successfully completes a recognized drug rehabilitation program. Students who are ineligible for federal aid may still be able to receive state or institutional aid.

If there is a recorded conviction for possessing drugs and the student has not completed a rehabilitation program, the federal government delays eligibility for federal aid as follows: one year after the date of conviction, or two years after the date of a second conviction for possession.

If there is a recorded conviction for selling drugs, eligibility is delayed for two years after the date of conviction.

Finally, if the student has convictions for both possession and sale, the eligibility date for financial aid is the *later* of the two dates on the worksheet.

A student who cannot answer "No" to the original question on the FAFSA must fill out the Drug Worksheet and mail it to the Department of Education along with the Student Aid Report form. The student must also notify the college or university of the calculated eligibility date.

If you have any uncertainty about how to fill out this form, consult a college financial aid office or an attorney. You may be able to receive free legal advice from local organizations or agencies.

Do you, the student, have children who receive more than half of their support from you?
Answer "Yes" if the student (and the student's spouse, if married) has children for which they provide at least half support. If the student or spouse is pregnant with a child expected to born before or during the school year, and if the student will provide more than half of the child's support from the date of birth through the end of the school year, the answer is also "Yes."

Do you, the student, have dependents other than your children/spouse who live with you and receive more than half of their support from you?

If another person—other than the student's spouse or children—lives with the student and will receive more than half of their support from the student through the end of the coming school year, the answer is "Yes."

Are both of your parents deceased, or are you or were you (until age 18) a ward/ dependent of the court?

A young person is considered a ward or dependent of the courts when he or she is under the protection or supervision of a legal guardian appointed by the court. A "Yes" answer here establishes the student as independent of the finances of parents.

Are you, the student, a veteran of the U.S. Armed Forces?

A student is a veteran if he or she served on active duty in the U.S. Army, Navy, Air Force, Marines, or Coast Guard. Veteran status is also granted if the student served as a member of the National Guard or Reserves and was called to service for purposes other than training, or was a cadet or midshipman at one of the service academies. The final element: the student must not have been dishonorably discharged.

The answer is "No" if the student has never served in the U.S. Armed Forces, or is currently in the U.S. Armed Forces and will still be in the service through the end of the coming school year. Veteran status is also *not* granted to a student who is currently in ROTC (Reserve Officers' Training Corps), is a cadet or midshipman at a service academy, or is a National Guard or Reserves enlistee activated only for training.

Have you, the student, completed a 20XX IRS income tax return or other income tax return?

If you had income from a job or investments above a certain level, or if you owe any special taxes—including Social Security or Medicare tax on tips you did not report to your employer, the alternative minimum tax, additional tax on a qualified retirement plan or health savings account, additional tax on a Coverdell or qualified tuition program, or any of a few dozen other liabilities to the government—you must file an income tax return. This doesn't necessarily mean you owe taxes to the government, but Uncle Sam (or at least the U.S. Department of Education) does demand a full accounting.

Even if you are not required to file, it may be to your advantage to send in a completed tax form if you had federal income tax withheld from your pay or if you qualify for the earned income credit, the additional child tax credit, or the health coverage tax credit.

If you have any doubts about whether you are required to file a form, consult a tax accountant or attorney (again, you may be able to receive free services from government agencies or local organizations) or contact the IRS.

One of the headaches of the FAFSA form is that most applicants fill it out early in the year, sometimes months before they actually file their income tax forms for the previous calendar year. The three choices here are: 1) that you have already completed the return (and thus have actual numbers from the IRS form to use on the corresponding lines of the FAFSA), 2) you will file a tax form later (in which case you will make good-faith estimates of income and tax questions posed on the FAFSA and follow up later with any necessary revisions or corrections), or 3) you will not file a return (in which case you will make good-faith estimates of income and asset questions on the FAFSA).

The federal government and colleges and universities have the right to ask applicants to verify the information provided on the FAFSA and may ask to see the actual IRS tax form once filed, or the documents used in preparing it or answering questions on the financial aid form.

What income tax return did you, the student, file or will you file for 20XX?
This is an informational question that the government can use to correlate your answer on the FAFSA to the tax form. The available answers are:

- **IRS 1040.** The standard tax form, with space for full listing of adjustments to income.

- **IRS 1040A.** A slightly simplified version of the 1040 form. The student or parent filing must earn less than $100,000 per year and not itemize deductions, not have any capital gains on investments, and not receive income from a business or farm, self-employment income, or alimony.

- **IRS 1040EZ.** An even simpler version of the 1040A with the same limitations plus a requirement that the student does not claim any dependents.

- **IRS 1040EZ TeleFile.** An electronic version of the 1040EZ, which can be filed using a touch-tone telephone.

- Foreign tax return.

- Tax return from Puerto Rico, Guam, American Samoa, the U.S. Virgin Islands, the Marshall Islands, the Federated States of Micronesia, or Palau.

If the student, student's spouse, or the parents of the student have filed or will file a foreign tax return, or a tax return from a U.S. Territory or possession, figures from that form are supposed to be converted to U.S. dollars on the date the FAFSA form is filed and used to answer questions about income and assets. The federal government uses the official exchange rates posted by the Federal Reserve Board at *www.federalreserve.gov/releases/h10/update*.

If you, the student, filed a 1040, were you eligible to file a 1040A or 1040EZ?

There is no penalty for filing the longer and more complex IRS 1040 form rather than the simpler 1040A or 1040EZ—if the student was eligible to use those forms (see the previous question)—but for the purposes of some financial aid programs, this question seeks to determine whether the only reason a 1040 was used was to claim a HOPE or Lifetime Learning Tax Credit.

Select "No" if your particular tax situation required use of a 1040 form, or "Don't know" if you are uncertain.

What was your, the student's (and spouse's), adjusted gross income for 20XX? Adjusted Gross Income is on IRS Form 1040-line 36; 1040A-line 21; 1040EZ-line 4; or TeleFile-line I.

The Adjusted Gross Income, or AGI, is total income less adjustments to income. AGI includes the total of your income, wages, dividends, interest, taxable capital gains, gains or losses from real estate if they flow through to page one of your tax return, and gains or losses from real estate, Subchapter S corporations, and partnerships.

Your total income also includes taxable Social Security payments you have received, unemployment insurance receipts, alimony you receive from others, and tax refunds. If you have a Subchapter S business, AGI also includes income that flows through to page one. Subtracted from AGI are items that are called adjustments to income, which include payments to a traditional (not Roth) IRA, Keogh contributions, and self-employed pension plans. You also get credit for half of your self-employment tax, moving expenses, and certain other items, including alimony you pay to others.

Adjusted gross income is the last line on page one of the 1040 or 1040A tax return. On the simpler 1040EZ form, AGI is in the middle of the Income section. On a 1040 form the result is then carried over to page two, where it is modified by standard and itemized deductions. Note that the line numbers refer to the 2004 IRS tax forms; the line numbers may change slightly from year to year but will be the summation line of the Adjusted Gross Income section of each form.

You must make an entry here unless the student will not file a tax return. If you have not yet filed a return, you need to make an estimate of the AGI based on W-2s and other papers you have received from sources of income. The online FAFSA and the printed FAFSA include worksheets to help you make an estimate. You may be able to obtain free or low-cost assistance in filling out IRS forms through state or local agencies or private organizations.

What was your, the student's (and spouse's), income tax for 20XX? Income tax amount is on IRS Form 1040-line 56; 1040A-line 36; 1040EZ-line 10; or TeleFile-line K(2).

Income tax paid is the summation of the amount of taxes you owed the government minus any or all of the following: foreign tax credit, credit for child and dependent care expenses, credit for the elderly or the disabled, education credits (including HOPE or Lifetime Learning Credits), retirement savings contributions credit, child tax credit, adoption credits, and certain other credits listed on IRS forms.

Note that line numbers refer to the 2004 IRS tax forms; the line numbers may change slightly from year to year but will be the summation line of the Tax and Credits section of each form.

If you have not yet filed a return, you need to make an estimate of the income tax amount based on W-2s and other papers you have received from sources of income. The online FAFSA and the printed FAFSA include worksheets to help you make an estimate. You may be able to obtain free or low-cost assistance in filling out IRS forms through state or local agencies or private organizations.

Enter your, the student's (and spouse's), exemptions for 20XX. Exemptions are on IRS Form 1040-line 6d or 1040A-line 6d. For Form 1040EZ, if a person answered "Yes" on line 5, use EZ worksheet line F to determine the number of exemptions ($3,100 equals one exemption). If a person answered "No" on line 5, enter 01 if he or she is single, or 02 if he or she is married. For Form TeleFile, use line J(2) to determine the number of exemptions ($3,100 equals one exemption).

A student who is listed as a dependent (and thus an exemption) on a parent's or guardian's tax form cannot claim himself or herself as an exemption on his or her own tax form. Similarly, if a student's spouse is listed as a dependent of someone else, the student cannot claim an exemption on his or her tax form.

If a married student and spouse have filed or will file separate tax returns for the previous calendar year, the FAFSA asks that you include both individual's exemptions even if they were not married until the current year. (In this section the FAFSA is, to some extent, forward-looking to expected income and taxes in the current year.)

If the student is currently divorced, separated, or widowed and has filed or will file a joint tax return, list only the student's portion of the exemptions for the current year.

Again, note that line numbers refer to the 2004 IRS tax forms; the line numbers may change slightly from year to year but will be the summation line of the Exemptions section of each form.

How much did you, the student (and spouse), earn from working (wages, salaries, tips, etc.) in 20XX? Answer these questions whether or not you, the student, filed a tax return. This information may be on your W-2 forms, or on IRS Form 1040-lines 7+12+18; 1040A-line 7; or 1040EZ-line 1. TeleFilers should use their W-2 forms.

If you filed a Form 1040A or Form 1040EZ, this is the sum of wages, salaries, and tips that are reported on a W-2 form received from your employer. If you filed a Form 1040, you also need to add in business income or loss from Schedule C or C-EZ plus farm income or loss from Schedule F.

Note that line numbers refer to the 2004 IRS tax forms; the line numbers may change slightly from year to year but will be the sum of the items listed above.

Questions Asked of Independent Students

If the student answers "no" to all of the following questions, he or she is still considered dependent upon parents.

Questions include:

- Were you born before January 1, 19XX? (1982 for the 2005–2006 form; the year increases by one with each successive academic year.)

- Are you working on a master's or doctorate or other graduate certificate?

- Are you married?

- Do you have any children who receive more than half their support from the student or the student and spouse?

- Do you have any dependents other than children or a spouse who receive more than half their support from the student and spouse?

- Are both of your parents deceased, or were you until age eighteen a ward or dependent of the court?

- Are you a veteran of the U.S. Armed Forces?

If you are filling out the FAFSA on the Web you will automatically be taken to the section of the form where you will need to fill in information about the finances of the parents. If you are using the printed copy of the form, the instructions will direct you to the fourth section of the form.

If your answers to questions in Step Three of the printed FAFSA or to the similar automated questions in the FAFSA on the Web identify the student as independent of his or her parents, further questions will focus on the student's household size and income. Among the questions asked are:

What is the student's household size? Include in your (and your spouse's) household: (1) yourself (and your spouse, if you have one), and (2) your children, if you will provide more than half of their support from July 1, 20XX through June 30, 20XX, and (3) other people if they now live with you, and you provide more than half of their support, and you will continue to provide more than half of their support from July 1, 20XX through June 30, 20XX.

The student's household size begins with the student and a spouse if there is one. Added to the total are any children and other persons if the student and spouse provide more than half of the cost of their support. Remember that two people or two households cannot both claim to provide more than half of someone's support.

What is the student's number in college? Always count yourself as a college student. <u>*Do not include your parents.*</u> *Include others only if they will attend at least half time in 2005–2006 in a program that leads to a college degree or certificate.*

This awkwardly phrased question is asking how many people in the student's household are currently attending college at least half-time. The number includes the student and spouse if there is one. It does not include the parents.

Questions About Assets and Investments of Students and Parents

Students and parents of dependent students are also asked to provide information about cash, savings, and investments. The FAFSA does not, however, include the principal residence of the student or parent in its calculation of net worth. (However, questions about the net value of the family home are included on the CSS/Profile, and some colleges will ask for documentation about home values in their calculation of financial aid.)

Here are some of the questions about assets:

As of today, what is the total current balance of cash, savings, and checking accounts?

As with other questions on the FAFSA, "today" means the day the form is actually filed. The question applies to the student (and spouse if married) and to the parents. I am in no way suggesting that you do anything illegal or even sneaky, but if you have a $20,000 bill that you must pay and you have $20,000 set aside for that purpose, you would probably be better off paying the bill (and reducing your current balance of cash or savings) before the date you file the FAFSA.

As of today, what is the net worth of current investments, including real estate (not your home)?

Net worth means the current value of a holding minus the outstanding debt on the specific investments listed; the information should be current as of the date the FAFSA is filed. Investments tracked here include real estate, mutual funds, stocks and bonds, options, money market funds, certificates of deposit, other securities, land sale contracts and mortgages issued to borrowers, commodities, and trust funds. Also included here are education savings plans such as Coverdell savings accounts and 529 plans.

Excluded from investments are your own home, the current cash value of any life insurance, retirement plans (including pension funds, annuities, retirement IRAs, and Keogh plans), and prepaid tuition plans.

If net worth is $1 million or more, report $999,999; if you owe more than the value of your investments, enter 0. (If your financial holdings are very large or very complex, you may want to involve a qualified tax preparer or attorney in determining whether it is worthwhile to file a FAFSA, and if so, to obtain assistance.)

As of today, what is the net worth of any current business and/or investment farms? Do not include a farm that a student or parent of a dependent student lives on and operates.

This question is asking about investment farms—owned and operated for profit but not the student or parent's principal place of residence or one where either participates in the operation. What is sought is the net worth as of the date of filing of the FAFSA; this is the current value of the land, buildings, machinery, equipment, and inventory minus any debt for which the business or farm was used as collateral.

If you, the student, receive veterans' education benefits, for how many months from July 1, 20XX through June 30, 20XX will you receive these benefits?

The answer is the number of months in the coming school year that the student expects to receive these benefits.

What VA benefits amount will you receive monthly?

The answer is the amount per month that the student expects to receive in the coming school year, the same period covered in the previous question. The question includes a list of programs accounted for here. Not included here are death pensions or Dependency & Indemnity Compensation (DIC), and a spouse's veterans' education benefits.

What is the student's parents' household size?

This is the parent's equivalent to the question asked of students. If the student is still dependent on the parent, even if he or she doesn't live with them, the student is included in the count. So, too, are the parents and their other children if they provide more than half of their support in the coming school year.

If you are using the automated FAFSA on the Web, the computer will take you to a worksheet that will assist in calculating the proper answer here. It will draw some of its information from previously asked questions, including the marital status of the parents and the student.

What was the amount the student's parents paid in income tax for 20XX?

See the similar question about the student's income tax, above.

Enter the student's parents' exemptions for 20XX.

See the similar question about the student's tax exemptions, above.

Questions Asked of Parents of Dependent Students

The questions asked of parents are in many cases identical or similar to those asked of the student. See the explanations earlier in this chapter for the following questions:

- Parents' adjusted gross income?
- Earnings from working (wages, salaries, tips, etc.) in 20XX? (Included in a parent's wages are earnings from any need-based employment as well as combat pay for members of the Armed Services. Follow the instructions on the form or Web page to determine how to deal with separated, divorced, or remarried parents.)

A Nonsupportive Parent

If you answered "No" to the dependency questions, you must provide financial and other information about your parents even if you did not live with them. When it comes to the FAFSA and financial aid formula, here are guidelines:

- If both parents are living and married to each other, answer the questions based on their joint finances.

- If your surviving parent is widowed or single, answer questions about that parent.

- If your widowed parent is remarried as of the date you file the FAFSA, answer questions about that parent and your stepparent.

- If your parents are divorced or separated, answer the questions based on the finances of the parent with whom you lived during the largest portion of the past twelve months. If you did not live with one parent more than the other, give answers about the parent who provided more financial support during the past twelve months. If you did not receive support from parents in the past year, answer the question about the parent who most recently provided support. If that parent is remarried as of the date you are filing the FAFSA, answer the questions about that parent and the stepparent.

- Grandparents and legal guardians are not parents.

What do you do if you are estranged from your parents and do not have access to their financial information or tax returns but are still considered legally dependent upon them? Short of enlisting a lawyer to force their cooperation—not often done because a parent, estranged or not, cannot be forced to pay for college—the best advice is to make estimates of income and assets and then be sure to make direct contact with the financial aid office of any school you attend or are applying to and make them aware of the fact that you are financially on your own. You may need to file an affidavit or other supporting statements.

FAFSA Worksheets A, B, and C

A section of the FAFSA dealing with various tax credits, welfare benefits, retirement savings, and education credits collects information from three separate worksheets you must fill out. (A sample of this section, on the sixth page of the FAFSA Pre-Application Worksheet, is on page 129.) If you are using a printed version of the FAFSA you'll have to enter the numbers, do the math, and transfer the results to the appropriate line on the form; if you are working on the FAFSA on the Web, the numbers will automatically be taken from the onscreen worksheet and placed into the form for processing.

Both the student and spouse, and the parents of dependent students must provide information on each of the worksheets. On the printed form, the student/spouse and parent information is entered in separate columns; for the online version, the questions are asked separately for each filer.

The calculations are summed at the bottom of each of the three worksheets, and just one number is entered on the FAFSA. The reason for this is that the complex federal methodology for calculating the Expected Family Contribution assigns different weights to various types of income. Also, state or institutional programs may have different ways of accounting for certain types of income in their own methodologies.

Worksheet A

This worksheet asks about the following sources of credits or benefits:

- **Earned income credit.** This refundable tax credit is available to persons who work but earn low wages. It is intended to offset the cost of other taxes such as those for Social Security and Medicare. As a refundable credit it can be issued to people who pay no taxes or pay taxes that are less than the amount of the credit, both of which result in a payment to the family. In order to be eligible, a low-income worker must maintain a home in the United States, with at least one child living there.

- **Additional child tax credit.** Every taxpayer with less than $110,000 in modified AGI is entitled to a tax credit for each child. The amount was $700 in 2005, and is scheduled to increase to $800 per child in 2009 and $1,000 per child in 2010. Very

145

low-income taxpayers—and those who have higher incomes and a large number of deductions that bring the modified AGI down to near zero—can also receive additional tax credits.

- Welfare benefits, including Temporary Assistance for Needy Families (TANF).

- **Social Security benefits that were not subject to tax (such as SSI) received by any household member.** For retirees and other recipients with relatively large amounts of personal income from other sources, a portion of Social Security payments received may be taxable. This question seeks to determine—for financial aid decision-making purposes—the total amount of those benefits that were not subject to taxes. For more information about untaxed Social Security benefits, consult the Social Security Administration by calling (800) 772-1213 or visiting *www.ssa.gov*. Excluded from this section are food stamps and subsidized housing payments.

Worksheet B

This worksheet is a grab bag of other sources of income and credits that are not specifically identified on some tax forms or in other questions on the FAFSA. In most cases, this is a situation in which the federal government is seeking to avoid giving double benefits to people who receive credits or payments that are not subject to tax; when it comes to calculating financial aid, that money will be taken into account when the U.S. Department of Education calculates the Expected Family Contribution.

For many financial aid applicants, many of these questions are not relevant.

- **Payments to tax-deferred pension and savings plans.** These include funds paid directly or withheld from earnings and reported on the student's or parent's W-2 Form. These might include 401(k) and 403(b) pension plans and tax-sheltered investments available through employers. If you have any uncertainty about this question, consult a qualified tax preparer, the IRS, or a financial aid office.

- **IRA deductions and payments to self-employed SEP, SIMPLE, and Keogh and other qualified plans.** The information sought here is the total amount of tax-deductible payments to private retirement accounts set up under qualified programs.

- **Child support you received for all children.** Child support is not taxable, but the financial aid formula takes it into account in determining the EFC. Do not include foster care or adoption payments in this total.

- **Tax-exempt interest income.** Some or all of the interest on certain governmental bonds and other special financial instruments are exempt from taxation.

- **Foreign income exclusion.** Certain U.S. citizens and residents living in foreign countries can deduct a portion of their living expenses or exclude from taxation some income received as compensation for work performed abroad. Although this may not be taxed by the IRS, this income is included in the calculation for federal student aid and must be reported here.

- **Untaxed portions of IRA distributions, and untaxed portions of pensions.** Certain withdrawals from an IRA or a qualified pension are not subject to taxation after a set age. Again, the financial aid formula is seeking to account for untaxed income in calculating financial aid. Do not include rollovers—the transfer of funds in one IRA or pension account to another account without a withdrawal to your personal funds.

- **Credit for federal tax on special fuels.** Certain nongasoline fuels used in motor vehicles on public highways (not on private property, including farms) are not subject to tax, and users are given a tax credit; some of these special fuels include diesel, kerosene, LPG (propane), CNG (compressed natural gas), and experimental fuels. If you received a credit for use of these fuels you are required to report it on IRS Form 4136, and the credit earned on that form is reportable here. The credit is considered untaxed income when financial aid is calculated.

- **Housing, food, and other living allowances paid to members of the military, clergy, and others.** Certain payments including living allowances or free room and board may not be considered taxable on IRS forms, but are of interest to the Department of Education in calculating financial aid. If a benefit, such as free room and board, was provided to a parent or student, the cash value of that benefit must be calculated and listed here. This line is not meant to account for rent subsidies received for low-income housing.

- **Veterans' noneducation benefits** such as Disability, Death Pension, Dependency & Indemnity Compensation (DIC), or VA Educational Work-Study allowances. Untaxed benefits are considered income when it comes to calculating federal financial aid.

- **Any other untaxed income or benefits not reported elsewhere on Worksheets A and B,** such as workers' compensation, untaxed portions of railroad retirement benefits, Black Lung Benefits, and disability. This is a catchall category seeking to account for *any other* untaxed income or benefits not reported elsewhere on the first two worksheets. Excluded from this question are student financial aid, Workforce Investment Act education benefits, or benefits from flexible spending arrangements (also known as cafeteria plans) in which workers are given a choice of cash or nontaxable benefits.

- **Money received, or paid on your behalf not reported elsewhere on this form.** If the student (not the parents) received cash support from a friend or relative other than parents, or if someone other than the student is paying some or all of the cost of rent, utilities, and other expenses while he or she is in school, that is considered untaxed income for purposes of calculating the EFC.

Worksheet C

The items accounted for here include education credits claimed on IRS forms, child support paid to other households, and taxable income from federal work-study and other employment programs.

- **Education credits.** The HOPE Education Tax Credit is a tax credit available to parents or students for the first two years of college or postsecondary education. The Lifetime Learning Credit provides a tax credit to parents and students at any time. As noted in Chapter 8, you cannot claim both credits for the same student in the same year.

- **Child support** you paid because of divorce or separation or by court order or other legal requirement. This amount does not include support for children in the student's own household, or in the parent's household.

- **Taxable earnings from need-based employment programs, such as federal work-study.** Also included are any need-based employment portions of fellowships and assistantships. Do not report any other sources of need-based income that are accounted for elsewhere on Worksheet C.

- **Student grant and scholarship aid reported to the IRS as part of adjusted gross income.** Included here are grants, scholarships, waivers, AmeriCorps benefits, and the grant or scholarship portion of fellowships. Note that the question is asking for that portion which makes its way into the AGI.

Federal School Codes

Applicants for financial aid need to inform the Department of Education of the code number of the school or schools to which they want the SAR and EFC sent. If you have already been accepted to a college and plan to attend there, you should enter only the code for that institution. If you are applying to more than one college or university, you should enter all applicable codes so that you do not miss any financial aid deadlines. The codes are available from the schools' financial offices, from Web sites, and as part of the FAFSA on the Web.

If you are using the FAFSA on the Web and are filling out a renewal of a form submitted in previous years, the codes used in the past will be automatically filled in. The first time you filled out the form you may have asked the government to send the data to more than one school; you should remove any schools that you are not planning to attend in the coming school year.

For each school code you will also be asked to indicate your expected housing plan: on-campus, off-campus, or with parent. Your selection here will affect the total cost of attendance and may be relevant to a particular school's institutional financial aid.

POSSIBLE FAFSA PROBLEMS

Here are some problems you may encounter in submitting your FAFSA form:

- **Wrong Social Security Number or Incorrect Name.** If you have submitted an application using an incorrect Social Security number or the wrong name, there is no recovery; you will have to fill out a completely new FAFSA form.

- **Name Change.** If your name changes because of marriage, adoption, or other reason, a previously submitted FAFSA cannot be deleted. You must resubmit a form with the new name, and then notify any college to which the information has been submitted that they may receive two applications under your name or Social Security number. Tell them which is correct.

- **Rejection Code 14, 15, or 16.** If your form is rejected and you receive one of these uninformative numerical codes, the system is telling you that it has not received an acceptable signature.

If you encounter a problem with your signature, you can take one of the following four steps to correct the problem: 1. If you have obtained a PIN you can electronically sign the application; on the *www.fafsa.ed.gov* page click on "Provide Electronic Signatures" in the section about filling out the form. 2. You can print out and sign the Student Aid Report (SAR) and mail it in. 3. You can print out a Signature Page from the FAFSA Web site and mail it in, again delaying processing for at least several days. 4. If you are currently enrolled in college, the institution's financial aid office may be able to assist in filing a signature electronically.

chapter 14

CSS/ FINANCIAL AID PROFILE

The CSS Profile is a second set of inquiries about the finances of the parent and student. It is intended to help colleges (mostly private) make permissible adjustments to the federal methodology for the calculation or make decisions on grants and scholarships outside of federal financial aid programs.

The CSS Profile is just like the FAFSA, only more so. Some of the same questions are asked, but in more detail. And there are some questions on the Profile that even the federal government doesn't consider to be its business.

You may find it easier to fill out the CSS Profile after you have completed the FAFSA, but there is no requirement to file them in any particular order.

You'll find a copy of the 2005–06 Profile Pre-Application Worksheet on pages 153 to 166. This form is used to organize the necessary information required to fill out the Profile online at *www.collegeboard.com* or *https://profileonline. collegeboard.com/index.jsp*, or in writing on a printed copy of the form.

2005-06 PROFILE Pre-Application Worksheet

Use this worksheet to help collect your family's financial information before you begin your online PROFILE Application. You can print instructions from the Help Desk by clicking on "Application Instructions." As you complete your online application, you will find more detailed online help.

This worksheet contains the questions found in the PROFILE Registration and application (Sections A through P). In general, these are standard questions that all families must complete.

• When you complete your online application, you may find questions in Section Q that are not found on this pre-application worksheet. Once you register, you should print the Supplemental Information Worksheet to obtain these questions. These are additional questions required by one or more of the colleges or scholarship programs to which you are applying. If your application does not contain a Section Q, it means that none of the colleges and programs to which you are applying require questions beyond those collected in Sections A through P.

• Based on the student's dependency status, you may not be required to complete all of the questions in Sections A through O. When you complete your PROFILE Application, questions that are not required will not be presented to you. For example, if the student is younger than age 24, you will not be asked to complete Questions 1 and 2, or Questions 24 and 25.

Do not mail this form to the College Board. It is a Pre-Application Worksheet and cannot be processed. Any worksheets received for processing will be destroyed.

Pre-Application Worksheet

Registration

Student's Social Security Number: ☐☐☐

Student's name: ☐ ☐ ☐
                Last name   *First name*   *M.I.*

Student's title   O Mr.   O Miss, Ms, or Mrs.

Student's email address: ☐

Student's date of birth: ☐ ☐ ☐
                     Month   *Day*   *Year*

Student's postal address location

O Domestic (U.S., Puerto Rico, U.S. Territories)   O Canada   O Other international

Student's permanent mailing address: ☐
(domestic addresses)   *Number, street, and apartment number*

           ☐ ☐ ☐
                     City   *State*   *Zip code*

Student's home telephone number: ☐ ☐ ☐
                              Area code

What will be the student's year in school during 2005-2006?

O 1st year (never previously attended college)	O 5th year or more undergraduate
O 1st year (previously attended college)	O First-year graduate/professional (beyond a bachelor's degree)
O 2nd year	O Second-year graduate/professional
O 3rd year	O Third-year graduate/professional
O 4th year	O Fourth-year graduate/professional

What will be the student's financial aid status during 2005-2006?

O First-time applicant, entering student (or transfer student)   O First-time applicant, continuing student
O Renewal applicant, continuing student

What is the student's current marital status?

O unmarried (single, divorced, widowed)   O married/remarried   O separated

What is the student's citizenship status?

O U.S. citizen
O Eligible non-citizen
O Neither of the above

If you answered "Neither" in the question above, what the student's country of citizenship? ☐

If you answered "Neither" in the question above, what is the student's Visa classification?

O F1   O F2   O J1   O J2   O G1   O G2   O G3   O G4   O Other

Is the student a veteran of the U.S. Armed Forces?   O Yes   O No

Are both of the student's parents deceased, or is the student or was the student (until age 18) a ward/dependent of the court?
O Yes   O No

Does the student have legal dependents (other than a spouse)?   O Yes   O No

Are the student's biological or adoptive parents separated or divorced, or were they never married? (Answer "no" if the student's biological or adoptive parents are living together, regardless of their current marital status.)   O Yes   O No

If you answered "yes" above, with which of the student's biological or adoptive parents did the student live with more during the past 12 months?   O Father   O Mother   O Neither parent

If you answered "neither parent" above, which parent provided more support during the past 12 months?   O mother   O father

Do the student's parents own all or part of a business, corporation, partnership, or farm, or is either parent self-employed?
O Yes   O No

Where will the student live while enrolled in college?
O On campus   O Off campus   O With parents   O With relatives

2

Section A - Student's Information

(Dependent students skip Questions 1 and 2.)

1. How many people are in the student's (and spouse's) household? <u>Always include the student (and spouse)</u>. List their names and give information about them in Section M. ▢

2. Of the number in 1, how many will be college students enrolled at least half-time between July 1, 2005 and June 30, 2006? Include the student. ▢

3. What is the student's state of legal residence? ▢

4. Where is the computer that the family is using to complete the PROFILE Application?

- O Home
- O Father's work
- O Mother's work
- O High School
- O College
- O Library
- O Community Center
- O Friend or relative's home
- O Other

Section B - Student's 2004 Income & Benefits

Questions 5-14 ask for information about the student's (and spouse's) income and benefits. If married, include spouse's information in Sections B, C, D, E, and F.

5. The following 2004 U.S. income tax return figures are: (Fill in only one oval.)

- O estimated. Will file IRS Form 1040EZ, 1040A, or Telefile. Go to 6.
- O estimated. Will file IRS Form 1040. Go to 6.
- O from a completed IRS Form 1040EZ, 1040A, or Telefile. Go to 6.
- O from a completed IRS Form 1040. Go to 6.
- O a tax return will not be filed. Skip to 10.

6. 2004 total number of exemptions (2004 IRS Form 1040, line 6d or 1040A, line 6d or 1040EZ or Telefile) ▢

7. 2004 adjusted gross income (2004 IRS Form 1040, line 36 or 1040A, line 21 or 1040EZ, line 4 or Telefile, line I) $ ▢

8. a 2004 U.S. income tax paid (2004 IRS Form 1040, line 56 or 1040A, line 36 or 1040EZ, line 10 or Telefile, line K) $ ▢

   b 2004 Education Credits - Hope and Lifetime Learning (2004 IRS Form 1040, line 48 or 1040A, line 31) $ ▢

9. 2004 itemized deductions (IRS Schedule A, line 28. Fill in "0" if deductions were not itemized.) $ ▢

10. 2004 income earned from work by student $ ▢

11. 2004 income earned from work by student's spouse $ ▢

12. 2004 dividend and interest income (2004 IRS Form 1040, lines 8a and 9a or 1040A, lines 8a and 9a or 1040EZ, line 2 or Telefile, line C) $ ▢

13. 2004 untaxed income and benefits (Give total amount for year.)

   a Social security benefits (untaxed portion only - see help) $ ▢

   b Welfare benefits, including TANF $ ▢

   c Child support received for all children $ ▢

   d Earned Income Credit (2004 IRS Form 1040, line 65 or 1040A, line 41 or 1040EZ, line 8 or Telefile, line L) $ ▢

   e Other - write in the total from the worksheet at the end of this document. $ ▢

14. 2004 earnings from Federal Work-Study or other need-based work programs plus any grant, fellowship, scholarship, and assistantship aid reported to the IRS in your adjusted gross income. Include AmeriCorps benefits. $ ▢

Section C - Student's Assets

Questions 15-22 ask for information about the student's (and spouse's) assets. Include trust accounts in Section D.

15. Cash, savings, and checking accounts (as of today) $ _____

16. Total value of IRA, Keogh, 401k, 403b, etc. accounts as of December 31, 2004 $ _____

17. Investments (Including Uniform Gifts to Minors)
   a What are these worth today? $ _____
   b What is owed them? $ _____

18. Home
   a What is it worth today? (Renters write in "0") $ _____
   b What is owed on it? $ _____
   c Year purchased   _____
   d Purchase price $ _____

19. Other real estate
   a What is it worth today? $ _____
   b What is owed on it? $ _____

20. Business and farm
   a What is it worth today? $ _____
   b What is owed on it? $ _____

21. If a farm is included in 20, is the student living on the farm?   O Yes   O No

Section D - Student's Trust Information

22. a Total value of all trust(s) $ _____
   b Is any income or part of the principal currently available?   O Yes   O No
   c Who established the trust(s)?   O Student's parents   O Other

Section E - Student's 2004 Expenses
(Dependent students skip Questions 23 and 24.)

23. 2004 child support paid because of divorce or separation $ _____

24. 2004 medical and dental expenses not covered by insurance $ _____

Section F - Student's Expected Summer/School-Year Resources for 2005-2006

25. Student's veterans benefits (July 1, 2005 - June 30, 2006)
   Amount per month $ _____
   Number of months   _____

(Section continues on next page.)

4

<u>**Section F - Student's Expected Summer/School-Year Resources for 2005-2006 - continued**</u>

26. Student's (and spouse's) resources (Don't enter monthly amounts.)

    Student's wages, salaries, tips, etc.

    a Summer 2005 (3 months) $ _____

    b School year 2005-2006 (9 months) $ _____

    Spouse's wages, salaries, tips, etc.

    c Summer 2005 (3 months) $ _____

    d School year 2005-2006 (9 months) $ _____

    Other taxable income

    e Summer 2005 (3 months) $ _____

    f School year 2005-2006 (9 months) $ _____

    Untaxed income and benefits

    g Summer 2005 (3 months) $ _____

    h School year 2005-2006 (9 months) $ _____

    i Grants, scholarships, fellowships, etc. from sources other than the colleges or universities to which the student is applying (List sources in Section P.) $ _____

    j Tuition benefits from the parents' and/or the student's or spouse's employer $ _____

    k Amount the student's parent(s) think they will be able to pay for 2005-2006 college expenses $ _____

    l Amounts expected from prepaid tuition plan withdrawals, other relatives, spouse's parents, and all other sources (List sources and amounts in Section P.) $ _____

<u>**Section G - Parents' Household Information**</u>

27. How many people are in your parents' household? <u>Always include the student and parents</u>. List their names and give information about them in Section M. _____

28. Of the number in 27, how many will be college students enrolled at least half-time between July 1, 2005 and June 30, 2006? **Do not include parents.** Include the student. _____

29. How many parents will be in college at least half-time in 2005-2006?   O Neither Parent   O One Parent   O Both Parents

30. What is the current marital status of your parents?   O Never married   O Separated   O Widowed

    (Fill in only one oval.)   O Married/Remarried   O Divorced

31. What is your parents' state of legal residence? _____

32. What is your parents' preferred email address? _____

Section H - Parents' Expenses

33. Child support paid because of divorce or separation

  a 2004 $

  b Expected 2005 $

34. Repayment of parents' educational loans

  a 2004 $

  b Expected 2005 $

35. Medical and dental expenses not covered by insurance

  a 2004 $

  b Expected 2005 $

36. Total elementary, junior high, and high school tuition paid for dependent children

  Amount paid (Don't include tuition paid for the student.)

  a 2004 $

  b Expected 2005 $

  For how many dependent children? (Don't include the student.)

  c 2004

  d Expected 2005

Section I - Parents' Assets

If parents own all or part of a business or farm, enter its name and the percent of ownership in Section P.

37. Cash, savings, and checking accounts (as of today) $

38. **a** Total value of parents' assets held in the names of the student's brothers and sisters who are under age 19 and not college students $

  b Total value of assets held in Section 529 **prepaid tuition** plans for the student's brothers and sisters (Do not include assets in Section 529 **savings** plans.) $

  c Total value of assets held in Section 529 **prepaid tuition** plans for the student (Do not include assets in Section 529 **savings** plans.) $

39. Investments

  a What are they worth today? $

  b What is owed on them? $

40. Home

  a What is it worth today? (Renters fill in "0" and skip to 40e.) $

  b What is owed on it? $

  c Year purchased

  d Purchase price $

  e Monthly home mortgage or rental payment (If none, explain in Section P.) $

41. Business

  a What is it worth today? $

  b What is owed on it? $

42. Farm

  a What is it worth today? $

  b What Is owed on it? $

  c Does family live on the farm?   O Yes   O No

43. Other real estate

  a What is it worth today? $

  b What is owed on it? $

  c Year purchased

  d Purchase price $

Section J - Parents' 2003 Income & Benefits

44. 2003 adjusted gross income (2003 IRS Form 1040, line 34 or 1040A, line 21 or 1040EZ, line 4 or Telefile, line I) $ _____

45. 2003 U.S. income tax paid (2003 IRS Form 1040, line 54 or, 1040A, line 36 or 1040EZ, line 10 or Telefile, line K) $ _____

46. 2003 itemized deductions (2003 IRS Form 1040, Schedule A, line 28. Enter "0" if deductions were not itemized.) $ _____

47. 2003 untaxed income and benefits (Write in the total from the worksheet at the end of this document.) $ _____

Section K - Parents' 2004 Income & Benefits

48. The following 2004 U.S. income tax return figures are: (Fill in only one oval.)

    O estimated. Will file IRS Form 1040EZ, 1040A, or Telefile. Go to 49.

    O estimated. Will file IRS Form 1040. Go to 49.

    O from a completed IRS Form 1040EZ, 1040A, or Telefile. Go to 49.

    O from a completed IRS Form 1040. Go to 49.

    O a tax return will not be filed. Skip to 53.

49. 2004 total number of exemptions (IRS Form 1040, line 6d or 1040A, line 6d or 1040EZ or Telefile)   [_____]

50.a Wages, salaries, tips (2004 IRS Form 1040, line 7 or 1040A, line 7 or 1040EZ, line 1) $ _____

    b Interest income (2004 IRS Form 1040, line 8a or 1040A, line 8a or 1040EZ, line 2 or Telefile, line C) $ _____

    c Dividend income (2004 IRS Form 1040, line 9a or 1040A, line 9a) $ _____

    d Net income (or loss) from business, farm, rents, royalties, partnerships, estates, trusts, etc. (2004 IRS Form 1040, lines 12, 17, and 18) To enter a loss, use a minus (-) sign. $ _____

    e Other taxable income such as alimony received, capital gains (or losses), pensions, annuities, etc. (2004 IRS Form 1040, lines 10, 11, 13, 14, 15b, 16b, 19, 20b and 21 or 1040A, lines 10, 11b, 12b, 13, and 14b or 1040EZ, line 3 or Telefile, line D) $ _____

    f Adjustments to income (2004 IRS Form 1040, line 35 or 1040A, line 20) $ _____

    g 2004 adjusted gross income (2004 IRS Form 1040, line 36 or 1040A, line 21 or 1040EZ, line 4 or Telefile line I). This entry is the sum of 50a to 50e, minus 50f. $ _____

51.a 2004 U.S. income tax paid (2004 IRS Form 1040, line 56 or 1040A, line 36 or 1040EZ, line 10 or Telefile, line K) $ _____

    b 2004 Education Credits - Hope and Lifetime Learning (2004 IRS Form 1040, line 48 or 1040A, line 31) $ _____

52. 2004 itemized deductions (2004 IRS Schedule A, line 28. Fill in "0" if deductions were not itemized.) $ _____

53. 2004 income earned from work by father/stepfather $ _____

54. 2004 income earned from work by mother/stepmother $ _____

(Section continues on next page.)

7

Section K - Parents' 2004 Income & Benefits (continued)

55. 2004 untaxed income and benefits (Give total amount for the year. Do not give monthly amounts.)

   a Social security benefits received for all family members except the student (untaxed portion
      only see help) $ _____

   b Social security benefits received for the student (See help.) $ _____

   c Welfare benefits, including TANF $ _____

   d Child support received for all children $ _____

   e Deductible IRA and/or SEP, SIMPLE, or Keogh payments (2004 IRS Form 1040, lines 25 and 32 or
      form 1040A, line 17) $ _____

   f Payments to tax-deferred pension and savings plans $ _____

   g Tuition and fees deduction (2004 IRS Form 1040, line 27 or 1040A, line 19) $ _____

   h Amounts withheld from wages for dependent care and medical spending accounts $ _____

   I Earned Income Credit (2004 IRS Form 1040, line 65 or 1040A, line 41 or 1040EZ, line 8 or Telefile,
      line L) $ _____

   j Housing, food, and other living allowances received by military, clergy, and others $ _____

   k Tax-exempt interest income (2004 IRS Form 1040, line 8b or 1040A, line 8b) $ _____

   l Foreign income exclusion (2004 IRS Form 2555, line 43 or Form 2555EZ, line 18) $ _____

   m Other - write in the total from the worksheet in the instructions at the end of this document. $ _____

Section L - Parents' 2005 Expected Income & Benefits

If the expected total income and benefits will differ from the 2004 total income by $3,000 or more, explain in Section P.

56. 2005 income earned from work by father/stepfather $ _____

57. 2005 income earned from work by mother/stepmother $ _____

58. 2005 other taxable income $ _____

59. 2005 untaxed income and benefits (See 55a-m.) $ _____

Section M - Family Member Listing

Give information for all family members entered in question 1 or 28. Only six family members are shown here but you will be able to enter up to seven family members in addition to the student on our website. If there are more than seven, list first those who will be in school or college at least half-time. List the others in Section P. **Failure to complete all information could reduce your aid eligibility.**

Question 60.

Student - Family Member 1

Full name of family member _____   Claimed by parents
                                               as tax exemption in 2004?   O Yes   O No

2004-2005 school year

Name of school or college _____   Year in school _____

Scholarships and grants $ _____   Parents' contribution $ _____

(Section continues on next page.)

Section M - Family Member Listing (continued)

Family Member 2

Full name of family member [_____]   Claimed by parents
                                            as tax exemption in 2004?   O Yes   O No

Relationship to student: O Student's parent   O Student's stepparent   O Student's brother or sister
Age: [____]   O Student's husband or wife O Student's son or daughter   O Student's grandparent
                           O Student's stepbrother/stepsister   O Other (explain in Section P)

<u>2004-2005 school year</u>
Name of school or college [_____]   Year in school [_____]
Scholarships and grants [$ _____]   Parents' contribution [$ _____]
<u>2005-2006 school year</u>
Attend college at least one term   O Full-time   O Half-time   O Will not attend
College or university name [_____]
Type: O 2-year public college   O 2-year private college   O 4-year public college/university
        O 4-year private college/university   O graduate/professional school   O proprietary school

Family Member 3

Full name of family member [_____]   Claimed by parents
                                            as tax exemption in 2004?   O Yes   O No

Relationship to student: O Student's parent   O Student's stepparent   O Student's brother or sister
Age: [____]   O Student's husband or wife O Student's son or daughter   O Student's grandparent
                           O Student's stepbrother/stepsister   O Other (explain in Section P)

<u>2004-2005 school year</u>
Name of school or college [_____]   Year in school [_____]
Scholarships and grants [$ _____]   Parents' contribution [$ _____]
<u>2005-2006 school year</u>
Attend college at least one term   O Full-time   O Half-time   O Will not attend
College or university name [_____]
Type: O 2-year public college   O 2-year private college   O 4-year public college/university
        O 4-year private college/university   O graduate/professional school   O proprietary school

Family Member 4

Full name of family member [_____]   Claimed by parents
                                            as tax exemption in 2004?   O Yes   O No

Relationship to student: O Student's parent   O Student's stepparent   O Student's brother or sister
Age: [____]   O Student's husband or wife O Student's son or daughter   O Student's grandparent
                           O Student's stepbrother/stepsister   O Other (explain in Section P)

<u>2004-2005 school year</u>
Name of school or college [_____]   Year in school [_____]
Scholarships and grants [$ _____]   Parents' contribution [$ _____]
<u>2005-2006 school year</u>
Attend college at least one term   O Full-time   O Half-time   O Will not attend
College or university name [_____]
Type: O 2-year public college   O 2-year private college   O 4-year public college/university
        O 4-year private college/university   O graduate/professional school   O proprietary school

(Section continues on next page.)

Section M - Family Member Listing (continued)

Family Member 5

Full name of family member [   ]   Claimed by parents
as tax exemption in 2004?   O Yes   O No

Relationship to student: O Student's parent   O Student's stepparent   O Student's brother or sister
Age: [   ]   O Student's husband or wife O Student's son or daughter O Student's grandparent
                            O Student's stepbrother/stepsister O Other (explain in Section P)

<u>2004-2005 school year</u>
Name of school or college [   ]   Year in school [   ]
Scholarships and grants $[   ]   Parents' contribution $[   ]

<u>2005-2006 school year</u>
Attend college at least one term   O Full-time   O Half-time   O Will not attend
College or university name [   ]
Type: O 2-year public college   O 2-year private college   O 4-year public college/university
         O 4-year private college/university   O graduate/professional school   O proprietary school

Family Member 6

Full name of family member [   ]   Claimed by parents
as tax exemption in 2004?   O Yes   O No

Relationship to student: O Student's parent   O Student's stepparent   O Student's brother or sister
Age: [   ]   O Student's husband or wife O Student's son or daughter O Student's grandparent
                            O Student's stepbrother/stepsister O Other (explain in Section P)

<u>2004-2005 school year</u>
Name of school or college [   ]   Year in school [   ]
Scholarships and grants $[   ]   Parents' contribution $[   ]

<u>2005-2006 school year</u>
Attend college at least one term   O Full-time   O Half-time   O Will not attend
College or university name [   ]
Type: O 2-year public college   O 2-year private college   O 4-year public college/university
         O 4-year private college/university   O graduate/professional school   O proprietary school

Section N - Parents' Information

(to be answered by the parent(s) completing this form)

61. a Select one: O Father   O Mother   O Stepfather   O Stepmother   O Father deceased (skip 62b - j)
                      O Mother deceased (skip 62b - j)   O Legal guardian   O Other (Explain in Section P.)
    b Name [   ]
    c Date of birth (MMDDYYYY) [   ]
    d Select if: O Self-employed   O Unemployed
    e If unemployed, enter date unemployment began [   ]
    f Occupation [   ]
    g Employer [   ]
    h Number of years employed by employer listed above [   ]
    i Preferred daytime telephone [   ]
    j Retirement plans (Check all that apply.)
       O Social security   O Civil service/state   O Military
       O Union/employer   O IRA/Keogh/tax-deferred   O Other

(Section continues on next page.)

Section N - Parents' Information (continued)

62. **a** Select one: ○ Father ○ Mother ○ Stepfather ○ Stepmother ○ Father deceased (skip 62b - j)

○ Mother deceased (skip 62b - j) ○ Legal guardian ○ Other (Explain in Section P.)

b Name

c Date of birth (MMDDYYYY)

d Select if: ○ Self-employed ○ Unemployed

e If unemployed, enter date unemployment began

f Occupation

g Employer

h Number of years employed by employer listed above

I Preferred daytime telephone

j Retirement plans (Check all that apply.)

○ Social security ○ Civil service/state ○ Military

○ Union/employer ○ IRA/Keogh/tax-deferred ○ Other

Parent Loan Information

The questions that follow are intended to provide the student's family with options for financing the parents' share of the student's college costs. Many families choose to borrow through the Federal Parent Loan for Undergraduate Students (PLUS) Program to supplement the financial aid offer. This program, as well as most private loan programs, requires a check of parent credit worthiness to qualify.

Families that answer the questions on this page will:

- get information about their eligibility to borrow through the PLUS program.
- learn what their monthly payment responsibilities would be, should they decide to borrow (a valid email address is required to receive financing guidance).
- learn about loan programs sponsored by the College Board.

By answering Questions **B-G** below, you are authorizing the College Board (or its agent), to use the information you provide below and the student's full name and Social Security Number to evaluate the parents' credit record and report the results of the credit evaluation to the parent whose information is provided below. A positive credit rating will mean that the parent is pre-approved to borrow a PLUS Loan from most lenders, including the College Board's PLUS Loan program, should additional financial assistance be necessary. (Most other lenders use the same criteria in approving families' applications for PLUS Loans.) The College Board will not share this information with the student, the student's colleges, or anyone else. Reporting of credit worthiness results will begin in February 2004 to ensure that your credit results remain valid when you are ready to apply for a PLUS loan. (The results are valid for only 180 days.)

You may skip the questions below if you are not interested in learning about your eligibility for the Federal PLUS program.

A. Does the parent want to be considered for an educational loan to cover college costs? ○ Yes ○ No

If you answered "Yes," complete Questions **B-G**.

B. Parent's name:

Last name   First name   M.I.

C. Parent's home address:

Number, street, and apartment number

City   State   Zip code

D. Telephone number:

Area code

E. Parent's social security number:

F. Parent's date of birth:

Month   Day   Year

G. Parent's email address:

Section O - Information About Noncustodial Parent

(to be answered by the parent who completes this form if the student's biological or adoptive parents are divorced, separated, or were never married to each other)

63. a Noncustodial parent's name:

   b Home address-street

   c Home address-city, state, zip

   d Occupation/Employer

   e Year of separation

   f Year of divorce

   g According to court order, when will support for the student end? (MM/YYYY)

   h Who last claimed the student as a tax exemption?

   i Year last claimed

   j How much does the noncustodial parent plan to contribute to the student's
education for the 2004-2005 school year? (Do not include this amount in 27g.)

   k Is there an agreement specifying this contribution for the student's education?   O Yes   O No

Section P - Explanations/Special Circumstances

Use this space to explain any unusual expenses such as high medical or dental expenses, educational and other debts, child care, elder care, or special circumstances. Also give information for any outside scholarships you have been awarded. If more space is needed, use sheets of paper and send them directly to your schools and programs. When online, please limit your responses to no more than 27 lines of information.

PROFILE Online 2004-2005 Worksheets

Question 13e

Complete the worksheet below and calculate the total at the end of the questions. Enter the total in question 13e. **Don't include:** *any income reported elsewhere on the PROFILE Application, money from student financial aid, food stamps, "rollover" pensions and "rollover" IRA distributions, Workforce Investments Act educational benefits, or gifts and support, other than money, received from friends or relatives.*

Deductible IRA and/or SEP, SIMPLE, or Keogh payments from IRS Form 1040, total of lines 25 and 32 or 1040A, line 17	$
Tax exempt interest income from IRS Form 1040, line 8b or 1040A, line 8b	+
Payments to tax-deferred pension and savings plans (paid directly or withheld from earnings), including but not limited to, amounts reported on the W-2 Form in Boxes 12a-12d, codes D, E, F, G, H, and S. Include untaxed payments to 401(k) and 403(b) plans.	+
Additional child tax credit from IRS Form 1040, line 67 or 1040A, line 42	+
Workers' Compensation	+
Veterans noneducational benefits such as Death Pension, Disability, etc.	+
Housing, food, and other living allowances paid to members of the military, clergy, and others (including cash payments and cash value of benefits)	+
Cash received or any money paid on the student's behalf, not reported elsewhere on this form	+
VA educational work-study allowances	+
Any other untaxed income and benefits	+
TOTAL =	$

Question 17

Complete the worksheet below and calculate the total at the end of the questions. Enter the total in question 17.

Uniform Gifts to Minors (or similar accounts)	$
Stocks, stock options (if less than $0, enter $0), bonds, savings bonds, & mutual funds	+
Money market funds	+
Certificates of deposit	+
Non-qualified (non-retirement) annuities	+
Commodities	+
Precious and strategic metals	+
Installment & land sale contracts (including seller-financed mortgages)	+
All other investments	+
TOTAL =	$

Question 39

Complete the worksheet below and calculate the total at the end of the questions. Enter the total in question 39.

Trust funds	$
Stocks, stock options (if less than $0, report $0), bonds, savings bonds, & mutual funds	+
Money market funds	+
Certificates of deposit	+
Coverdell savings accounts	+
Section 529 college savings plans	+
Non-qualified (non-retirement) annuities	+
Commodities	+
Precious & strategic metals	+
Installment & land sale contracts (including seller-financed mortgages)	+
All other investments	+
TOTAL =	$

Question 55m

Complete the worksheet below and calculate the total at the end of the questions. Enter the total in question 55m. **Don't include:** *any income reported elsewhere on the PROFILE Application, money from student financial aid, Workforce Investments Act educational benefits, gifts and support, other than money, received from friends or relatives, or veterans educational benefits.*

Untaxed portions of IRA distributions (excluding "rollovers") from IRS Form 1040, lines 15a minus 15b or 1040A, lines 15a minus 15b or 1040A lines 11a minus 11b	$
Untaxed portions of pensions (excluding "rollovers") from IRS form 1040 lines 16a minus 16b or 1040A lines 12a minus 12b	+
Additional child tax credit from IRS Form 1040, line 67 or 1040A, line 42	+
Veterans noneducational benefits such as Disability, Death Pension, Dependency & Indemnity Compensation	+
Workers' Compensation	+
Cash received or any money paid on your behalf (Don't include child support.)	+
Black Lung Benefits, Refugee Assistance	+
Credit for federal tax on special fuels	+
Untaxed portions of Railroad Retirement benefits	+
Any other untaxed income and benefits	+
TOTAL =	$

14

Question 47

Complete the worksheet below and calculate the total at the end of the questions. Enter the total in question 47. Give total amount for the year. Do not give monthly amounts. **Don't include** *any income reported elsewhere on the PROFILE Application; money from student financial aid; Workforce Investment Act educational benefits; gifts and support, other than money, received from friends and relatives; or veterans educational benefits.*

Social security benefits received for all family members except the student (untaxed portion only)	$
Social security benefits received for the student	+
Welfare benefits, including TANF	+
Child support received for all children	+
Deductible IRA and/or SEP, SIMPLE, or Keogh payments from 2003 IRS Form 1040, lines 24 and 30 or Form 1040A, line 17	+
Payments to tax-deferred pension and savings plans	+
Tuition and fees deduction from 2003 IRS Form 1040, line 26 or 1040A, line 19	+
Amounts withheld from wages for dependent care and medical spending accounts	+
Earned Income Credit from 2003 IRS Form 1040, line 63 or 1040A, line 41 or 1040EZ, line 8 or Telefile, line L	+
Housing, food, and other living allowances received by military, clergy, and others	+
Tax-exempt interest income from 2003 IRS Form 1040, line 8b or 1040A, line 8b	+
Foreign income exclusion from 2003 IRS Form 2555, line 43 or Form 2555EZ, line 18	+
Untaxed portions of IRA distributions, excluding "rollovers," from 2003 IRS Form 1040, lines 15a minus 15b or 1040A lines 11a minus 11b	+
Untaxed portions of pensions, excluding "rollovers," from 2003 IRS Form 1040, lines 16a minus 16b or 1040A lines 12a minus 12b	+
Additional child tax credit from 2003 IRS Form 1040, line 65 or 1040A, line 42	+
Veterans non-educational benefits such as Disability, Death Pension, or Dependency & Indemnity Compensation	+
Workers' Compensation	+
Cash received or any money paid on your behalf (Don't include child support.)	+
Black Lung Benefits, Refugee Assistance	+
Credit for federal tax on special fuels	+
Untaxed portions of Railroad Retirement benefits	+
All other untaxed income and benefits	+
TOTAL =	$

PREPARING FOR YOUR PROFILE

Here's what you need to prepare for the worksheets:

- The previous calendar year's tax return, if completed. For the 2006 Profile this would be the 2005 tax return.

- The as-filed tax return of two calendar years previous. For the 2006 profile this would be the 2004 tax return.

- W-2s, 1099s, and other forms that report money earned in the previous year.

- Records of untaxed income in the two previous tax years.

- Current bank statements.

- Current investment statements including records of stocks, bonds, trusts, and other holdings.

- Current mortgage information.

- An appraisal or estimate of the value of real estate owned by the parents or student.

If you have not yet filed the tax form for the previous year, you will be asked to estimate income and benefits using income and tax records from the previous two years. If after you file the Profile you determine that your estimates were significantly incorrect, you must correct the data by directly contacting scholarship programs and financial aid offices at schools.

Even if you are not required to file a federal tax return, you must report income and other information on a Profile in order to be considered for financial aid from participating institutions. Foreign students must convert income, assets, and expenses into U.S. dollar equivalents as of the date the Profile is submitted.

Many colleges and institutions will ask families to supply photocopies of tax returns as filed, and may ask for additional information. Such requests will come directly from the financial aid offices of schools in which the student intends to enroll. (You may also receive requests from schools at which the student has been accepted but has decided not to attend; you do not have to respond to those requests, but as a courtesy you might want to call or send a letter to the admissions office to advise them of your plans.)

The worksheet is divided into sections about the student, the parent, and general inquiries about the family. In this chapter, we'll concentrate on questions that are significantly different from those also posed on the FAFSA.

Section C—Student's Assets/ Section I—Parents' Assets

The Profile collects additional information about assets held by the students and parents, although not all colleges and institutions place the same weight on the data as others.

Students (and their spouses if married) are asked to list:

- The total value of liquid assets held as cash, savings, and checking accounts.

- The total value of IRA, Keogh, 401(k), 403(b) and other retirement accounts held in the student's name as of December 31 of the previous calendar year. This is an area that significantly differs from the FAFSA, which only looks at distributions made from retirement assets and not their untapped value.

- The total value of investments (including accounts registered following the guidelines of the Uniform Gift to Minors and Uniform Transfer to Minors acts), minus any loans.

- The value of a home owned by the student and spouse and the amount owed in mortgages and other loans against it. This section also asks the year purchased and its purchase price; this is a way for the financial aid office to gauge whether the home may have a recently inflated value because of a run-up in real estate values or is a long-held asset. In some markets there are many people who own very valuable homes but are not otherwise wealthy.

- The value of other real estate owned, and the amount owed on it.

- The value of a business or farm owned by the student and spouse, and the amount owed against it. If there is a farm, the Profile also asks if the student lives on the farm; if the student does not, the farm is presumed to be a business investment.

Parents are asked a similar set of questions, expanded to include family assets:

- The total value of cash, savings, and checking accounts.

- The total value of any assets owned by the parents but held in the names of the student's brothers and sisters who are under age nineteen and not college students. This question obviously intends to keep parents from sheltering assets in the names of younger children as older ones head off to college and seek financial aid. Not all institutions assign the same weight to this information in the same way.

- The total value of assets held in 529 Prepaid Tuition Plans for the student's brothers and sisters. (This does not include 529 Plan savings accounts.)

- The total value of assets held in 529 Prepaid Tuition Plans for the student applying for financial aid. (This does not include 529 Plan savings accounts.)

- The value of the parents' investments, and the amount owed against them.

- Today's value of the family home, and the amount owed against that value in mortgages and other loans. (Renters should enter a zero here.) This section also asks the year purchased and the home's purchase price. Finally, parents are asked the amount of their home mortgage payment (principal and interest only, excluding property taxes).

- The value of any business owned by the parents, and the amount of any loans or other obligations against it.

- The value of any farm owned by the parents, and the amount of any loans or obligations against it. Parents are also asked if the family lives on the farm.

- The value of any other real estate owned by the family, the amount owed on it, the year purchased, and the purchase price.

If parents own all or part of a business or farm, they are asked to explain more about it in the "essay question" in Section P. Similarly, if parents own a home or live in a residence without making mortgage or rent payments, they are asked to explain the arrangement in the same section.

Section D—Student's Trust Information

A trust exists when there is cash, an investment, or property held by one person (the trustee) for the benefit of another (the beneficiary). This sort of arrangement is sometimes set up for a minor child by a relative.

This section asks for the total value of all trusts and whether any income or part of the principal is currently available to the student. It also asks whether the trust was established by the student's parents or by another person or persons.

If there is income or principal available to the student, some institutional methodologies will count that as income or assets in determining financial aid.

Section E—Student's Expenses/ Section H—Parents' Expenses

Students who are not dependent upon their parents should skip this section.

Independent students (and their spouses, if any) are asked:

- The total amount of child support paid because of divorce or separation, which means this applies only to a child born of a spouse or former spouse and paid to that person for support of a dependent child.

- The total amount of medical and dental expenses not covered by insurance, including insurance premiums. The amount should be left blank if parents paid the student's medical and dental expenses in the previous year, or if the expenses amount to less than 3 percent of the previous year's income.

Parents are asked:

- The amount of child support paid to a former spouse for support of a dependent child in the previous calendar year, and the amount expected to be paid in the current year.

- The total amount of education loan repayments (for their own education, for the student, or for the student's siblings) in the previous calendar year, and the amount expected to be paid in the current year. Note that the question is asking about payments made against the outstanding balance of the loans, not the total amount owed.

  This line does not include any loans that the student or siblings have obtained for their own education, even if the parents have agreed to repay that debt.

- Medical and dental expenses not covered by insurance for the previous year and the amount expected to be due in the current year, including the cost of insurance premiums.

  The lines should be left blank if the expenses amount to less than 3 percent of the previous year's income or are expected to be below that level in the current year.

  If the parents itemized deductions on their federal income tax return, the amount listed here should be the same as reported on line 1 of Schedule A.

- The total cost of tuition paid for elementary, junior high, and high school tuition for dependent children in the previous year and expected in the current year. Not included here is tuition paid for the college-bound or college-enrolled student. Also not included here are any preschool or college tuition expenses.

  Note that the question is asking for the amount of tuition (not room, board, books, fees, and other costs). This line should also exclude tuition that is paid by scholarship money.

Section F—Student's Expected Summer/School-Year Resources for the Upcoming Academic Year

This section seeks to account for income the student will receive in the three months of summer leading up to the coming academic year plus income expected in the nine months of that academic year. Questions include:

- The student's veterans' benefits on a monthly basis, plus the number of months when the benefits are expected to be received, for the period from July 1 of the current year through June 30 of the coming year. Not included here are any veterans' benefits received by the student's spouse if the student is married.

- The student's and spouse's expected three-month total of wages, salaries, tips, and other income for the summer period before the academic year.

- The student's and spouse's expected income for the nine-month period of the coming academic year including wages, salaries, and tips. Not included here are any earnings from Federal Work-Study programs.

- Other taxable income for the summer and school year for both the student and spouse.

- Any untaxed income or benefits for the summer and school year for both the student and spouse.

- The total of all grants, scholarships, and fellowships from sources other than the college or university where the student is applying or enrolled. Details of these funds must be explained in Section P.

- Tuition benefits received from the parents', the student's, or spouse's employer. If the benefits are in some way limited so that they cannot be used at all schools, this must be explained in Section P.

Also in this section are two questions that call for estimates or guesses; students and parents should make their best efforts to give an accurate response and figure on the possibility of questions from the financial aid office about any number that seems out of line with other information. The questions ask:

- The amount the student's parents think they will be able to pay for college expenses in the coming academic year.

- The amount the student expects to be able to apply toward college expenses from withdrawals from prepaid tuition plans, and from contributions from other relatives, the spouse's parents, and any other sources. Details must be listed in Section P.

Section G—Parents' Household Information

Questions here are straightforward and generally self-evident, with the possible exception of:

- Parents' state of legal residence.

  The answer here is the state in which the parents make their permanent home as of the date the Profile is filed. The various states have different definitions for legal residence; it's not as simple as the place where you are registered to vote or the place where you own a home if you also have another residence. You may be able to obtain assistance from a college's financial aid office or the Secretary of State's office in the state where you may or may not have legal residence.

  If a parent's students are separated or divorced, this question applies to the parent who makes the larger contribution to the living and college expenses of the student and is thus filling out the parent's portion of the Profile.

Sections J and K— Parents' Income and Benefits for the Past Two Years

Section J asks about adjusted gross income, federal income tax paid, itemized deductions, and untaxed income and benefits from the as-filed tax return of two years previous.

Section K asks the same questions, in more detail for the most recent tax year. If you have already filed your tax return, filling in most of these questions amount to a deconstruction of a 1040 form.

The second part of Section K concentrates on untaxed income and benefits. None of the entries here should be reflected anywhere else on the Profile. Also excluded from this section is money received as student financial aid, gifts other than money received from friends or relatives, and veterans' education benefits including those received under the GI Bill.

Questions here include:

- The untaxed portion of Social Security benefits received for all family members except the student. Basically, this is seeking any part of Social Security that is not part of the adjusted gross income.

- Social Security benefits received for the student and not part of adjusted gross income.

- Welfare benefits including Temporary Assistance for Needy Families (TANF), excluding food stamps and subsidized housing.

- Child support received for all children, excluding foster care and adoption payments.

- Deductible payments to IRA, SEP, SIMPLE, or Keogh retirement plans.

- Payments to tax-deferred pension and savings plans made directly or withheld from earnings.

- The amount of the tuition and fees deduction claimed on the federal tax return. IRS regulations put an income cap on this deduction, and it cannot be claimed in the same year a taxpayer takes a HOPE or a Lifetime Learning credit for this student.

- Amounts withheld from wages for dependent care and medical spending accounts. These benefits are usually recorded on W-2 forms given to employees by employers.

- The amount of the Earned Income Credit claimed, if taken. This credit is aimed at low-income workers and can result in a payment from the government even if taxes are not due.

- Housing, food, and other living allowances received by military, clergy, and others. This includes cash allowances and the cash value of benefits.

- Tax-exempt interest income, such as earnings generated by municipal bonds or funds that hold this sort of bond. Not included here is interest earned on an IRA or Coverdell Education Savings Account.

- The amount of any foreign income permitted to be excluded from the adjusted gross income and reported on IRS Form 2555 or 255-EZ.

- An "other" catchall line that enters the total from a special worksheet aimed at accounting for other sources of income such as untaxed portions of IRA distributions (excluding rollovers); untaxed portions of pension distributions; additional child tax credit; noneducational veterans' benefits such as disability, death pension, and dependency and indemnity compensation; workers' compensation; Black Lung Benefits; Refugee Assistance; credit for the federal tax on special fuels; the untaxed portion of railroad retirement benefits; and any other untaxed income and benefits.

Section L—Parents' Expected Income and Benefits

In this section parents are asked to estimate the total income and benefits they expect to receive in the current calendar year, including earnings from work, other taxable income, and untaxed income and benefits.

If the total is expected to be $3,000 or more higher or lower than last year, this needs to be explained in Section P. This gives parents an opportunity to explain why last year's income was unusually high (special bonuses, unusual sales, or other one-time events) or to explain why the coming year may be an anomaly (a reduction in income because of a change in job, a one-time bonus or profit received, and the like).

Section M—Family Member Listing

In this section the parents are asked to disclose the amount of scholarships and grants received by every member of the immediate family and the amount of the parents' contribution to those members' educational costs. Excluded from the contribution are withdrawals from 529 Plan Prepaid Tuition programs.

Section N—Parents' Information

Information here begins with a clarification of the relationship of the parents to the student: father, mother, stepfather, stepmother, or legal guardian. The applicant can also indicate that the father or mother is deceased. The form needs to be filled out even if the parents were never married to each other or are separated or divorced. An "other" category could apply if another family member serves in the role of a parent; that would need to be explained in Section P.

In this same section is a subsection called Parent Loan Information. The questions in this section are aimed at providing options for loans through various federal programs, including the federal Parent Loan for Undergraduate Students (PLUS) program, as well as some state and private loan programs. To be eligible for these programs, parents must agree to an assessment of their creditworthiness.

If you choose to answer these questions you will receive information about eligibility for the PLUS program and other loan programs sponsored by the College Board. Some private colleges will also provide information about plans they administer or endorse.

The key question in this section is the parent's Social Security number and date of birth. This information, together with an affirmative answer to the question that asks whether the parent wants to be considered for an education loan, gives the College Board permission to check your credit record.

You do not have to accept a loan if one is offered.

Section O—Information About Noncustodial Parent

If the student's biological or adoptive parents are divorced, separated, or were never married to each other, this section seeks information about the noncustodial parent—the parent who does not have parental control over a dependent child.

If information about a noncustodial parent is not available to the parent who is filling out the form, this needs to be explained in Section P.

Section P—Explanations/Special Circumstances

This relatively small open box is intended to allow filers of the Profile to explain any unusual circumstances for the family and explain any answer that does not fit into a check box on the form. Use the space to your best advantage to explain unusual job-related, health-related, or financial events in the family.

If you are filling out the form on paper, you can attach additional pages to explain your situation if needed. If you are working online, you have only twenty-seven lines of characters to explain special circumstances. In either case, though, you can also send a detailed letter to the financial aid office of the college or university where the student has applied or is enrolled.

Section Q—Supplemental Information

Some private schools and certain programs within some schools will ask specific questions about family finances and family makeup to assist them in making financial aid decisions. If you are working online, this section may appear based on the school selection you made in initiating the Profile; if you are working from a paper copy of the Profile, you may receive a request for supplemental information directly from the college.

chapter 15

TIPS
FROM THE
INSIDERS

Among the fascinating insider tips you'll learn in the roundtable of experts in this book is the suggestion that you take advantage of geographical differences. A strong but ordinary history in your backyard may be appealing and exotic elsewhere in the country—or in a foreign country.

In this chapter I'll also tell you strategies for SAT and ACT tests that may help you gain admission to highly competitive colleges or earn a merit scholarship. And I'll pass along some warnings and advice from the pros about early decision, waiting lists, and "senioritis."

EARLY DECISION CUTS BOTH WAYS

Many major colleges and institutions offer applicants an "early decision" option; by some estimates the option is available at more than 20 percent of all schools. Applicants submit their paperwork to an early deadline, and the institutions promise to respond months earlier than usual.

Here's the hitch: students can only seek an early decision from one college, and they must promise to enroll at that school if they are accepted. For their part, the colleges promise to offer a "sufficient" level of financial aid.

Here's the good part about an early decision application:

- Most college admission offices pay special attention to the early applicants because the student is directly saying, "Your school is my first choice." At a time when many students apply to half a dozen schools (under regular admission deadlines), colleges look differently—and sometimes just a bit more charitably—at applicants who commit to attend if accepted.

Overall, a much higher percentage of early admission applicants are accepted than those who apply under regular admission deadlines. One reason for the higher rate is that students and academic advisers may be much more selective in their applications, matching their GPA and SAT or ACT scores to published averages from the schools. It does not make sense to apply for early admission to a school that has a much higher threshold than the student can expect to pass.

Here are the most significant not-so-good parts about an early decision application:

- You will not be able to compare financial aid offers from multiple colleges. Although schools promise to offer a "sufficient" amount of aid, that does not mean that the bottom line at different colleges will not vary significantly.

- By applying for early decision, you may end up at the back of the line at other schools (where financial aid amounts are smaller) if the first school does not grant admission.

WHEN MONEY MAY MATTER: WAITING LISTS

One area in which it may be to your advantage to be too well-off to receive financial aid is the admissions waiting list.

There are three possible outcomes to an application to college: acceptance, denial, or a place on the waiting list. The first two are definite answers; the third is an area of uncertainty made all the more difficult by current trends that see students applying to five, six, or more colleges. Obviously they will attend only one, but schools have to find a way to fill every seat and dorm room.

It's very much like the dance that airlines go through, overselling seats on some flights with the expectation that some customers won't show up. Based on past experience, colleges know that a certain percentage of accepted students will choose to decline the offer. Here's what could happen:

1. If the admissions office is exactly right in its estimate, then precisely the predicted number of acceptances will be declined and the school will be left with just enough incoming freshmen for the next school year.

2. If too many students accept the offer of admission, the college faces a dilemma. It may have to squeeze more students into dorms and classrooms than it had planned; in recent years we have seen situations in which schools have had to house students in hotels and private apartments. Alternatively, the school might make a special offer to some students: put off the start of school for a semester or even a full year in return for a larger discount on the list price for college.

3. If not enough students accept the offer of admission, the college has a different sort of problem: not enough customers

to pay the salaries of the professors, the support staff, the dormitory workers, and the foodservice staff.

Because of this uncertainty, most schools maintain a waiting list. It doesn't cost the college a great deal of money to send out a few dozen or a few hundred or even a few thousand letters saying, "We cannot offer you acceptance at this time, but if you're still interested in June or July we may give you a call if a space opens up."

As a student, a place on the waiting list for his or her number one choice can be an uncomfortable perch. When a student is admitted, most colleges ask for a nonrefundable deposit of as much as $500 by May 1. That's the date when the admissions office knows whether its estimates were accurate or way off the mark. In most cases, students will have to make that payment and plan to attend the school that was their second or third or fourth choice—and then wait for that phone call from the school they really want to attend.

And who do you think the school is likely to call from the waiting list? Consider the situation: The financial aid office has dispensed all of the money it has planned to give to students in need, and may be able to redistribute some money to students who could use some more aid.

Unless the school is firmly "need-blind" in its acceptance policies, the most likely students to be chosen from the waiting list are those who are able to pay their own way and will not be receiving financial aid. (You will learn more about acceptance policies that are "need-blind" and "need-aware" in Chapter 19.) If the school wants to maintain a claim that it accepts any qualified student without regard to need, it may just work its way down the waiting list . . . but offer no financial aid.

Whether they admit it publicly or not, colleges are a business. Also, whether or not the colleges admit it, at most schools early admits and regular admits get the first crack at available financial aid. By the time names are taken from the waiting list, the pantry is bare.

BONUS DOLLARS

If the opportunity is there, consider charging college bills on your credit card and then immediately paying off the charges from savings or a line of credit.

In this way you can earn airline miles or bonus points or whatever special program is associated with your credit card.

One warning: Some colleges charge a fee for payments by credit cards. Be sure you know the details before going down this path.

You should also consider taking advantage of interest-free installment plans offered by some colleges. Doing this allows you to spread out your payment over a year's time, helps to level out some of the effects of fluctuations in the value of your investments, and allows you to earn a bit more on your money before you pay it out.

STATE EXCHANGE PROGRAMS

Unless you are receiving a free-ride scholarship to a private university, in many cases, the best deal on higher education is at a state college in the state where you are a resident. The deals are usually not quite as good for out-of-state residents, who are usually charged a higher tuition.

But what if your state does not offer the program of study you want? One solution, available to many students, is to take advantage of reciprocity or exchange programs set up between individual states or among state colleges in a region of the country.

Most programs allow residents of one state to enroll in a nearby state's college with a partial or full waiver of the nonresident tuition charges.

To find out about available reciprocity agreements, contact the admission office at a state college in your home state.

Here are a few such programs:

- **Idaho-Washington Reciprocity Program.** A limited number of exchanges between the two states' programs. Contact the Idaho or Washington institution the student wants to attend or the Washington Higher Education Coordinating Board at (360) 753-2210.

- **Midwest Student Exchange Program.** Residents of Nebraska, Kansas, Michigan, Minnesota, and Missouri are eligible to enroll in designated programs at participating colleges and universities outside their home state, paying substantially less than nonresident tuition rates—usually about 150 percent of regular in-state tuition. For information, contact the Midwestern Higher Education Compact at *www.mhec.org* or individual schools in the region.

- **Minnesota-North Dakota Tuition Reciprocity; Minnesota-Wisconsin Tuition Reciprocity.** Students who qualify pay the established reciprocity fee for course work that is available at public institutions in the neighboring state. Contact state colleges for information or consult the Minnesota Office of Higher Education at (651) 642-0533 or *www.mheso.state.mn.us*.

- **New England Board of Higher Education's Regional Student Program (RSP).** Certain undergraduate and graduate degree programs are available at reduced out-of-state tuition to residents of Connecticut, Maine, Massachusetts, New Hampshire, Rhode Island, and Vermont. For information, contact the New England Board of Higher Education at (617) 357-9620 or consult *www.nebhe.org*.

- **SREB (Southern Regional Education Board) Academic Common Market.** Students in the sixteen SREB member states who want to pursue degrees in fields that are not offered by in-state institutions can enroll in regional universities that offer the specialized degree programs; the students pay only the in-state tuition rates. Participating states are Alabama, Arkansas, Delaware, Florida, Georgia, Kentucky, Louisiana, Maryland, Mississippi, North Carolina, Oklahoma, South Carolina, Tennessee, Texas, Virginia, and West Virginia. For information, contact the SREB at (404) 875-9211 or consult *www.sreb.org*.

- **Utah-Idaho Scholarship.** A limited number of Idaho residents can attend Utah State University with a full waiver of nonresident tuition. Additional partial waivers are offered to students in Idaho who live within 100 miles of USU. For information, contact the Recruitment and Enrollment Services Office of Utah State University at (435) 797-1129 or consult *www.usu.edu*.

- **Western Interstate Commission for Higher Education.** The Western Undergraduate Exchange is a cooperative program for undergraduates, graduates, and students at professional schools in 15 states: Alaska, Arizona, California, Colorado, Hawaii, Idaho, Montana, Nevada, New Mexico, North Dakota, Oregon, South Dakota, Utah, Washington, and Wyoming. Most programs offer a tuition rate of 150 percent of in-state charges. For information, consult the state colleges or *www.wiche.edu*.

- **National Student Exchange.** Students at 177 member campuses around the United States and in Canada are able to enroll for courses or semesters at participating schools; they pay either their home-state tuition rate or the in-state tuition rate of the host school, plus room and board. For information, contact the NSE at (716) 878-4328 or (260) 436-2634 or consult *www.nse.org*.

THE CANADIAN ALTERNATIVE

Why go to college in Canada? We like Canada. It's a very attractive country with very friendly people. And there are several dozen first-class schools of higher education including a few that would rank with the best in the United States. But the real reason is money.

The same can be said of schools of higher education in a number of other English-speaking countries, including Australia, the Republic of Ireland, and England, and students who are fluent in a foreign language will find savings almost anywhere. But the advantage of Canadian schools include proximity to the United States and the fact that most courses of study are easily transferable to American colleges or job requirements.

The cost to an American to attend a Canadian college can be about $10,000 to $20,000 less per year. According to the Association of Universities and Colleges of Canada, the average cost of tuition and living costs in that country in 2004 was about $18,841 Canadian; that's approximately $15,000 in U.S. dollars. The same association estimates a total cost for an American private college at about $34,500 per year.

(The gap is not quite as large as this, though, when you add in the cost of travel and the fact that some American federal grants are not available for study in a foreign country. College loans, though, are available.)

Most Canadian universities are accredited by the U.S. Department of Education as eligible institutions for the HOPE and Lifetime Learning tax credits, and the Student Financial Assistance Programs (including Stafford Loans). To check whether Americans are eligible for such assistance at a Canadian college, check to see if it has a Federal School Code. The school's office of admission may be able to assist.

In general, undergraduate tuition for foreign students in Canada ranges from about $5,000 to $16,000 per year. The lowest rates are in the country's midsection, in Manitoba. The highest rates are in the most populous provinces of Quebec, Ontario, and British Columbia.

There are more than 125 colleges and universities in Canada; many are quite large. Most experts consider the best Canadian schools to be McGill University, the University of Toronto, and the University of British Columbia. Several of the schools give instruction in French, marked here as [F], but most are English-speaking institutions. Here are twenty-five of the best:

Carleton University: Ottawa, Ontario

Concordia University: Montreal, Quebec

Dalhousie University: Halifax, Nova Scotia

McGill University: Montreal, Quebec

McMaster University: Hamilton, Ontario

Memorial University of Newfoundland:
St. John's, Newfoundland

Queen's University: Kingston, Ontario

Simon Fraser University: Burnaby, British Columbia

Université de Montréal: Montreal, Quebec [F]

Université de Sherbrooke: Sherbrooke, Quebec [F]

Université Laval: Quebec City, Quebec [F]

University of Alberta: Edmonton, Alberta

University of British Columbia:
Vancouver, British Columbia

University of Calgary: Calgary, Alberta

University of Manitoba: Winnipeg, Manitoba

University of New Brunswick:
Fredericton, New Brunswick

University of Ottawa: Ottawa, Ontario

University of Saskatchewan: Saskatoon, Saskatchewan

University of Toronto: Toronto, Ontario

University of Victoria: Victoria, British Columbia

University of Waterloo: Waterloo, Ontario

University of Western Ontario: London, Ontario

University of Windsor: Windsor, Ontario

University of Winnipeg: Winnipeg, Manitoba

York University: Toronto, Ontario

Student Visas and Job Opportunities

In the new world of tight border security, travelers need a valid passport, even for Canada. In addition, depending on your country of origin and the type and length of planned studies, you may require a temporary resident visa and a study permit. The province of Quebec also requires students to obtain a CAQ (*Certificat d'acceptation du Québec* / Quebec Acceptance Certificate).

For information about immigration issues, consult the Citizenship and Immigration Canada site at *www.cic.gc.ca* or the private Web site at *www.studycanada.ca*.

Foreign students can work part-time while attending college in Canada if the job is on campus or is part of a course of study including cooperative programs with employers. After graduation, foreign students can work in a study-related job.

In order to work off campus, students will need employment authorization from Citizenship and Immigration Canada.

Applying to Canadian Schools

The process of applying for acceptance to a Canadian school is similar to that of American schools, although application deadlines (and acceptances)

187

may not be perfectly in sync with domestic colleges. Most colleges make offers of admission before May 1.

In some Canadian provinces, a single common application is used for all colleges. A small number of scholarships are offered to foreign students who show academic excellence; the dollar amount is usually less than the full cost of attendance.

SAT PREPARATION

Does it really make sense to spend between $1,000 and $3,000 for a professional tutor or a formal course on SAT or ACT preparation? In a word, maybe.

The most important thing is that your student spends the time to become thoroughly familiar with the format of the test and the type of questions that are asked. There are numerous books that include copies of actual previously administered tests or re-creations of similar exams.

You can also sign up for preparation courses that are delivered over the Internet, with immediate response and tips.

Most of the major companies offering tutoring, including Princeton Review and Kaplan, claim their graduates earn a boost in SAT score of at least 100 points. Private tutors might offer the same sort of claim. Similar increases are promised for the ACT, used by some colleges as an alternative to the SAT.

There is no way to know if your child could not produce that sort of gain through self-study or with your assistance. But this much I do know: Scores are almost certain to be better for a student who has spent the time to prepare than they will be for someone of equal ability and background who walks into the test center without any preparation.

Here's what I suggest:

Part One

- Buy one or more copies of books of previous exams.
- Re-create a test environment, with a quiet room, a straight-back chair and a desk. Have your child take a test completely cold, following all of the rules: you can be the proctor, timing the various components and enforcing silence.

- Score the test using the answer key, and make a record of the verbal and math scores.

- Sit with your child to review all of the incorrect answers and work through the proper response. Many test books give definitions or mathematical explanations.

Part Two

- School your child on the testing tips available from the College Board, from SAT or ACT prep books, from online sources, and through many high school guidance offices.

  Key among the tips are suggestions that advise students against reading the answers to verbal questions before trying to come up with responses of their own. (This helps guard against being trapped by trick answers.) On the reading comprehension sections, students are generally advised to skip the sample paragraphs and begin with the questions, working backward to find the answer. And depending on the test (and varying from section to section) it often makes sense to skip over questions where the student cannot eliminate one or two obviously incorrect answers before making a guess.

- After studying test-taking techniques, have your child take a few tests in informal sessions.

- Administer another formal test, coming as close as possible to the actual test environment. Score the test using the answers provided in the preparation books.

Part Three

- Compare the scores between the original "cold" test and the second formal test.

  If your child has improved by 100 points or more, you may have accomplished the same results he or she would have received by taking an SAT or ACT prep course. Remember that the prep courses concentrate more on strategy than on content; more about this later.

If the score has not improved much between the cold test and the formal test, your student may benefit from some professional tutoring on test-taking strategies.

- Consider your child's weaknesses and strengths outside of the SAT or ACT test. If he or she has significant problems with algebra or reading comprehension it might be a more worthwhile use of your money to hire a tutor to concentrate on those skills. As I noted above, the SAT or ACT preparation courses concentrate on test strategies and not content.

It was my family's experience that tutoring works well. My son breezed through all things verbal, but had difficulty with math all through high school. We hired a math teacher to come to our home and work with him on algebra and geometry, beginning with basic concepts and then moving on to sample math tests from the SAT. The weekly courses extended for several months leading up to the test. The final results: a high verbal score, a slightly above average math score, and an academic scholarship that reduced the four-year cost of a very good private university by $32,000.

BEWARE THE PRICE OF SENIORITIS

The SATs came out fine. Recommendations from teachers and community leaders were effusive in their praise. And acceptance letters—complete with financial aid and academic excellence grants—are in from all six colleges.

Now's the time to blow off steam. Slack off on studies, let loose the inner Dennis the Menace, and paarrttyy! It's called "senioritis," and it was not invented in the twenty-first century.

Harmless gags such as soaping the principal's windows or taking part in a coordinated senior class silly-hat day are not going to harm anyone; as they want you to believe about Las Vegas, (most of) what happens at the old high school stays at the old high school.

HOW HIGH IS TOO HIGH?

Most admission offices at colleges make a real effort to look at the complete picture presented by applicants. A student whose high school transcript shows very poor math grades, even though the SAT or ACT tests present a very high score, may set off alarm bells. At the very least, the student may be asked to explain the discrepancy; at worst, the college may choose to place more emphasis on the transcript.

That's another reason why parents may want to hire a tutor for their child early in the student's junior high school or high school career to help boost grades in math or language courses. A good result here could have a double benefit, also improving standardized test scores.

There are some things, though, that don't stay a secret. Most colleges make their primary acceptance decisions on the basis of high school transcripts through the end of the junior year and sometimes including the first semester of the senior year. However, many will ask to examine the complete senior year transcript even after students have been accepted.

The schools are looking for students who slacked off in their final year in high school, dropped the more difficult courses, or even failed to complete courses. And of course, if mischief turns to misdemeanors or suspensions, the schools want to know about that too.

In most cases the warning is right there on the acceptance letter: admission is contingent on satisfactory completion of the senior year and receipt of a high school diploma.

In the worst of circumstances, a college reserves the right to withdraw its offer of admission to any student who shows a senior year performance that is much less impressive than the years that preceded. The admissions office also can take away or reduce any academic-based grant.

In the best case, the school may require a student who is guilty of serious slacking off to attend a summer school class or to take remedial courses in the freshman year of college.

191

chapter 16

DIRECT FROM THE EXPERTS:
A COLLEGE ROUNDTABLE

I was greatly assisted in my research for this book by a roundtable of experts on economics, personal finance, admissions, financial aid, and accounting. Read the interviews in the following six chapters for an insider's view of the business of college, the process of saving for higher education, a tour inside the admissions and financial aid office of a prestigious college, the view from a high school guidance counselor's desk, the perspective of a director of financial aid, and sage advice from a tax accountant.

Why do colleges charge so much money? Because they can get away with it, says Richard Vedder, distinguished professor of economics at Ohio University and an expert on the business of colleges. Consumers who may spend weeks researching the price of a car or months pondering the purchase of a house pay almost no attention to the true bottom line of the cost of four years of higher education for their children. We'll hear more from Dr. Vedder in Chapter 17.

Start saving early and don't stop, says Patrick Curtin, an accomplished financial planner and broker with Bank of America. And though your heart may tell you to put every dime into junior's college account, the smartest strategy may be to start funding your own retirement before you think about your children's education. Curtin discusses long-term and short-term financial planning in Chapter 18.

How does a prestigious college sort through a huge pile of applications to find the pearls amongst the . . . not-so-pearly? In Chapter 19, Monica Inzer, dean of Admission and Financial Aid at Hamilton College, explains how her office looks for the right match.

Thom Hughart, director of guidance for the 1,200-student Wellesley High School in Massachusetts, says that students should look beyond their region for bargains. In Chapter 20, he talks about the college search from the point of view of high school advisers and students.

Ken Kogut, former director of financial aid at Hamilton College, explains in Chapter 21 what it is like to be on the receiving end of applications for assistance and appeals for special circumstances. Financial aid offices are not selling cars, expecting families to try to shake them down for another $500 off the list price, Kogut says, but applicants with a good case for more aid will receive a sympathetic ear.

Americans are not very good at making sacrifices, says Robert Klein, an experienced CPA in New York City. He has clients who spend like billionaires but have nothing in the bank. You can read his advice—on taxes, savings, and the best gift you can give your children—in Chapter 22.

chapter 17

THE ECONOMICS OF THE COLLEGE INDUSTRY

Richard Vedder, distinguished professor of economics, has taught at Ohio University in Athens for more than forty years. He began teaching at OU in 1965 after receiving his Ph.D. in economics from the University of Illinois. Among his specialties is studying the economics of a one-of-a-kind industry: the American college and university business.

According to your research, in 1958 college expenses were about the equivalent of two months of a typical family's income, and today it has reached about six months of annual earnings. Why does college cost so much?

One answer is because colleges can get away with it. They can get away with raising the costs because the consumers have not been as sensitive to the price of higher education as they are to the price of most other things they buy in their lives.

Today, automobiles cost roughly the same as a year in college. People will haggle over car costs. They will change brand names to get the better deal. They will certainly change dealers. But they seldom will do that to the same extent with colleges.

Another reason colleges get away with raising the cost of education is that third parties are paying part of the bills, at least in the short run. In particular I'm talking about the federal government through its various loan and grant programs, and also the colleges themselves through private scholarship programs.

And colleges can get away with it because still, even with the high cost, it is a pretty good investment. The typical consumer who goes to college and earns a college degree will end up making more money, usually more than enough money to recoup the cost of going to college.

There are exceptions to this and they are growing in number, particularly when you consider that 35 percent or more of the kids who go to college don't graduate or at least don't graduate within six years. Some of those people, and particularly those who run up debt, are disadvantaged pretty severely.

But for the majority of people, college is still a pretty good deal.

Why do you suppose that consumers of college education will make careful spending decisions when it comes to buying a car or a house, but not for college?

It may well be that people think the more they spend on college, the better the education their kid's going to get, and from a purely financial point of view the better the job the student is going to get after college.

Although there hasn't been a lot of work done on it, it is probably true that the typical graduate of a quality private university makes a good bit more than the typical graduate of a public university. So that sort of compensates for the additional cost of going to a private school.

Similarly, the graduate of a public university makes a good bit more money—and we can document this—than do kids who graduate from a two-year community college.

Can this sort of situation continue without change?

As prices get higher and higher, people are starting to become more sensitive to costs. We are seeing some people trying to find ways around the high cost of education.

Perhaps they might send their child to community college for two years and then on to a four-year university for the last two years. That reduces the costs but still gets the prestige of the degree from the four-year school.

Taking courses online is another strategy. Taking courses in high school to get some credits out of the way at a lower cost is another.

The numbers are still very small, but some students are going to foreign countries, to Canadian or British or Australian universities, for example.

You say one of the reasons colleges are not price-sensitive is because there is so much government involvement. But there is a great deal of inequity in the formula, isn't there? People who are relatively poor are supported, people who are very wealthy don't have to worry about the cost, and then there is the great middle class that gets little or no help and has to pay the whole bill.

There are certainly some inequities in the system, and it's true that access to the system varies a good bit across the economic spectrum even with the various scholarship and loan programs. Many people in the middle class are getting gouged, particularly those in the upper middle class. People who are not super-rich but are reasonably affluent are still finding themselves paying pretty much the whole bill for college.

What the colleges are doing is taking money from these people and redistributing some of it to families of lower income, or in some cases as scholarships to talented students who may be from very wealthy families.

Is the system fair to those of us in the middle?

It is a difficult decision today to know what to do about preparing for college for kids.

The family that saves and saves and saves and does everything right, sacrificing their own personal consumption for many years to build up big savings accounts for their children for college, may find that they have enough money to pay for college but they won't get any of the discounts or breaks given to people who live more ostentatiously. People who don't save much for college and don't have many assets will probably get larger amounts (of assistance).

Colleges are (in effect) imposing an income or wealth tax on people. It is not a normal tax like one imposed by government, because the amount you pay for college depends on the amount you have; the more you have, the more you pay. Savings that you do put aside are going to be dissipated in having to pay a higher total cost for college.

One could question whether that is a good thing from a fairness point of view or even socially for the country.

You also point out in some of your writing that colleges are really not held accountable for their financial decisions, especially in a seller's market.

That's right. Colleges are unique and peculiar institutions. Many things about academia are quite different than the regular economy.

They even define things like an hour or a year differently. You might say, "I went to Stanford for a year," but what you really mean is you went to Stanford about the first of September and you left the end of May and took off a couple of weeks in December. You spent about eight months at Stanford; the twelve months that most of us think of as the definition of a year doesn't apply in academia. And an hour is usually about fifty minutes.

Colleges and universities are almost all not-for-profit institutions whether they are private or public, and there is very little incentive to keep costs down and to try to minimize costs, or to maximize the quality of what they do in order to get more revenue. The profit motive that is an instrument of accountability in most of society is missing from colleges and universities.

And even when we look at state universities, we see that the political process, which often provides accountability for government institutions, is more muted; state systems are given a high degree of independence from the government even though they receive government subsidies.

College boards of trustees tend to be part-time people who come on the campus maybe three or four times a year and are not familiar with what is going on. They usually hear one side of the story from the university administration.

Is there a top? Will we reach a point at which the cost of going to college will be too high to justify for all but the super-rich?

What we have now is an unsustainable trend. It is fine for the cost of college to rise even faster than the inflation rate; that could go on forever, at least in theory. But you can't have the cost of college rising so much faster than inflation that it is rising faster than people's income.

If it takes six or seven months to pay the bill at a college today and it used to take two months, maybe we can afford that. But if it takes two years to pay for a year of college, that gets to be pretty steep, particularly if you have two or three different kids, and if it gets to be five years or ten years it becomes an impossible financial burden. And if it ever got to that point—I don't think it would—people would just say, well, we just can't afford college. And we will have to do something else.

The piece of paper that you get from a college is an indication to employers that this person is reasonably intelligent, reasonably literate, probably speaks fairly articulately, is probably going to show up for work most of the time, and is probably not crazed with drugs or other disabilities. It is not necessarily proof of learning a lot in college. Learning happens, but that is almost incidental to other characteristics that are associated with that piece of paper.

There are other ways you can certify skills other than getting a piece of paper that is a diploma. We certify skills all the time with things like CPA exams and various licensing exams. Microsoft oversees exams [Microsoft Certified Professionals] to attest to competency on their software, and so do Oracle and Novell and several other companies. If you can say "I am Oracle-certified," that is a way of showing employers that you have a skill.

Are too many high school graduates going off to college? Is that part of the problem?

I don't know what the optimal amount is, but at the least one can conceptualize that there is an optimal number of students who ought to receive college education. Maybe we have exceeded that.

One thing is for certain: If you have attrition rates of 35 percent or more, as we do now, there are an awful lot of kids who enter college but never finish, and there are a lot of resources that are at least partially wasted. Although, I might add, going to college for two years and then dropping out doesn't mean it is a totally wasted investment. But it is a sign that many people are not achieving their expectations. Some of those students perhaps should never have entered in the first place.

chapter 18

DO SOMETHING *NOW* ABOUT COLLEGE SAVINGS

Patrick Curtin, financial adviser and vice president for Bank of America Investment Services, is an intense and dedicated steward of the investments and savings of his clients. Working on Nantucket Island in Massachusetts—one of the richest areas in America—he advises multimillionaire investors (and plumbers) as well as young account-holders just starting out with a few hundred dollars in the bank.

A graduate of Dickinson College in Pennsylvania, he worked for Morgan Stanley as a financial adviser and then Quick & Reilly as a senior financial consultant before that company was purchased by Bank of America. (The Pacific National Bank, where he works, draws its name from the eighteenth-century whaling industry that made Nantucket famous; the island, in the North Atlantic off Cape Cod, sent ships all the way around Cape Horn and into the South Pacific and up to Alaska in search of whales. The bank is the oldest business on the island, and its locations are the only two branches of nearly 6,000 branches of the company that do not have the Bank of America logo displayed outside.)

A young couple in their early twenties have just had their first child. They don't have a lot of extra money floating around, but they can look far enough into the future to know that they are going to have to find a way to pay for one—or two or three—children going off to college some eighteen years from now. What is the first step they should take?

The first thing I would say is this: don't focus solely today on funding your child's college education.

You need to think about what your goals are for the short term, intermediate term, and long term. It wouldn't be prudent for me to say, "If you have a few hundred or thousand dollars, allocate that for college for your child." It may be appropriate to set aside a portion of that for college, but you might also want to use some or all of it to fund an IRA for your own retirement.

I always recommend to parents that they not sacrifice their retirement assets to fund college because it is a lot easier for their child to fund college through borrowing and grants and loans and scholarships than it is to try to fund retirement through borrowing.

You're suggesting to young parents that they think first about their own retirement forty or so years down the road before they worry about paying for college in twenty years?

Yes. Many parents come to me full of all the horror stories. College tuition is going up anywhere from 5 to 10 percent a year, depending on which study you look at. They read an article that tells them in twenty years it is going to cost $100,000 a year to send their kid to school, and they feel they are going to need that kind of money in an account in order to make it happen. Well, that's not true.

The likelihood is they are not going to be able to save that kind of money no matter what they do between now and when the child is eighteen. And if they do focus solely on college they may be short-changing themselves when they are sixty-five or sixty-two or whenever they decide to retire.

As far as I am concerned, you've got to engage in a regular process over the years, as opposed to saying, "Give me $2,000 and we will stick it in a 529 plan and send you on your way."

I would encourage this young couple to focus on starting a systematic savings plan that disciplines them to set aside money. Put $50 a month in a 529 or a Roth IRA or a mutual fund or a savings account—it doesn't matter what the vehicle is—but just get something started.

Don't focus on the vehicle before you get the process under way. If you get into the habit of putting away $50 a month, you're going to save $600 a year that you wouldn't have otherwise set aside. Put away more if you can, but start early.

As a financial adviser, though, it's part of your job to recommend a vehicle or type of investment. For a long-term goal like a college savings fund, should you look for an aggressive, speculative investment or a more conservative type of asset?

Parents have to understand the ramifications of putting money in something that you might call speculative or aggressive; I prefer to use the word "volatile." These are investments where the principal is likely to fluctuate from month to month or year to year.

I don't get too carried away with whether or not we are trying to achieve 5 percent or 10 percent or 1 percent a year; whether the money goes into a savings account paying 1 percent or a balanced mutual fund with a goal of maybe 6 or 7 percent over an eighteen-year period is not the big issue.

I think the reason many people are not successful with retirement and college savings is that they do not have a disciplined approach to it. They put a couple of thousand dollars in an account and hope that they are going to have another couple of thousand somewhere down the line. If they have three, four, five, six, or more years where they don't put anything in, they are really not much better off than when they started.

I used the figure of $50 a month even though I know that is way too little. But I have found that if you start with a small amount that is comfortable, it is very easy to increase it over the years.

A great tool is to set up withdrawals that automatically come out of your checking account each month as if it were a day-to-day expense.

The same thing goes for retirement savings. Let's say the IRA contribution maximum this year is $3,000; it is a lot easier for many people to put aside $250 a month for twelve months than to come in with $3,000, because by the end of the year that full amount has usually been already spent on something else.

Putting aside a fixed amount of money each month into an investment is one way to even out the fluctuations in price for some investments, isn't it?

Yes. It is called dollar cost averaging if you are investing in something that is going to vary in price. You are potentially going to get much better pricing over a ten- or twenty-year period by putting in money every month.

If you were to instead invest in a bond fund that has very little fluctuation but pays a dividend, dollar cost averaging is still going to work because of fluctuations in the interest rate as it compounds.

Obviously there is no way to predict how the stock market or any other volatile investment is going to perform over time, but investment advisers have a pretty good sense of long-term averages, correct?

Yes. If we look back over history, over any particular ten-year period you can expect a positive rate of return. If we're looking at stocks, the rolling average will vary depending on the type of capitalization the company has.

[Capitalization refers to the market value of its outstanding shares; it is calculated by multiplying the stock price by the number of shares the company has put on the market. In relative terms, analysts talk about large-cap, mid-cap, and small-cap companies.]

Over a ten-year period, large-cap stocks have typically yielded between 9 and 11 percent, with small caps doing slightly better, anywhere from 10 to 12 percent. Within a 529 plan there are usually options where a client can opt to go with a single strategy if they want to put money into a small cap growth fund, which you could expect to be more volatile than a balanced fund that is composed of large cap, growth, and value stocks, and also bonds. The theory here is that they will get more return over time if they accept more volatility. If they have a short-term need, they may lose more.

Let's be realistic: Are you really expecting a proud new mom and dad to put their own retirement planning ahead of their child's college funds?

I think it is going to be much harder for people to retire in the manner that they envision because of inflation and other things going on in the world, and the amount of money that people spend. Most households spend more than they earn, and they expect that level of standard of living when they retire. That is just not feasible.

That is why you should put more of your finances toward retirement than college planning. But I do understand that many or even most parents and grandparents feel like they need to be doing something to be good parents.

I meet with people who want to dump all kinds of crazy money into college plans at the potential expense of their retirement down the road, or the goal of buying a house. They are going to worry about sending junior to Princeton before they buy a house.

Maybe junior can go to a good state college. And in any case, not every kid is going to be able to go to Harvard or Yale or Princeton or Duke. And there is nothing wrong with sending your child to a state college or a community college for two years and then transferring into a private school.

I think our society has some mistaken goals if we believe that every kid should strive to go to a $40,000 institution when the parents make $50,000 a year. There has got to be a compromise somewhere. I would like to have a Ferrari, but I don't because I can't afford it or I can't justify spending money that I should be putting away for retirement instead.

One of the advantages of many retirement plans Is that the funds you invest or the interest you earn may be exempt from taxes for some period of time.

Most retirement accounts allow you to make pretax contributions, or in the case of a traditional IRA, allow you to claim contributions as a deduction on your tax return, provided you meet certain criteria including income thresholds and that you are not an active participant in somebody else's plan.

A Roth IRA is an example of a plan in which you invest post-tax dollars but don't pay tax on the interest. Gains accrue in the account tax-deferred and then can be withdrawn tax-free if the IRA is at least five years old and you are at least fifty-nine years and six months old.

What are some dollar-smart ways to reduce a huge college bill?

Just as you should do with any other major purchase or investment, you need to investigate the product from all angles. One very good way to save a lot of money is to go two years to a community college and then transfer. A college is not good or bad because it is a two-year school rather than a four-year school. What is important is the quality of the professors.

Another way to save a lot of money is to go to a state school in your home state. Many parents don't want to restrict their children to going to a state school. You could argue all day long about whether or not a student will get a better education at a private school or a public school. I have taken classes at both; at the community college where I took a couple of summer courses, the professors were just as good if not better than the school that charged $30,000 a year.

Let's talk now about parents who have diligently put away as much money as they could for fifteen or eighteen years and their child is now ready for college. Let's say they have put some of that money into a retirement fund, some into the purchase of a house, and some into a college fund. What is the best strategy now that they face a $35,000-a-year bill?

Whatever you have done over the years, when it comes time to send your child to school you should consider the economy and your personal finances at that moment. If interest rates are low—like they were in 2004—real estate prices usually rise. That combination makes it easy and relatively inexpensive to borrow against the equity in your house.

Under the current tax code, in addition to mortgage interest, the first $100,000 of interest in a home equity line or home equity loan is deductible. [A line of credit has a variable amount of debt and interest rate, while a loan has a fixed amount and rate.]

Borrowing against your home in this situation is an efficient way to gain access to funds to use for college without sacrificing your retirement. You are leveraging assets of the bank or financial institution—other people's money.

[Warning: The downside to borrowing against the equity in your home is that you are putting the roof over your head at risk. Don't borrow more than you can reasonably expect to repay, and keep your college and other expenses as low as possible.]

Another way to borrow against your assets is to tap into a brokerage account; that's called borrowing on margin. It is a bit more speculative than using the equity in your home, and requires a bit more sophistication. You have to know that if something dramatic happens to holdings in your brokerage account, you may have to immediately repay the money you have borrowed.

You don't have to borrow from just one place, either. You can take some in equity and some on margin, for example. I think the reason more people don't seek multiple sources is that it requires more effort on their part.

Too many people want an easy fix: Give me the money to pay for the tuition. They don't want to sit down and spend an hour or two to make sure it is done as efficiently as possible. It's the same way with retirement funds and other investments; most people focus less on those details than on clipping coupons to go to the grocery store. That's why they are not really getting the most out of their situation.

The first house I bought, back in 1981, came blessed with an 18 percent mortgage rate. The cost of borrowing may not reach that level again in our lifetimes, but how would you deal with a return to double-digit interest rates?

If you are worried about the prospect of a big spike in interest rates, then you would go with a fixed product such as a home equity loan where your payment and interest are structured similar to a traditional mortgage.

And if rates are already too high to allow you to reasonably borrow against your home or brokerage account, then I think you should go back to a reconsideration of how much you can afford to pay. How much is it worth to go to a $30,000-a-year institution versus $15,000?

What about student loans? Is it fair to saddle a youngster with debt before he or she has earned the first dollar from a full-time job?

It really comes down to a judgment call from the parents. How much of the bill do they want to foot, and what is the message they want to send to their children?

I think balance is the name of the game. If you are going to borrow for college, some of the debt should be yours and some the student's; obviously, in most cases, the bigger weight should probably go on the parents.

Having students bear some of the debt also teaches them the value of what you are spending. I don't think the average child has any conception of how much it is going to cost to go to school. I know I didn't at first. Then one day I divided all the hours of tuition and I realized that if I missed a class it was like $240 thrown away forever.

Is any particular student loan program better than another?

There are differences, and both the parents and the students have to educate themselves about how they work. In any program there is a debt that needs to be paid back, on time. You could ruin or damage your credit rating early by not paying those debts back.

These are good programs, but a student cannot walk away from college with a degree and a $20,000 debt and ignore it; five years later their credit rating is really weak and they'll have a hard time getting a loan to buy a car or getting a mortgage to buy a house.

I still have student loans I am paying every month. It was a pact that my father and I had: when I chose to go to an expensive private school instead of a free state school, I agreed to pay a portion of the cost. It empowered me to make that choice, and it worked out for me.

Where do 529 plans fit in college planning?

A 529 is a savings plan defined under the IRS section 529 of the tax code. Each state oversees its own plan, outsourcing the management to companies like Vanguard, Fidelity, Franklin Templeton, and others.

As with any investment, the success of a particular plan is mostly due to the quality of the people managing the money. Don't focus too much on whether one plan has higher fees or expenses than another; it is much more important to choose a good management company.

One of the benefits of a 529 plan is that they have a very high limit, typically in excess of $300,000. Anybody can contribute to it: parents, grandparents, siblings, and friends. Taxes are deferred (meaning they do not have to be paid) on dividends and interest that accrue in the account, and then ultimately the gains are tax-exempt if they are withdrawn to pay for qualified educational expenses.

Obviously, the fact that you pay no taxes on gains is powerful. On the downside, the fees and costs are usually higher than they would be on most mutual funds; the state takes a fee, the money manager has a fee, and then a portion of that is sent to somebody like myself if there is an adviser involved.

But I think if it is managed properly you are going to get a nice benefit out of it, especially if you have time. If the child is fifteen or sixteen years of age that may be too late to get much advantage from it, but for a child who has seven or ten years or more before college it could be very useful. And it is really a great vehicle if you start it when the child is born and put money in every month for eighteen years.

Many of the plans allow the parents or guardians to set up a set of investments within the plan that changes as the child grows older and closer to attending college. For example, it might concentrate in the younger years on stocks, but as the child gets older it shifts to a more balanced approach with a greater percentage of fixed income and money market investments. There are also allocations that can be put together using specific mutual funds, and if someone wants to be really conservative they can just use the money market fund within the plan.

The money is under the control of a custodian, and it is necessary to report it on the FAFSA as part of the parent's assets and not the child's.

Parents with a lot of money don't have to worry about finding funds to pay for their child's college education, and parents with very few assets can expect—or at least hope—for substantial financial aid. The great middle class, though, has to scrape, save, and borrow.

Because the FAFSA and other financial rating mechanisms used by colleges pays a lot of attention to liquid assets of the parents (excluding retirement funds) and those held by the student, doesn't it make sense in some cases not to put money aside for college?

That's an argument you can talk about all day long. Would you rather play the roll of dice and hope to get more money in financial aid, or is it better to save and invest on your own? I lean toward trying to do both.

You don't want to depend on getting student aid and not getting what you anticipate. If you put money away for ten or eighteen years, you can at least guarantee yourself that some amount of money is there to use.

Financial aid assessments will take into account all of your assets as a parent except for retirement funds; some schools and programs also do not look at the value of your principal home.

That is why it makes a lot of sense to maximize those [retirement] accounts first. If your goal is to get as much financial aid as possible, you want to make sure you have put away as much as possible into retirement accounts and whole life insurance and things of that nature, which are relatively illiquid.

And doesn't that also argue in favor of putting as much money into your home as possible at a young age because it doesn't count—in most cases—as an asset when financial aid eligibility is calculated? And it gives you something to borrow against.

That's right.

Many states now offer prepaid college plans where you invest money over the years and lock in tuition and some other costs at current or even discounted levels and don't have to worry about inflation and rising costs. Some of the plans are limited to just a specified group of colleges in a single state, but increasingly we're seeing reciprocal agreements between various states to honor each other's plans.

This sort of plan may work for some parents and some students, but they might turn out to be pretty inflexible. What do you do if your child, at age seventeen, decides he doesn't want to go to school in your home state? What if she wants to attend a private school not on the list?

How on earth are you going to be able to gauge where an elementary school child wants to go to college ten years from now? Are you going to tell them that they have to go to UMass because that's where they are prepaid, and not to Syracuse, where they want to go?

This goes back to my original suggestion that parents encourage their children to go to a good state school or a community college at least for the first year or two. I know most parents don't want to make that suggestion, so why does it make sense to enter into a prepaid tuition plan where you are almost financially locked in to particular schools? The fact that some plans are now transferable between some states is a good thing.

But whether you like it or not, one wrong assumption in this country is that people think they are entitled to whatever they want whether they can afford it or not.

The first step . . .

Do something. Procrastination is the biggest enemy to any financial goal you have. If you put it off for one day, it becomes two, then four, then a month, then a year, and then two years. You've got to understand and take advantage of the power of time in investment: compounded interest and long-term gains.

People don't act for all kinds of reasons, but I think one of the most common is this perception that it is going to cost $200,000 to go to school. They say to themselves, "There is no way in hell we can afford it, so we are not even going to try."

But if you break it down and show them that if they can put aside a couple of hundred dollars a month and earn 7 percent a year for eighteen years, it can be done. If I can show that to people in that way, it becomes a more reasonable goal.

You can hope for more, and you might get less, but historically, over a ten- to eighteen-year period you can expect a 7 percent gain on a careful investment. At 7 percent, any particular investment doubles roughly every ten years. Financial advisers and bankers use something that is called the Rule of 72 and it works like this: Take the interest rate [expressed as a percentage, as in 6 percent] and divide it into seventy-two to determine roughly how long it will take your money to double. [For example, money earning 6 percent a year will take twelve years to double, as seventy-two divided by six equals twelve. The formula is a rough estimate, and also assumes that earned interest is compounded over the years.] That doesn't take into account inflation or taxes, but you try to deal with those factors in other ways.

So let's do some numbers. Show us a plan for eighteen years.

If you were to put away $300 or $400 a month for eighteen years, at the end of the process you would have invested something close to $100,000, and the investment should be worth close to $200,000 with just modest or average growth.

Now where are you going to come up with $300 or $400 a month for a college fund?

Well, let's start with the fact that most of us have car payments that are higher than that, so we're already able to set aside that kind of money. Do you really need a second car? Do you need to buy a new car every three years, or can you hold on to a vehicle for twice that time? Can you get by with a Corolla instead of an Expedition? How about buying a used car and putting the difference into a college fund?

Coming up with a $400-per-month investment takes $12 to $15 a day. If I break it down to those terms, you can sometimes see the light go on. Mom and Dad will look at each other and say, "that's easy."

It is easy, but you have got to do it in a systematic fashion. The best way to do it is to link your college fund to your checking account and have the money taken out on the first of every month. If you do it that way, you are going to ensure yourself a much better chance of success than if you leave it to random investments.

I know that if people wait until the end of the year to bring me their retirement investment, many will miss a year.

Unfortunately, many people are already in debt when their children are born. They may have student loans of their own, or a car payment, or a large credit card debt. In theory, that debt—especially consumer debt like the credit card—should be paid off first because it is so expensive.

That's correct, but I would advocate setting up a structured payment plan toward paying off the credit card as well as one toward a college savings plan.

I have to learn about the people I am advising. If I feel that I'm working with someone who is determined not to get into debt again, I might suggest they pay off the credit card bill before putting aside money for college. One of the things people have to guard against is something like this: Someone has

$10,000 in debt and they work hard to pay it off, and when they do they feel that they have a free pass to do it again and pretty quickly they have another $10,000 in debt . . . and no college fund.

The way out is to set up an automatic withdrawal plan from your checking account to pay off the credit card bill and to fund the college plan.

Some people are perfectly capable of handling debt—using other people's money—to leverage their own assets or earning abilities, while for others it is a dangerous, slippery slope. As an adviser, how do you tell what is right for a particular client or family?

If someone has a large credit card debt, I worry that they are not doing a good job of managing their finances. And that is where the refinancing and home equity line of credit or loan boom can be dangerous; if they use the value of their house to pay off a credit card bill and continue to run up debt, sooner or later they can end up in a situation where they are endangering the roof over their head—and not dealing with college funding.

And you have to pay attention to the fact that by the end of 2005, the Federal Reserve had begun raising rates pretty steadily. So rates for equity loans or lines of credit may start to become less attractive, and as interest rates go up real estate values sometimes slow their increase, which could reduce the amount of equity you have in your home. You and your financial adviser have to watch all these things.

The more cash value you start taking out of your house, the less flexibility you leave yourself. If a bank offers you 80 percent of the value of your house, that's a ready source of cash, but if there is a "correction" in the price of real estate you could end up being "under water" or "upside-down." [These two terms—one from the financial world and the other from real estate and car financing—mean the same thing: owing more on an asset than it is worth. In other words, you might owe $100,000 on a house that if sold would bring in just $80,000, and you would have to come up with the difference from other sources.]

Investments don't always go up, and different types of investments may be heading in different directions at the same time. When stocks go down, bonds may rise in value; when interest rates rise, home values may decline or stagnate. How do you guard against that?

Historically, every class of assets will fluctuate over time, going up, down, or sideways—staying level in value. That's even true of real estate.

The answer here is *balance*.

Invest your money carefully, on a regular basis, and in complementary types of vehicles.

Try to fund college from many different places. Don't do it just from a 529 account, and spread out the type of investments held within that account. Don't just plan on borrowing from your home equity.

When it comes to borrowing, I'd like to see a balanced approach, too. Don't become overextended with debt and don't sacrifice your potential standard of living down the road. Don't put too much on your child's shoulders when they are done with college. The parents should decide how much they are willing or able to pay, and how much they expect the child to pay in loans.

I think the child should be asked to get a job and put aside some money for living expenses while they are in high school. And he or she should seek academic, sports, or financial aid scholarships wherever possible.

All of this requires more involvement from the parents and the student, and a lot communication between them. It also takes more effort from someone like myself. Some of the advice I am giving here is not something that is going to earn me, as a financial adviser, a commission. But it is going to help the family's overall finances.

·How should someone choose a financial adviser? What should make you stay, and what should make you run away?

I think you should run out the door if an adviser wants to push a single solution on you without really getting to know your situation and your personality. I don't need to spend ten hours with somebody to get the feel for what I think they should do, but I would want forty-five minutes to an hour and two or three appointments before any firm decisions were made.

Unfortunately a lot of people, a lot of parents, want me to just give them the easy, quick fix. They might come in and say, "We want to set up a 529 plan, and here is $1,000 to fund it." I'd want to say, "Look, this is not enough to do it for you unless you keep adding to it." Sometimes parents get angry with me when I tell them they have to keep working at a plan month after month, but if they don't it's going to be hard for them to send their child to school.

If an adviser tries to shuffle you in and out quickly because you don't have a lot of money, I would look to someone else for assistance.

Most financial advisers earn much of their income from commissions, and 529 plans are not going to pay them very well. But that should not matter: somebody who is not willing to spend some time with you cannot have your best interests at heart.

We've been concentrating on systematic investment over time as a way to build up a college fund. There is also a strategy that is front-loaded: If you were to find a way to invest $50,000 in a college fund on the day your child was born, it should double in value twice by the time he or she is ready to enroll.

That strategy makes sense, but the reality is that most young parents are not in that situation. But the grandparents might be.

One of the advantages of a 529 plan is that grandparents or anybody who wants to can use five years of their gift tax exclusion at once and do it again in five years. In 2005, the amount of money a family member could give as a tax-free gift was $11,000, and so under that situation they could put $55,000 into a 529 plan. If there are two sets of grandparents involved, they could each put that amount into the plan.

If you put that sort of money into a balanced fund and earn a reasonable 7 percent a year on the money over eighteen years, the youngster should be in great financial shape when it comes time to go to college. Remember that gains in a 529 plan are tax-free while they are in the account, and withdrawals for educational purposes are also free of taxes.

And for the grandparents, a 529 plan can also be an estate planning tool because (in our example here) it removes $55,000 or $110,000 out of their estate, which is going to be left to junior and junior's parents anyway, and it does so without payment of taxes. In 2005, anything in the estate over $1.5 million is taxed as high as 45 percent, so this sort of early gift is a very valuable one.

But this sort of scenario is a hard one to make happen, even when I deal with people who have a lot of money. It is a communications thing. What I need to do to make this happen is to have all of the parties in the same room at the same time and we need to talk about money. The problem is that often the parents don't want to ask the grandparents for money, or the grandparents don't want to discuss their finances with their children.

If I get the chance to speak with them, I will ask grandparents if they have thought about funding their grandkids' education. That's a very nice way to do it.

It really takes a special relationship for all involved—the financial adviser, the grandparents, and the parents—to get a family meeting going. It's an important and difficult discussion to get going. It's part of overall estate planning, where the goal is to try to pass along as much of the grandparents' assets to the children and grandchildren as possible without giving it to the government.

If parents of a newborn went to their parents and said, "Our financial adviser said if you gave your new grandchild $40,000, that will pretty much take care of college in eighteen years," most people who have that kind of money would give it. Especially if they are shown that there are no tax implications.

We've talked about the 529 plan's advantages over some of the state-specific plans. How flexible is an investment in a 529?

The plans are pretty flexible. You can change the beneficiary so that if child A doesn't go to college you can switch it to child B. The money in the account can even be used if one of the parents wants to go back to school.

And in fifteen years if the grandparents or the parents suddenly find they need the money for retirement or health care or whatever—you name the scenario—they can also take the money out and pay a penalty and income tax on it should they choose. The fact is that if the plan has been in place for a while, the penalty over time is still relatively small.

The 529 account is under the control of the custodian, which could be the parents or the grandparents or someone else. The children do not have the right or the chance to get into the account and spend it by themselves.

You mentioned that one relatively painless way to come up with the monthly set-aside for a college fund is to buy a less expensive car and put the difference away in an investment. Any other tips?

Parents and grandparents who have life insurance with a cash value (usually in the form of a whole life policy) may be able to take out some of that money—tax free—as a loan to use for tuition. Billions of dollars are sitting in these policies, and most people never access any of it; when they are dead it goes to a death benefit. This is a very underutilized, tax-free source of funds for tuition.

Whole life policies may be somewhat less popular for today's baby boomer generation and their children, but more common among those a bit older.

What about the grandparents taking out a reverse mortgage as a source of tuition funds, drawing on the equity while continuing to live in their home?

I look at that as a last resort because you are giving up an appreciating asset. If it's a case where older people really don't need the money to make ends meet, then it is a strategy that is sometimes employed, but I would say ninety-nine times out of 100, let's try to borrow somewhere else.

Have you ever given thought to a different sort of scenario: Instead of sending a child off to college, handing him or her a check (or an investment account) worth $100,000 and suggesting they go off and get a job?

I said that to my dad when I was in high school, but the truth is that if you look at statistics about average income for a graduate with a four-year degree versus a two-year degree versus a high school diploma or a trade school certificate, it makes sense to go to college. For someone with a college degree today, the average income is somewhere from $70,000 to $90,000 per year, while those with a high school diploma average something like $25,000 to $30,000. If you spread that out over thirty years in the workplace, that makes a huge difference in the standard of living.

That doesn't mean you won't have people like Michael Dell of Dell Computers or Bill Gates of Microsoft who drop out of college and make billions of dollars. In my family, I have a relative who is a millionaire several times over from real estate; he never finished high school but has worked hard all his life.

There is always going to be a need for skilled trades; local plumbers and electricians charge as much as $100 an hour. In some places there are millionaires mowing billionaires' lawns. There is nothing wrong with that either.

It depends on the family and the student. It's one thing to say "I want to be an actor," or "I want to spend the next ten years walking across Europe." Those might not be realistic or productive goals. But just as an example, if you have a very good knowledge of computers it doesn't matter how many degrees you have; you can earn a very good living. If you are entrepreneurial, it doesn't matter how many degrees you have.

But if you want to be a physician or an attorney you have to go to a formal educational program.

So, as they say in financial circles, what's the bottom line?

One thing to take away from all of this is that there is no single solution for everyone. It is an ever-changing process because family dynamics may change over time. There may be more than one child over the years. There may be changes in earning power—up or down. There may be divorce.

I think the biggest issue for today's younger generation and their children is that the amount of money that will be required to maintain the same standard of living in retirement is going to be huge. Then add the fact that we are living to eighty-five or ninety years of age. The thing that really hurts retired people is unexpected health-care costs. So in addition to retirement planning, you should also have health insurance and possibly long-term care insurance before you start worrying about saving for college.

I am also a proponent—for people in the middle between wealth and ordinary means—of purchasing long-term care insurance. A long-term care policy bought at the right time and in the right amount will save the day for many people financially.

Leverage the resources you have around you. If you don't have a financial adviser, get one; if you have an attorney and an accountant, get them into the mix. Establish a relationship at your bank, especially if you are involved with a loan or other form of credit. Many people have all those parties in place, but they never have them talk to each other.

I don't speak with very many of my client's accountants and estate planners, and I wish I had the chance. There is this conception that everybody knows everybody's job. What an accountant does is very specialized. What the attorney does is very specialized. Yes, there is overlap, but I could not imagine doing taxes and legal work on top of what I do. I always tell people to watch out for anybody who is trying to do all of these jobs.

chapter 19

A DEAN OF ADMISSIONS SORTS THROUGH THE MAIL

Monica Inzer is dean of admissions and financial aid at Hamilton College in Clinton, New York. The prestigious liberal arts college places an emphasis on individualized instruction and independent research. Founded in 1793 as the Hamilton-Oneida Academy, it takes its name from Alexander Hamilton, first secretary of the U.S. Treasury and one of the original members of the board of trustees of the college.

What makes a particular student's application for admission and financial aid stand out from the pile?

Here at Hamilton College, we receive 4,000-plus applications each year and enroll about 470. How do I decide which ones to admit? Do we just want smarter kids every year?

The answer is we want more applications so that we can be more selective. We want higher quality. We want more diversity: geographic and ethnic. We want to win some football games. We want to be kind to the children of alumni because we are in a capital campaign, and if we can come in on target and not spend too much money that would be good too.

But before we even look at students who are interested in scholarships or aid, we look for the most attractive candidates.

At Hamilton we have selective college admissions, and that was also true at the colleges where I worked before. I was dean of admissions and student financial services at Babson College in Wellesley, Massachusetts, and before that director of admissions at Worcester Polytechnic Institute in Worcester, Massachusetts. So I have been at a business management, engineering, and now a liberal arts school, but all of them had selective admissions.

What are the school's goals?

[Each year] we decide what is most attractive to us. At Hamilton we have gone up incredibly in quality in the last three years, with average SATs up more than 100 points. Right now our goals are geographic and ethnic diversity, while we maintain quality. And then we are going to look at a number of other variables.

Of course, if you push a button in one place something is going to pop out the other side, so you can't do everything at once.

So a priority for us is geographic and ethnic diversity. That's going to make somebody more attractive for admissions.

At each of the schools I have been affiliated with, the basic way that you run your admission operation is like this:

- You gather a pile of applications from the people you would love to have on your campus—rock stars in every way. They may bring geographic diversity, ethnic diversity, be academic superstars, or they may be the great kicker on the football team.

Whatever their attributes, these are the people you know you want to have in your community. Other people are going to want to come to your school because of them. This is usually a small number.

- Then you set aside the applications from people who are obvious "denies." If we feel you can't do the work here, we are not going to admit you.

No matter how diverse—even if you come from North Dakota (nobody can get students out of North Dakota), or even if you are a great kicker—if we know you can't do the work at a college like Hamilton [we're not going to admit you].

- And then we have this huge pile in the middle, and you can only take so many. Any of them could do the work at our college or others. What we have to do is choose which ones to select, and that's where institutional priorities come into play.

We look for applicants who rise to the top because they meet various criteria we are looking for. We have conversations with families all the time where we have to say: Our denial doesn't mean your student can't do the work. It doesn't mean your student isn't equal to other students who are admitted based on whatever measurements you want to use. It just means the student didn't rise to the top because of selective college admission.

Let's talk about how a student rises to the top of that middle pile.

Coming from a state from which we don't have any students can make a difference. In 2004, our average SAT for admitted students was 1380. We are not going to go much lower than that for a kid from upstate New York who is not an athlete and needs financial aid, because he or she would not be bringing anything new to the community. But we may dip a little lower on the SAT scores for a student from Iowa or North Dakota because we don't get many students from there.

As we read applications we are constantly evaluating how attractive the student is to us, and that is not just based on academics.

So if you are a common commodity in one place and a rarity in another, it makes sense to consider applying to colleges where you will expand their diversity?

[If a family is shopping for the best financial package without a particular college in mind] they should consider looking at schools that are out of their own region. They may be more attractive to those schools; it may help them not only with admission, but if the school has only so many dollars to give out they may be more willing to spend it on someone who is going to bring them geographic diversity rather than someone who is from their own home state.

So at this point you have looked at academics and diversity. The question of whether the student or parents can afford tuition and room and board has not yet been examined.

The first lens is academic. Can the student do the work here? We get rid of those for whom we think the answer is "no," no matter who they are.

The next lens is: What do they bring to this community?

[After that] we try to achieve consistency [within a particular group]. Just as an example, we may get twelve applicants a year from Phillips Andover Academy in Massachusetts; we want to be consistent within the school because they are all getting their decisions in the same mailroom.

And then we look at financial aid, and here we consider ourselves need-aware or need-sensitive.

We look at the group of students we want to admit and ask: "If we admit them all, how much will it cost us in terms of their financial need?" And if we see we would need to put out more dollars than we think we should, we pull back some decisions at the lower end. That is the hardest part of what we do.

Hamilton is different from many other colleges in its declared process in that it is need-aware in its admission policies. Some schools may have so much money available in financial aid that they can admit anyone they want and still have enough aid to support them all.

Other schools keep the admissions process completely separate from financial aid, but when it comes time to total up the financial requirements of students they may end up having to offer reduced aid or no aid at all to some needy applicants.

Among college administrators, you will hear talk about admission processes that are "need-blind" and those that are "need-aware." Hamilton is the most selective college I have worked at, and it is the first place I have worked at that is need-aware.

At my previous colleges, we didn't consider whether a student was applying for financial aid as a factor in the admission process; we absolutely didn't. We admitted who we were going to admit.

However, we still had only so much in the financial aid budget. We had to spread the available financial aid among the students we were going to admit; we had to do what we called "gapping." If someone needed $20,000, we might only be able to give them $15,000 and hope they would make up the rest with a loan.

How does a need-blind process work?

Need-blind colleges are schools that make admission decisions without any consideration of whether or not a family is applying for financial aid or what they need. After that they see if they can afford to give aid.

There are some need-blind colleges that will let their admission decisions stand, while others will use some kind of rating system. If it is on a fifty-point scale, they might decide that they will meet the needs for everyone ranked forty and above; people who fall in the next group will be admitted but may not have all of their needs met, and there is a bottom group of people who are lucky enough to be admitted but might not receive any financial aid.

There is an inside-baseball term college administrators sometimes use: *admit/deny*. You are admitting someone because he or she earned it, but you are denying financial aid. And you know you are not going to get many of those kids to come, but you don't feel it is fair to not admit them.

Sometimes they spread out the pool of money so that at the end of the day they might be meeting 90 percent of the need of all the students who were admitted, but some students might be getting 80 percent of their need met and other students 100 percent. I've worked at colleges where we had what we called differential or preferential packaging based on how attractive the student was.

Hamilton is on the other side of that coin. Our philosophy is this: We don't want to admit students and then not give them financial aid if they are in need. That's just not fair and it doesn't feel good. And selfishly, it hurts our own ranking among colleges if we are throwing out admission offers to kids who can't come here.

No college will want to admit it, but a lot of what we do is to help ourselves in the rankings. We have to pay attention to that. It doesn't feel good to admit kids we can't give financial aid, so why don't we as a last step before we finalize our admissions decision look at what the family's need is.

And so we will get all the people we want to admit, and if we don't have enough money to go around we will not admit some of the students at the bottom of the list who have high needs. We'll admit some of the students who can afford to pay in their place, and we'll change the others to a deny or wait list in case we have more money later.

Is being need-aware a matter of philosophy, or is it simply related to the amount of money that you have available for financial aid?

It is an institutional decision. There may not be many other schools of our caliber that have been working in this way for as long as we have, or are as honest about it.

But I feel we owe it to families to let them know. The reality is that we are running a business. Nobody wants to talk about it like that, but at the end of the day we have a budget to balance, and it is getting harder and harder for colleges to balance their budget.

Many colleges have these lofty goals to make sure that they are accessible to students from lots of backgrounds—diversity is a huge initiative right now for almost every college, and especially here. You want to provide access to students who are first-generation college, particularly at private colleges, yet we have a limited number of dollars to go around. We have to figure out a balance, and so we factor in financial need when we make admission decisions.

Are the schools with the largest endowments need-blind? In 2004, Harvard announced that applicants whose families make less than $40,000 will not be expected to contribute to tuition costs at all—if they are accepted on an academic basis. [The schools with the largest endowments are Harvard University, Yale University, University of Texas System, Princeton University, Stanford University, Massachusetts Institute of Technology, Emory University, Columbia University, University of California, and the Texas A&M University System.]

We have a huge endowment but we have to be responsible with the money we have. Harvard is need-blind.

But I would guess there are many colleges that are tinkering around the edge of being need-aware whether they would admit it or not. At Hamilton we have been out there for more than ten years saying we consider financial need as a factor.

All that said, 52 percent of our students were on financial aid in 2004. We spent more than $5 million on the freshman class last year. We have more than $18 million (allocated) to our entire student body.

Here's another inside-baseball term: We are operating at a 30 percent discount rate, a higher rate than many of our peers. The discount rate is the gross tuition dollars for the number of students you have, less your financial aid budget.

The average private college discount rate was a bit higher than other schools, probably because the most selective colleges attract more students from families with more money. Most of our competition ranges between 25 and 30 percent.

Even though we are need-aware, we are giving out more financial aid than most of our peers. Some of that is because of decisions we have made. We have attracted a higher quality student. We have raised our SAT average by more than 100 points in recent years. We are moving up the rankings.

What do you know about the decision-making process amongst applicants to a highly selective school like Hamilton?

We are more selective than we have ever been. We are not the top choice for every kid who applies here, but 50 percent or a little bit less of our incoming class will be early decision applicants where we are the top choice.

225

When we look at students who apply for a regular decision, our yield is about 18 percent [from that larger pool].

Of the regular admission applicants, it is hard to know whether we are their first choice or their eighth choice; some students are applying to ten or twenty schools.

At Hamilton, are students who apply for early admission more likely to get financial aid than those who seek regular admission?

No. They are not more likely to get their need met, but they are more likely to get admitted because they have applied early decision. The preferential treatment they are getting is with admission.

We are pretty up-front about our process: if you want Hamilton, apply early decision. It is the only way to let us know. We want to fill the school with people who love us.

At some schools, though, it may make sense to apply early to get a better shot at the bucket of financial aid.

That is correct. There are places that are need-blind where they run out of money for the last admits, and at those schools it is definitely a financial advantage to apply early decision.

At Hamilton, it is to your advantage to apply early decision as far as getting admitted, but we are going to give the same financial package to the early decision person as we will to a regular decision applicant.

In general, not just at Hamilton, what is the best strategy when you consider early admission?

There is some controversy about early decision, with claims that it puts families who need money at a disadvantage. There are some colleges that will criticize admission deans like me who say, "If you want Hamilton, apply early decision," because it puts too much pressure on students to make a decision early.

Very often the neediest students are the first generation in their family to go to college. They may not be as sophisticated in the process. They may not be able to make that top choice and get the application in by October. They may not have been able to travel and visit the schools. They may need more time to make a decision and shop for the best financial aid package. And so they end up applying in the regular decision process and some people feel they end up being shut out.

It is harder to get into the places they want by the time regular decision comes around, and that's a fair argument. I am not sure aid is endangered, but because they wait to shop for aid they may be putting themselves at a disadvantage on the admissions side.

Turning the question around, doesn't it make sense for some people to apply to six or eight schools, hope to be accepted to all of them, and then wait to see which one offers the best financial assistance or the lowest bottom-line cost?

That might be the smart thing for families to do if the student is not determined to go to one particular school and is willing to lower the likelihood of getting into one of the more selective schools. That's the chance they take if they are going to be shopping.

Do I hope for a better offer and run the risk of not getting admitted to my top choice? It's tough for families.

I am working right now with a recruited athlete in a situation that gives a whole new layer to this. At Hamilton we don't give athletic scholarships, but coaches are pressuring kids to go early decision because they want to lock them in. They do not want other schools competing for these kids. Here we have an athlete who has SATs over 1500; he is a star athlete and a smart kid, one of the best applicants we will see this year.

We gave him a terrific financial aid package based on need, admitting him early decision. Now the dad is calling and saying he is not sure it is enough. "Other schools and coaches are telling me they are going to give me more financial aid," he said. "We might get a merit scholarship above and beyond our need. And I have another son and I have $80,000 worth of loans. And so I may need to sit around and wait for these other packages."

I told him, "You made a commitment to us [by applying for early admission]."

Here is a kid who would have been admitted to Hamilton early or during regular admission; we would have been lucky to get that kid. The dad tells us his son's top choice is Hamilton but there may be someplace else that might give more money. I don't want to identify the other schools, but they are not in the same league as Hamilton.

So what I am saying to the dad is: Those schools may give you more money, but they are a tier below where we are, and you need to weigh value. Is it worth $4,000 more a year for your son to graduate from Hamilton?

Many of the supposed experts on college financing advise people to call up the dean of admissions or the financial aid office and lobby for more aid. Does that work?

We call that "dialing for dollars." It happens and it is embarrassing for those of us in the profession, because we would like to think that everybody is making their best offer up-front and that we are doing the best we can for students we have admitted because we want them to come.

But there are some schools out there that will tell the parent, "Send me the package from [the other school] and we will take a look and see if we can match it."

I don't want to completely stereotype the situation, but it is usually something that a less selective college will do. Some of it has to with survival. They might go out with a little less money than the family needs, and if they hear from a prospective student they might add to the offer.

But places like Hamilton are not about negotiating packages. I always want to hear from a family if they think we are way off from what they need. And that's what we tell them, that's what we advise them. I have had families calling me trying to negotiate and trying to play hardball with me and I just say you need to go someplace else.

Financial aid is based on a formula, and sometimes there are situations where families don't fit the formula or we might have missed something. In that situation, you should call the school: "Mom just got cancer and she is not going to be working next year even though the tax return shows her income." We want to know that.

We don't typically like families to call and say, "We have four other packages that are better than yours," and ask us to match them. However, we do understand when they do, because there are other colleges who say to do just that.

But just to clarify: If parents or students call and ask for an improved financial aid package, it's not going to result in the college withdrawing its offer of admission?

No. We only withdraw offers of admission if we question moral character, honesty, academic integrity, or if a student doesn't do well in the final semester of high school.

Some families can fill out the FAFSA form easily because one or both of the parents have a steady salaried job with easily documented assets. And then you have people whose stream of income is less regular. They may be between jobs, or going through a divorce; they may be self-employed with great fluctuations in income from year to year. How should they deal with the financial aid office?

The package is the package and the formula is the formula unless there are extenuating circumstances. In any nontraditional situation, a family should always come forward and speak with the financial aid department. There are supplements for people who own their business or are self-employed. There are supplemental forms for farm owners. There are supplemental forms for people who are divorced or separated.

We try to capture as much as we can with forms but usually there is some story to tell, and in order to help the student the financial aid office needs to know about it.

If most schools work from the FAFSA information, how come different schools — with similar levels of available funds from endowments and other sources — may offer different amounts of aid?

At Hamilton, and at many other schools, we have our own formula. We don't just go by the FAFSA. Schools use the federal methodology or an institutional methodology or some combination.

The important thing is that it is consistent at a particular school. A better essay on the application is not going to get someone a better financial package [when we're offering need-based aid].

So a great essay, a spectacular set of recommendations, and a compelling personal story is not going to earn you a higher financial aid offer?

Well, first of all that might make the difference on whether or not a student is admitted. And that would be what we would look at for a merit scholarship.

But I'll go back to the rating of applicants: We have only so many spots and we can only take so many people, and sometimes someone is taken off the table because of their high financial need. But sometimes someone from that bottom rung gets included even though they have high financial need because they represent something to the college that we don't already have.

What else can you do to raise your visibility on the admission and merit scholarships?

One thing that helps your chances of admission and possibly receiving a merit scholarship is to make a visit to the college. Schedule an interview if they offer that opportunity—unless you think you would interview poorly.

There are students where an interview will backfire on them because they arrive unprepared and don't know anything about the college. They are only there because mom and dad want them to be there, and they don't do well. In those cases the interview is going to work against them when we sit down in an admission committee.

But if they think they can interview reasonably well, it always communicates to the college that this is a student who is truly interested in attending. We want to admit kids who want to come. We want to offer scholarships to students we like.

The best way we can get to like them and get to know them is not just their transcripts and their SAT scores. Often it is other things like a recommendation, a really good essay that gives us insight into the student, and an interview where they really connect with the interviewer. All those little things around the edge can add up to make a difference.

What is the key to getting a merit scholarship?

[If you're looking for a merit scholarship you should do the research about colleges and apply to schools where you will be highly valued.] At Hamilton, if you are within our expected profile—in the SAT range of 1350 to 1400 and an A- student in an honors program—you shouldn't expect to receive a merit scholarship. You would have to be head and shoulders above that.

But if you were to look at schools just one rung below, which might not be quite as selective, you might be very happy and be considered a star student there. Are there huge differences in the education you would receive at places like Skidmore or Hamilton? No. I think they are both outstanding places; I went to Skidmore.

But Hamilton is ranked higher, is going to get more applications, and is a little more prestigious. So the same applicant who may not get a merit scholarship at Hamilton may get money at Skidmore or another school.

Before we took our son to visit colleges, we put a sport coat on him and sat him at a desk and role-played an admission office interview. He hated it, but later on when he came out of the real thing he told us we had done a great job preparing him for the process. And he received a four-year merit scholarship at a good school.

It is always good to prepare children for the interview process because it is unnatural for teenagers to talk about themselves. They really haven't had to sell themselves before. They haven't gone through formal job interviews like the rest of us.

A good interview can help with the admission process and merit scholarships. At some schools, like Babson, once you make the first cut for a merit scholarship (based on your application) they invite you to the campus for an interview. So much hinges on that interview, and you have got to be ready.

What are the most common sort of questions asked at a college admissions interview?

There are schools that will ask if you could be any kind of plant what would it be, or something stupid like that. Or they might ask which three people from history you might invite to dinner. Those are the exceptions, and they get talked about a whole lot more than they probably should.

By and large we are trying to get to know the student and we are going to ask them about themselves. We are going to ask them why they are interested in coming to our college. Why do they think it is a good fit? We'll ask them about their academic strengths. We'll ask them what they like to do.

Basically, the question is: Tell me why we should admit you.

The student should know about the school where they are applying. They should know enough about themselves to explain why they think the college is a good fit, and be able to articulate it.

I say it like it is so easy, but I know it is tough. I tell families all the time that the answer to why a school is a good fit is sometimes a gut feeling.

Sometimes they don't know why they like the colleges they like. You probably went through this with your own kids: you choose a school based on guidebook ratings and you make a visit and as soon as you drive on the campus the student says, "We should go home. I don't want to be here." They probably can't tell you why. And then they love other places you never thought they were going to like, and they can't tell you why. It is just a feeling.

And then the student goes into an interview and they have to describe why it is a good fit and they'll try to talk about the courses and the faculty. I think it's okay to talk about feelings, because we go on that feeling sometimes when we are admitting students. Yes, it's scientific; yes, it's mathematical; but part of it is an art—a feeling.

What would be a home-run answer to the question: Why are you applying here?

It depends on the college, but it comes back to knowing something unique about the school.

Here at Hamilton I would take note of the fact that the college has a very unique curriculum. Almost every other liberal arts college has a core curriculum with required courses. Hamilton is different because we don't. We tell students to take what they want. You decide your own path; we are not going to prescribe it for you.

We are really careful in our advising and we want students to be in a classroom only with those who want to be there and not with students who are required to take that class. I want people I interview to know about that, and I want to know from them if that's a good fit for them. I want them to be choosing us for what is different about Hamilton.

Beyond that, I want them to feel that our school is a place where they will be happy and thrive. If it turns out they are a fish out of water or if they are there because mom or dad went there and told them they had to go, they are likely to be unhappy and not do well, and I will have to replace them later.

Another thing is that at Hamilton we are in the middle of nowhere in upstate New York. I like it here and most of the students who choose us love it here. They love the sense of community. It's not the college for those who want a Division I basketball team or Boston or the ocean.

I interviewed a woman for a job in my office last week and she was doing really well until I asked her, "What is your dream job if you could do anything in the world?" She said she would love to be a pastry chef. And I thought: wrong answer.

But kids say things like that in admissions interviews. They say, "I would love to be a nurse." And I think to myself: We don't have a nursing school at Hamilton. It's over.

So, research the school where you are applying and interviewing. Know enough about it to be able to speak thoughtfully about it, and why you think it is a good match for you.

Even with early admission and regular admission deadlines and letters of commitment and deposits, schools are never 100 percent sure who is going to begin classes in September until they show up.

There is this phenomenon we call "summer melt" in the business. We want 470 students to show up in September and we may receive more than 500 deposits. We know that we are going to lose some over the summer. It's unfortunate, but sometimes kids will pay deposits at two colleges and take the summer to decide. Sometimes they're caught in the wait-list game: They paid their deposit at Hamilton but their top choice is really Middlebury, and when Middlebury calls in July and says they have a spot, they jump and leave a vacancy at Hamilton.

So we will over-enroll on purpose to account for that summer melt. It's not like I have extra spots or extra money. I overspend on financial aid because I know that not everybody is actually going to show up.

That's one of the most popular questions we get. Families who don't get merit scholarships will call and ask, "If the students who were offered merit scholarships don't come in September, is there money left over for the rest of us?" And I have to tell them we issue more merit scholarships than we have in the budget, knowing they are not all going to come. If they all come I am in trouble.

It is the same thing with financial aid. We go out with three times as many admission offers as we have space for and twice as much money as we have; if they all came I would be in trouble.

When deposits are due I don't sleep very well; what if enough don't sign up, or what if too many come? But I always say that April is the students' revenge on admissions people. We put them through hell with the whole process of choosing colleges to apply to, and come April the process is over and they are waiting on pins and needles. We finally give them a decision and then the roles reverse. They can shop. They can choose where they want to be, and it is the colleges that are on the waiting end.

Precisely because of what you just outlined—summer melt—some advisers tell enrolled students to reapproach the financial aid office in September to see if more funds have opened up. Is that good advice?

Yes and no. There's still only a limited pool of money. But as I said, when you first receive a financial aid package if you feel it isn't going to be sufficient, talk to us then. If, as it gets closer to September, it feels that way, talk to us. If in your junior year you feel you can't pay the book bill come talk to us, and we will try to find a way to work with the family and map out a payment plan. This is all especially true at smaller communities like Hamilton.

It doesn't mean we are going to say, "Oh, we will just pay for you the rest of the two years because you said you can't pay." But once you make a commitment to a school you should always work with them and talk to them and be honest and map it out.

My daughter was accepted at an excellent, very expensive major private university and offered almost nothing in financial aid. And she was also accepted at a small college and offered the highest merit scholarship they had available: free tuition for four years with the requirement that she maintain a 3.5 average. All we would have paid for was room and board and books. We tossed and turned for weeks because we were talking about the difference between a $150,000 bill for four years versus

perhaps $30,000. We ended up declining the merit scholarship because we felt the educational experience quality was not equal.

I think that happens all the time, although the range of money here is probably bigger than most. You've told me the two schools involved, and I would say they are several tiers apart in quality and prestige.

For some families, if the difference between schools is razor thin, you would be crazy not to take the scholarship, but if the student wants to go to a much better school and if you can afford to pay for it, that becomes a much harder decision.

Part of our thinking was that it would be huge pressure to maintain a 3.5 average at any quality school and we weren't sure it would be fair to our daughter to give her that assignment. My son also received a merit scholarship and his required a 3.0, which he was able to maintain for his entire undergraduate career. We felt that the 3.5 requirement was like a bait-and-switch sale.

I would hate to accuse a college of bait-and-switch, but it is hard to maintain a 3.5 average at a good school; 3.0 is usually the norm for a merit scholarship.

She would want to challenge herself and have the best experience she could have in college, and there would always be this pressure to keep the scholarship. I think that is too much to put on most kids; perhaps a 3.0 or 3.2 is more reasonable.

Actually, here at Hamilton, we have no GPA requirement for merit scholarships.

When I was at Babson we required a 3.0 for merit scholarship recipients, and we were pretty firm on that. If someone was right below that level they would probably have lost whatever scholarship they had; we would generally allow an appeal, and we would have given them another semester to come back above the minimum.

It's not really about the money, because the college has committed the funds to the family. It's more about academic integrity. A school is saying you are one of our best coming in, and if there are other kids who are getting 3.9 without a scholarship [it isn't fair]. We expect you to be one of our best.

235

Is it a reasonable strategy to accept a scholarship from a second-choice school and attend for two years before transferring to a college that would be at the top of the student's list? One of the financial advisers I spoke with for this book suggested things like attending a community college for two years to cut the cost of college roughly in half.

I think it is a reasonable strategy for families who are really struggling with the finances. I hate to see it, but I understand the reality when a family says we are only going to pay so many dollars.

As the student and the family decide where to apply and how much schools cost (with or without a merit scholarship), the parents have to be up-front and say we are going to pay for whatever you want, or we are only willing to pay a certain amount. If you get too far in the process and the kid falls in love with a school that might be beyond the family budget—that's when it gets difficult.

I think these sorts of conversations have to happen before the packages are out on the table.

How high is up? Can tuition and room and board continue to increase at the rate they have for the past decade?

Ten years ago I didn't think we would still be seeing increases. Fortunately, our financial aid budgets are usually tied to the tuition increases. But for families who don't qualify for financial aid, it is out of control.

I don't think it can continue to rise. Colleges have to kick in more because federal funding isn't going up, and in order to do that they have to raise tuition, and it just keeps escalating out of control. It is obscene. It is embarrassing. But as long as people continue to pay the bill, colleges will continue to [raise rates]. I think if students stopped coming, we would have to say rates are too high now.

chapter 20

A HIGH SCHOOL DIRECTOR OF GUIDANCE ADVISES US

Thom Hughart is director of guidance at Wellesley High School, a 1,200-student school. The town is an affluent suburb of Boston best known as the home of Wellesley College, one of the top-ranked liberal arts schools in the nation and perhaps the best of the exclusive Seven Sisters women's colleges. Hughart has been at the high school for fifteen years; he has master's degrees from University of Massachusetts Boston and Assumption College in Worcester, Massachusetts, and an undergraduate degree from Merrimack College in North Andover, Massachusetts.

As a high school guidance counselor, what are the hot-button issues faced by students and parents these days?

The more competitive colleges have become more selective than ever because there are more students and they can afford to be more selective. The anxieties of getting into a "good college" is beginning earlier, in the junior year and before.

One thing I don't hear a lot about from students is cost. It is a concern for parents, but for the kids that is not even a factor. Wellesley is quite affluent and a lot of parents have not taught them but instead have protected them, so they don't have to worry about the financial end of things.

You were quoted in a newspaper article saying that students can find good schools and good bargains by looking outside of their own region. As an example, you said students in New England should consider heading south of the Mason-Dixon line or to head west of the Hudson. How are you received in Wellesley when you suggest they consider going out of the area instead of attending a name-brand school in Boston?

When I first said this, probably about fifteen years ago, people looked at me as if I had two heads. The tradition had been pretty much that 80 percent of the class stayed within 500 miles of Boston. But gradually, over time, people have begun thinking about it. A lot of factors have entered into the decision other than just the money. Today demographics as well as economics have made it a real option.

And [it's also worth considering going north] because Canadian schools are a great buy right now: McGill College in Montreal or Queen's University in Kingston, Ontario, or York University in Toronto, or other schools.

Your own son and daughter both attended the University of Mary Washington in Virginia, a public college. How did that come about?

My son's guidance counselor, who had a real good sense of him, suggested he look at Mary Washington. Both of my children had an [interest in] international affairs or political science. My son was accepted at a number of schools and chose Mary Washington for his own particular reasons; kids decide because they like the music playing in the dorm that day or because the sun was shining or the right number of kids were playing Frisbee on the front lawn. He chose that school and it was a great find for him. Actually, he had his own process. He interviewed people in the political science department.

Finances were not the primary driving factor, but I knew from my own research that we were looking at out-of-state tuition at a state school. When he started it was probably about $17,000 to $18,000 for everything [which is still a relatively good deal].

Then my daughter visited him down there. She had her own list, and Mary Washington may have been the only school my son and daughter had in common. She decided she liked it down there, and it was big enough that they wouldn't be bumping into each other all the time.

The irony is that my son went there because he wanted to be challenged. He eventually went into economics and it was really challenging. My daughter wanted a college that was very demanding but where she could also take it easy and have a good time and they both ended up at the same school. They were both perfectly happy. And of course, it was fine come parents weekend, when my wife and I didn't have to split or make two trips.

What do you advise parents when the subject turns to the cost of higher education?

What I advise many parents to do is to have a frank discussion with your child at the end of their high school junior year. "This is now much money we can afford to pay for college," you say. "You are welcome to go to any college you want, but if it goes beyond 'X' amount then you are going to have to make up the difference in loans and [scholarships] and things like that."

We had that discussion with our children, and fortunately they both came in within the ballpark of what we felt we could afford. So they didn't leave with a lot of debt. My son was very aggressive about getting scholarships, and he probably brought in $5,000 or $6,000 through different applications he made.

Monica Inzer, dean of admissions and financial aid at Hamilton College in New York, says that if a student applies with 1400 SATs and a 3.5 grade point average and all the right references and you come from upstate New York you'll be a good candidate, but just one of the crowd. But if you are the one applicant from Iowa, suddenly you're

239

much more interesting. And, she said, it works the other way too: a student from New York applying to a school in Iowa may earn a few points for diversity. Is that your experience as seen from the high school end of the process?

Absolutely. We tell the kids and the parents exactly that when we go through the search process. We tell them, look at which colleges have the least number of students from Massachusetts and apply there; it is a good way to hedge some bets.

It's not the case everywhere, though. I was down in Tulane not too long ago and I noticed that something like 39 percent of their student body was from the northeast, so I am not sure how big a factor that would be down there, as an example.

The other thing is that some high schools are well known at certain colleges. [The admissions directors may know the guidance counselor] or they may know the school's reputation, the curriculum, and the rigor of the education.

More and more students are choosing to apply to college under early decision programs. What's your advice?

That's a toughie. [First of all, in all my years as a counselor] I have only had one case of a student who got accepted early decision to a school he didn't want to attend. He went and did fine.

The advice we give is that early decision [ED] is fine for students who have found a school they love and if accepted, they would go. And the students also have to be organized enough to meet the deadlines.

There's also something called early action [EA] that benefits the student because they can still hold off until May 1 for their decision.

It gets a little complicated because ED is binding and we have to make sure students are only applying to one school. And now we have a handful of schools offering early action single only; it is not binding, but you are not allowed to apply to any other school on an early deadline.

[Some schools are using things like early action single only] to recruit more of the stronger students, and they have added a few enticements like guaranteed housing, first choice at courses, and there may be a $2,000 scholarship or something on that order if you get accepted on the early program.

In general, early decision has been great for those of our students who use it; I would say we have close to 40 to 45 percent and maybe even more who apply in an early program or rolling admission.

At the end of junior semester we meet with all our students in seminars, and the whole purpose for that second semester is the college search process. So by the time they come back for senior year they have done a lot of the preliminary work in terms of search and getting applications and making visits. So when they get here in September, a lot of them are ready to roll.

How do you counsel a student who receives a merit scholarship that is extremely demanding in its requirements? I use as an example my daughter; she is a good student, and one small school offered her a full four-year tuition scholarship but required her to maintain a 3.5 GPA to keep the grant.

Ow!

With a great deal of pain, we ended up deciding that was too much pressure to put on her shoulders.

Absolutely.

The federal financial aid system requires that students earn at least a 1.7 average the first semester and 2.0 after that.

It depends on the student. I would know the student's academic record, maturity, and work ethic, and if I felt it was going to be a risk I would counsel the parent and the student to maybe rethink that one. Do they really want to make that commitment and, as you said, accept that kind of pressure?

One of the things we are focused on at the high school is alleviating stress for students and parents. I would encourage students to be very cautious, to think about the expectations and what their life is going to look like if they are trying to maintain something like the 3.5 GPA asked of your daughter.

You said that because of the general affluence of Wellesley, the issue of the cost of college is not always paramount. At the same time, you said that parents should sit down with their children and tell them how much money the family has available for college and ask the children to make the decision whether to stay within that range or accept debt. Financial planner Patrick Curtin gives the same advice, but he has no children; I said to him what he was saying makes eminent sense but probably goes against the heart of most parents.

Yes, because it puts limits and restrictions on their children. But we do recommend that parents try to give the student some idea that there are some financial restrictions.

The other thing we tell students and parents is that it is okay to apply to a $40,000-per-year college. Fill out the FAFSA and fill out the Profile and see what the Expected Family Contribution says. Sometimes it isn't going to take all your money.

Colleges tell the students that, too. "It costs a lot of money to go here, but only 20 percent of our students are paying the full ride, so go ahead and apply for the financial aid."

If money is not an issue, you don't need to have that conversation. Every year I also have a number of students who have trusts; grandparents may have set it up and the kids are fully covered. But sometimes the parents want to shield that from the college and I have to say, "Wait a minute: it was left for them to pay for college, so pay for college."

chapter 21

A DIRECTOR
OF FINANCIAL AID
LOOKS AT THE
NUMBERS

Kenneth Kogut retired at the end of the 2005 academic year after thirty-three years as the director of financial aid at Hamilton College. He had held a similar position before then at Utica College in New York. He has undergraduate and master's degrees from the University of Buffalo.

How is it that one school decides that its admissions office will be need-blind while another chooses to be need-aware?

Need-blind is when you are like Princeton University and you have more money available than you can spend for every kid. They can afford to be need-blind.

Being need-aware means that your priorities are the most attractive candidates. When all the rest of the candidates who are admissible begin to look like they are the same, it would be foolish to give preferential treatment to someone who can afford to pay.

When the endowment for scholarships is sufficient to take care of everybody, you don't have to be need-aware.

Here at Hamilton, and at most other schools—whether they admit it or not—admissions pays attention to the financial needs of applicants. Beyond that, though, the schools handle distribution of aid in all sorts of ways. Let's say someone applies to Hamilton with all of the right credentials: a high SAT, a strong high school transcript, great recommendations, and a strong and appealing personal story. At the financial aid office do you just plug in the FAFSA numbers and print out an automatic offer?

No. We look beyond the numbers and adjust the FAFSA results both upward and downward depending on other things that we might hear from the family, see on the tax return, and comments from others.

In what kind of situation would you adjust the FAFSA numbers down—which is another way of saying adjusting the possible financial aid upward?

Let's say we had a situation where a mother became widowed recently. She was a stay-at-home mom. The father had a decent job and there was half a million dollars in life insurance.

If you look at a half a million dollars in cash one way, you might think they can afford to pay college tuition. But she may be telling us she has to depend on the interest income to help support the family while she acquires skills to go out and get a job, or maybe she is unable to get a job. So we would treat that case a little more leniently than the traditional formula would.

The same thing goes for families who might report assets other than cash. The instructions on the FAFSA ask: What is the value minus the debt? In many cases—especially if the assets are sizable—there might be tax consequences if you sell some of those stocks. That is in effect a debt against the asset. Having $250,000 in the bank in cash [is not the same as] having $250,000 in your portfolio at your brokerage firm.

Another example where we might adjust the FAFSA results downward could be the result of unemployment or job change on the part of the parent.

By the same token, if a family makes us aware that they are going to be much better off in the future, we would tend to look at estimated income so it doesn't come as a shock the following year if we increase their expected contribution. We don't like to play games and do a bait-and-switch and have a low contribution year one and then elevate it for years two, three, and four.

Where might you adjust the FAFSA numbers upward, reducing the financial aid offer?

Someone who is self-employed may enjoy certain perks. People who own rental property enjoy depreciation write-offs. We might add those sorts of things back to income.

Or let's take as an example a family where the FAFSA formula calls for a $50,000 parent contribution. If they have two kids in school, the family would be expected to spend $25,000 on each, but if the second kid is going to a community college part-time, it is not a 50/50 split. We might say there is no eligibility.

What percentage of parents actually call the financial aid office to discuss the package they are offered? And are many of them making a valid case?

Probably 25 percent of families call.

If they can afford the [expected family] contribution, why contact the financial aid office? We are not selling cars and expecting the families to come back and try to shake us down for another five hundred or a thousand bucks.

From the financial aid office point of view, how do you react if a parent calls up and tells you they have received better offers from other schools and asks you to meet or beat those offers?

I read where one major school in Pennsylvania tells parents, "Send us a copy of your award letter from other schools and we will match it." We don't necessarily do that, but given the nature of the information on the FAFSA, we recognize it doesn't always give you the full story.

In some cases we feel the FAFSA formula is inappropriate because there is no minimum expectation from the student. The student contribution from income doesn't kick in until they make more than $2,400 a year. We think the priority shouldn't necessarily be on a cell phone and an automobile. A $900 minimum contribution from student earnings is realistic in most cases. In some cases, living out in the boondocks, they are lucky to find a job.

Is there a spreadsheet or a financial formula that you apply to the numbers to adjust them to Hamilton's view, or is this just done on the basis of institutional experience?

There is a methodology that we do use. It is very easy when you are looking at the forms in front of you to decide whether you should adhere to the formula as written or whether it should be amended in some way, and then you go about amending it.

As an author, my income, like that of many self-employed people, can vary greatly from one year to the next. It's not fair to judge my earnings on any particular week, month, or year. How do you deal with that sort of situation?

We would ask you to provide three or four years' worth of documentation, and we may take an average.

Someone might tell us he is in sales working on commission and had a great year but the past three years or whatever were relatively not as good. Or we had a lot of overtime at the mill and it's probably not going to happen again soon. We would say immediately: get us documentation for the last couple of years.

You try to do what is right. The law allows us to exercise professional judgment; it doesn't mandate good judgment. So there are calls you make today that maybe a week down the road you wished you wouldn't have. But based on the available documentation, you try to do what is right.

Staying on the right side of the law, is there any strategy for filling out the FAFSA or Profile forms that works to your advantage as a parent?

On the income side, your income is your income and we can verify that through a copy of your tax return.

As far as noncash assets [you should] report the amount of those assets less the debt and the potential tax liability.

Families should not have established custodial accounts with their children. There really is not much of a tax advantage to doing that; the money should be in the parents' name and not the kids'.

Opening a custodial account with your minor children, or putting an account just in their name, has the advantage of having income taxed at the child's presumably lower tax rate. But when the child reaches age eighteen, he or she could choose to spend that money on a car or a cool stereo system.

It also works against you because of the way the financial aid formula looks at assets. The Expected Family Contribution will take 35 percent of the student's assets but only 6 percent of the parents', at most.

Are you on the lookout for families who try to adjust holdings after a child has been admitted? For example, if the FAFSA shows a custodial account with $100,000 for the freshman year but by the sophomore year the account is down to zero, does that set off an alarm?

Absolutely. If you are expected to take 35 percent a year you are left with something at the end, so we may adjust for that internally.

So when you make a financial aid offer to a student you are basically opening an account for this kid, saying we expect this student to be here for four years and this is our rough estimate of what we're going to be able to offer for each of the next four years, allowing for the occasional unusual circumstance.

That's right. For most students the financial need doesn't spike like that. [We look forward for four years] and that makes it a bit easier for the family to plan, and for us, too.

What other things on the FAFSA might set off an alarm at the financial aid office?

There are some questions that sometimes get incorrect answers, which leads to forms being rejected.

- Frequently, families will report federal income tax withheld as opposed to the amount actually owed or paid. We do check for that.

- If there is more than one child in college, we want to know where that second family member is going to college.

- If there is an adjusted gross income on the student's side of maybe $1,000, but under student earnings the number is zero, then you know the money must have been generated from some unearned income. So you look to see if there are any assets on the student's side.

This all comes from years of experience looking at the form and using your brain a little bit.

One of the areas in which the FAFSA differs from the CSS and other profiles is that the FAFSA doesn't ask for the value of your home. What is your take on that?

When we get the Profile we do look at the value of the home. [But the numbers usually work out about the same when it comes to financial aid.] The Expected Family Contribution from the Profile is usually less than the FAFSA's number. If we add in the value of the home, they frequently are the same.

When the Department of Education took over and made FAFSA a federal system, they got rid of the home equity but they expected more out of income, so it didn't really change much.

In today's economy, many people are house-rich. Their home has appreciated hugely in value even though their income has not increased. To put it another way, many people are living in homes they could not afford if they had to buy them based on current income.

If you are talking about really inflated home values, we would take that into consideration. The Profile tries to address that in some way by capping home equity based on the family's income.

What are some good ideas for parents on how to structure their finances in the years leading up to applying for college?

Most of what we would recommend is not so much aimed at decreasing a family's expected contribution, but instead making the contribution more affordable.

An important thing to do is minimize your debt and pay your taxes. Many times we get letters from parents saying the IRS is garnishing my wages, or that the family has $35,000 in credit card bills.

That kind of tells me you are going to be an accounts payable problem in college, and it is not our job to give you an opportunity to come for nothing so you can pay the IRS.

As we have discussed, Hamilton is need-aware, but the admissions and financial aid processes are separate. At need-blind schools the wall is supposed to be impenetrable. Either way, though, is there anything you can do as an applicant on the admissions side that would benefit you on the financial side?

Yes. Try to be one of the top candidates in that admission pool. Get 1600 SATs and all As and be a National Merit Scholar. And understand that a college also looks at a lot of other things. We like to enroll good athletes, but we also like good artists and good writers.

Is there any advantage in making a personal visit to the campus and meeting with someone at the financial aid office in addition to the admissions office?

249

Establishing a rapport with the financial aid office gives us an opportunity to tell the family how we would look at various scenarios. There might be an advantage in that.

How does the financial aid office look at scholarships the student may receive from organizations at home, or from businesses, unions, or associations?

We have to keep things in balance if we can. We subtract the first $500 from what we call self-help, meaning a student loan or a work-study job. Then we would do a fifty-fifty split between their college award and their self-help until the self-help was exhausted. Finally, we take as much as 100 percent from the remaining scholarship we would be offering. Typically no one gets to that point, so if you look at a $1,000 outside award, the kid benefits by about $750.

Isn't it also true that the college may not be aware of all outside scholarships earned by a student?

It depends on how the award was made. Frequently it comes to the school, so we have to know about it.

But if they don't tell me, what can I do? I am not an investigator.

Are the parents and the students ethically required to notify the college of outside scholarships?

We ask that they do, but I am sure some forget.

In some ways, colleges are run like airlines: selling more tickets than they have seats because they know a certain percentage will not show up. Should parents or the student contact financial aid again in the fall to see if there is some unallocated money sitting around?

On occasion we do make a redistribution of financial aid that may be available. There may have been some late admits where we told them we couldn't promise them anything now but we will do what we can after registration.

Or if something happens in the summer where a parent becomes unemployed, we will typically wait until September or the early part of October to see if there is any way we can make accommodation for that.

Any time there is a change we would want to know, even during the school year. We would rather not have you be a receivable with a problem.

Can you see a ceiling on tuition and other college costs, or will they continue to rise?

I don't see any end in sight. I have been doing financial aid since 1967. There has never been a year I haven't experienced an increase in tuition.

The only good news is that I am sure financial aid will float up with it.

Fortunately or unfortunately, my two children do not qualify for any significant financial aid. I sat down and figured out that for eight years of private school the cost will total more than a quarter million dollars. How many parents actually work out the numbers?

There are many that do. Many families want their child to share in the risks and rewards, and they may say we will pick up three-quarters of the total and you pick up one-quarter of it in some way such as a loan program.

Do you think that helps the kid, or puts him or her in a deep hole at the very start of their independent life?

It all depends on the family and the kid. For some families it may be a good idea. I wouldn't do it to my kid.

Some studies have said that students who take jobs in work-study programs—one form of financial aid—tend to end up with better grades than those who do not.

I have heard that, but I have never really done a study to verify that claim. I go back to my older brother, who went to college in the late '50s; he played football at the University of Buffalo and he told me he did better during the season because he had to be more focused, so it very well may be true.

One of the things that I found unusual at Hamilton was that merit aid comes with no strings attached—there is no minimum GPA required.

Merit aid could be character-related, recognizing someone who has contributed to the community. Or it could be academic.

But we are not going to entice someone with a merit award and then say you've got to do this or it's gone.

Again, we don't want to get into bait-and-switch. As long as the faculty gives you a vote of confidence that you can come back, then we ought to continue the service we provided upon entry.

chapter 22

ACCOUNTING FOR YOUR CHILD'S EDUCATION

Robert Klein is a savvy certified public accountant in New York. A graduate of Baruch College, he does accounting and tax preparation for companies and individuals and works with financial and estate planners for his clients. He has put two children through college.

Speaking as a tax accountant, what's the best thing parents can do to prepare themselves to pay for sending their children to college?

Before you even become a parent, you should marry into money. Failure to do that brings you into crisis.

Basically, anyone who is middle class gets the shaft when it comes to scholarships and financial aid.

Do you think the average Joe out there making $50,000 to $100,000 and owning a house can afford $40,000 a year for his kid to go to school?

The norm in this country is to live hand-to-mouth, or worse. If you earn X, you spend X plus 10 percent, or 20 percent. People drive around in expensive cars that are leased. They have no equity and they are living over their heads.

I have people as clients who you would think were multibillionaires but they don't have anything to their name.

But the answer to your question is this: People who want to do something about college have to start at an early age. It is very tough to put money away for children when you are living on a very tight budget yourself, but that's what you have to do.

You have to make sacrifices, and unfortunately the American way is not to make the sacrifice. "I will worry about it next year," they say. Or "I will worry about it in ten years." And then they have a major problem.

Financial adviser Patrick Curtin agrees with you about the need for an early start, but he also says he becomes very concerned when young parents come in and say they are going to throw all their available savings into a college education fund and not into their own retirement fund. He says that is backwards.

There is an argument for that.

And you could also say, "I have a very intelligent child and I am going to spend $250,000 to get him through grad school and that kid is going to flourish and get a great job and he is going to be my retirement."

In my case, my wife and I have been very conservative when it came to our money, putting savings and investments aside and self-financing everything but our home.

The ordinary guy is the one who has a large amount of credit card debt and has no equity. He leases new cars not because he needs them, but because he wants them.

Some college advisers suggest that students consider changing their state of residency to qualify for a public college at the in-state rate. For tax purposes, how do you establish residency in a new state?

If there is a state income tax, people who earn income there have to file a state tax return whether or not they reside there. If general, if you are living in, let's say, Massachusetts and actually paying rent there, that's your residence and you are required to file a state tax return as a resident. If you are not deemed to be a resident, you would file a return as a nonresident

Just because you file a state return doesn't necessarily mean that you are now a state resident there, enabling your child to go to that state university. Each state has different criteria as to what constitutes residence for college purposes. In most cases it is living there as your principal residence for a period of time. In some cases, that period of time is vague.

One strategy that makes some sense—if the parents or the grandparents have some money—is to put aside $40,000 or $50,000 in something like a 529 plan when a child is born and leave it there for the next eighteen years. Done right, the parents don't have to talk about college financing again.

First of all, that means someone has $40,000 or so available. And there are a lot of grandparents out there who have that money but don't wish to be part of this to the extent that he is talking about. You are talking about parting with money. People have different priorities.

The greatest gift one can give their child is to allow them to graduate debt-free from college.

My son goes to a school where there is a lot of money, and he may be the poorest kid on campus.

And for the record, you are a successful CPA.

I will give you that point at times. But he appreciated more than anything what we have done to enable him to go without loans.

If you look at it, you can see how college debt has choked people beyond being able to survive. It's terrible.

It all boils down to what are your priorities in life. There are people who are so self-centered; they always say someone else will deal with it. They'll tell their kid, "I had to work 27,000 hours to pay for my own college."

Times are different.

a final note:

SEE SHARP, OR BE FLAT

If you didn't know this before you began this book, you do now: planning and paying for college is hard work and requires a great deal of time and attention. That's the reality.

But it should also be clear to you now that there are dozens of ways to cut the cost of college and soften the burden of paying for an education. And there's one more thing to keep in mind: not everyone pays the same amount for the same product.

The fact is that those of us who are willing to take the time to prepare, and those of us who spend the effort to structure our income and savings, can get a better deal. And like it or not, those of us who do are subsidized by those who do not.

And finally, all of the experts I consulted (to which I add the experiences of my wife and myself) agree on this: parents and families who can help their children get a college degree without receiving a huge "payment due" bill on graduation day are making one of the greatest gifts possible. And even if you are unable to completely wipe the slate clean, every dime you can save puts your student a dollar ahead of the rest of the class.

Appendix A

STATE HIGHER EDUCATION AGENCIES

Here is the contact information for higher education funding agencies in each of the states and U.S. territories. Also listed is a sampling of special state programs for residents. Consult the Web sites or call the agencies for details about state-specific programs as well as administration of federal grants and loans.

Alabama

Alabama Commission on Higher Education
P.O. Box 302000
Montgomery, AL 36130-2000
Phone: (334) 242-1998, (800) 960-7773 in Alabama
Fax: (334) 242-0268
Web: *www.ache.state.al.us*
Programs include: Alabama GI Dependents' Educational Benefit Program, Alabama National Guard Educational Assistance Program, Alabama Nursing Scholarship Program, Alabama Scholarships for Dependents of Blind Parents, Alabama Student Assistance Program, Alabama Student Grant Program, American Legion Auxiliary Scholarship Program, American Legion Scholarship Program, Junior and Community College Athletic Scholarship Program, Junior and Community College Performing Arts Scholarship Program, Police Officer's and Firefighter's Survivor's Educational Assistance Program, Senior Adult Scholarship Program, Two-Year College Academic Scholarship Program.
Alabama Prepaid Affordable College Tuition Program. (Fully paid undergraduate tuition at any public junior college, college, or university in Alabama. Alternatively, an amount equivalent to the average cost of Alabama public tuition is provided for students who attend an in-state private college or an out-of-state institution.)

Alaska

Alaska Commission on Postsecondary Education
3030 Vintage Boulevard
Juneau, AK 99801-7100
Phone: (907) 465-2962, (800) 441-2962
Fax: (907) 465-5316
E-mail: *customer_service@acpe.state.ak.us*
Web: *www.state.ak.us/acpe*

259

Programs include: AlaskAdvantage Financial Aid, AlaskAdvantage Education Grant Program, AlaskAdvantage Education Loan Programs (Stafford Loans, Alaska Supplemental Education Loan), AlaskAdvantage Family & Parent Loans (PLUS, Alaska Family Education Loan).

Arizona

Arizona Commission for Postsecondary Education
Suite 550
2020 North Central Avenue
Phoenix, AZ 85004-4503
Phone: (602) 258-2435
Fax: (602) 258-2483
Web: *www.azhighered.org*
Programs include: Arizona Leveraging Education Assistance Partnership (LEAP), Arizona Private Postsecondary Education Student Financial Assistance, Tribal Higher Education Grants.

Arkansas

Arkansas Department of Higher Education
114 East Capitol
Little Rock, AR 72201-3818
Phone: (501) 371-2000
Fax: (501) 371-2001
Web: *www.arkansashighered.com*
Programs include: Academic Challenge Scholarship, Arkansas Student Assistance Grant Program, Arkansas Health Education Grant Program, Governor's Scholars Program, Law Enforcement Officers Dependents Scholarship Program, MIA/KIA Dependents Scholarship Program, Second Effort Scholarship.

California

California Student Aid Commission
P.O. Box 419027
Rancho Cordova, CA 95741-9027
Phone: (916) 526-7590, (888) 224-7268
Fax: (916) 526-8004
Web: *www.csac.ca.gov*
Programs include: Cal Grant Entitlement Awards, Assumption Program of Loans for Education, Child Development Grant Program, Law Enforcement Personnel Dependents Grant Program.

Colorado

Colorado Commission on Higher Education
Suite 1200
1380 Lawrence Street

Denver, CO 80204
Phone: (303) 866-2723
Fax: (303) 866-4266
Web: *www.state.co.us/cche*
Programs include: College Access Network (Colorado Student Loan Program), CollegeInvest, College Achievement Scholarship, Governor's Opportunity Scholarship, Early Childhood Development Professional Loan Repayment Program, Western Interstate Commission for Higher Education.

Connecticut

Connecticut Department of Higher Education
61 Woodland Street
Hartford, CT 06105-2326
Phone: (860) 947-1800, (800) 842-0229
Fax: (860) 947-1310
E-mail: *info@ctdhe.org*
Web: *www.ctdhe.org*
Programs include: Capitol Scholarship, Connecticut Aid for Public College Students, Connecticut Independent College Student Grant Program, Connecticut Special Education Teacher Incentive Grant, Tuition Set-Aside Aid, Connecticut Family Education Loan Program.

Delaware

Delaware Higher Education Commission
Fifth Floor
Carvel State Office Building
820 North French Street
Wilmington, DE 19801
Phone: (302) 577-3240, (800) 292-7935
Fax: (302) 577-6765
Web: *www.doe.state.de.us/high-ed*
Programs include: Scholarship Incentive Program, Academic Memorial Scholarships (merit-based to University of Delaware or Delaware State University), Diamond State Scholarship, Legislative Essay Scholarship, Delaware Nursing Incentive Program, Christa McAuliffe Teacher Scholarship Loan, Critical Need Scholarship, Delaware College Investment Plan.

District of Columbia

State Education Office (District of Columbia)
Suite 350 North
441 Fourth Street, NW
Washington, DC 20001
Phone: (202) 727-2824, (877) 485-6751
Fax: (202) 727-2834
Web: *http://seo.dc.gov/main.shtm*

Programs include: DC Tuition Assistance Grant, DC Leveraging Educational Assistance Partnership Program (DC LEAP), DC Adoption Scholarship Program.

Florida

Florida Department of Education
Office of Student Financial Assistance
1940 North Monroe Street, Suite 70
Tallahassee, Florida 32303-4759
Phone: (888) 827-2004
Web: *www.firn.edu/doe*
Programs include: Florida Bright Futures Scholarship Program, Florida Student Assistance Grant, Jose Marti Scholarship Grant, Florida Work Assistance, Mary McLeod Bethune Scholarship, Children of Deceased or Disabled Veterans, Critical Teacher Shortage Tuition Reimbursement.

Georgia

Georgia Student Finance Commission
State Loans Division
Suite 230
2082 East Exchange Place
Tucker, GA 30084
Phone: (770) 724-9000, (800) 505-4732
Fax: (770) 724-9263
E-mail: *info@mail.gsfc.org*
Web: *www.gsfc.org*
Programs include: Lottery-funded Teacher Scholarship Loans, Agriculture Education (Service-Cancelable Stafford Loan), Destination Teaching, Allied Health Professions (Service-Cancelable Stafford Loan), Northeast Georgia Health System Nurse Program, Nursing Facility (Service-Cancelable Loan) Program, North Georgia College & State University Military Scholarship Loan, Georgia Military College State Service Scholarship Loan, Georgia Military/ North Georgia Military Transfer Scholarship Loan, Georgia National Guard (Service-Cancelable Education Loan), Scholarship for Engineering Education.

Hawaii

Hawaii State Postsecondary Education Commission
Room 209
2444 Dole Street
Honolulu, HI 96822-2302
Phone: (808) 956-8213
Fax: (808) 956-5156
Web: *http://doe.k12.hi.us/bulletin15*
Programs include: University of Hawaii Computer-Assisted Scholarship Help, Hawaii Community Foundation.

Idaho

Idaho State Board of Education
P.O. Box 83720
Boise, ID 83720-0037
Phone: (208) 334-2270
Fax: (208) 334-2632
Web: *www.idahoboardofed.org*
Programs include: Promise Scholarships, Freedom Scholarship, Public Safety
Officer Dependent Scholarship.

Illinois

Illinois Student Assistance Commission
1755 Lake Cook Road
Deerfield, IL 60015-5209
Phone: (847) 948-8500, (800) 899-4722
Fax: (847) 831-8549
Web: *www.collegezone.com*
Programs include: Monetary Award Program, Illinois National Guard Grant
Program, Illinois Veteran Grant, Bonus Incentive Grant, Student to Student
Grant, Merit Recognition Scholarship Program, Minority Teachers of
Illinois Scholarship, Illinois Future Teacher Corps, Illinois Special Education
Teacher Tuition Waiver, Golden Apple Scholars of Illinois, General Assembly
Scholarship, Department of Rehabilitation Education Benefits.

Indiana

State Student Assistance Commission of Indiana
Suite 500
150 West Market Street
Indianapolis, IN 46204-2811
Phone: (317) 232-2350, (888) 528-4719 in Indiana
Fax: (317) 232-3260
Web: *www.ssaci.in.gov*
Programs include: Higher Education Awards, Frank O'Bannon Grant, Academic
Honors Diploma Grants, Core 40 Grants, 21st Century Scholars Scholarship,
National Guard Supplemental Grant, Hoosier Scholar Grant, Nursing
Scholarship.

Iowa

Iowa College Student Aid Commission
Fourth Floor
200 10th Street
Des Moines, IA 50309
Phone: (515) 242-3344, (800) 383-4222
Fax: (515) 242-3388
Web: *www.iowacollegeaid.org*

Programs include: State of Iowa Scholarships, Iowa State Fair Scholarships, Iowa Tuition Grants, Iowa Vocational-Technical Tuition Grants, Iowa Grants, Iowa National Guard Educational Assistance Grants.

Kansas

Kansas Board of Regents
Curtis State Office Building
Suite 520
1000 SW Jackson Street
Topeka, KS 66612-1368
Phone: (785) 296-3421
Fax: (785) 296-0983
Web: *www.kansasregents.org*
Programs include: Kansas Ethnic Minority Scholarship, Kansas Teacher Service Scholarship, Nursing Service Scholarship, State Scholarship, Kansas Comprehensive Grants, Vocational Scholarship, Tuition Waiver for Foster Children, Tuition Waiver for Dependents of Slain Public Safety Officers.

Kentucky

Kentucky Higher Education Assistance Authority
P.O. Box 798
Frankfort, KY 40602-0798
Phone: (502) 696-7200, (800) 928-8926
Fax: (502) 696-7496
Web: *www.kheaa.com*
Programs include: Kentucky Educational Excellence Scholarship, College Access Program, Kentucky Tuition Grant, KHEAA Teacher Scholarship, Early Childhood Development Scholarship, Kentucky Education Savings Plan Trust.
Kentucky's Affordable Prepaid Tuition

Louisiana

Louisiana Office of Student Financial Assistance
P.O. Box 91202
Baton Rouge, LA 70821-9202
Phone: (225) 922-1012, (800) 259-5626
Fax: (225) 922-0790
Web: *www.osfa.state.la.us*
Programs include: Tuition Opportunity Program for Students (TOPS), Rockefeller State Wildlife Scholarship.

Maine

Finance Authority of Maine
P.O. Box 949
Augusta, ME 04332-0949
Phone: (207) 623-3263, x313, (800) 228-3734

Fax: (207) 623-0095
Web: *www.famemaine.com*
Maine State Grant Program.

Maryland

Maryland Higher Education Commission
Suite 400
839 Bestgate Road
Annapolis, MD 21401-3013
Phone: (410) 260-4500, (800) 974-1024 in Maryland
Fax: (410) 974-5994
Web: *www.mhec.state.md.us*
Programs include: Guaranteed Access Grant, Educational Assistance Grant,
Senatorial Scholarship, Delegate Scholarship, Loan Assistance Repayment
Program, Distinguished Scholar Award, Maryland Teacher Scholarship, Science
and Technology Scholarship, Tuition Waiver for Foster Care Recipients.

Massachusetts

Massachusetts Board of Higher Education
Room 1401
One Ashburton Place
Boston, MA 02108
Phone: (617) 994-6950
Fax: (617) 727-6397
Web: *www.mass.edu*
Programs include: Paul Tsongas Scholarship, Tomorrow's Teachers Scholarship,
CommonWealth Futures Grant, MASSGrant, Massachusetts Cash Grant,
Massachusetts Public Service Grant, Categorical Tuition Waiver, Need-Based
Tuition Waiver, Massachusetts No-Interest Loan.
Massachusetts Educational Financing Authority (*www.mefa.org*) administers
college loans, college savings plans, and prepaid tuition plans.

Michigan

Michigan Higher Education Assistance Authority
Office of Scholarships and Grants
P.O. Box 30462
Lansing, MI 48909-7962
Phone: (517) 373-3394, (888) 447-2687
Fax: (517) 335-5984
Web: *www.michigan.gov/mistudentaid*
Programs include: Gear Up Michigan Scholarship, Michigan Competitive
Scholarship, Michigan Merit Scholarship, Michigan Nursing Scholarship
Program.

Minnesota

Minnesota Higher Education Services Office
Suite 350
1450 Energy Park Drive
St. Paul, MN 55108-5227
Phone: (651) 642-0567, (800) 657-3866
Fax: (651) 642-0675
Web: *www.mheso.state.mn.us*
Programs include: Minnesota State Grant, Minnesota Child Care Grant, Minnesota Public Safety Officer's Survivor Grant, Alliss Opportunity Grant Program, Grants for Dislocated Workers, Minnesota Academic Excellence Scholarship, Minnesota Indian Scholarship, Minnesota Educational Assistance for War Orphans, Minnesota Veterans' Dependents Assistance Program, Education Vouchers for Former Youth in Care.

Mississippi

Mississippi Office of Student Financial Aid
3825 Ridgewood Road
Jackson, MS 39211-6453
Phone: (601) 432-6997, (800) 327-2980 in Mississippi
Fax: (601) 432-6527
Web: *www.mississippiuniversities.com*
Programs include: Mississippi Tuition Assistance Grant, Mississippi Eminent Scholars Grant, Critical Needs Teacher, Mississippi Teacher Loan Repayment.

Missouri

Missouri Department of Higher Education
3515 Amazonas Drive
Jefferson City, MO 65109-5717
Phone: (573) 751-2361, (800) 473-6757
Fax: (573) 751-6635
Web: *www.dhe.mo.gov*
Programs include: Missouri Higher Education Academic Scholarship, Missouri College Guarantee Program.

Montana

Montana University System
2500 Broadway
P.O. Box 203101
Helena, MT 59620-3101
Phone: (406) 444-6570
Fax: (406) 444-1469
Web: *www.montana.edu/wwwoche*
Programs include: Indian Student Fee Waiver, Honorably Discharged Veteran Fee Waiver.

Nebraska

Nebraska Coordinating Commission for Postsecondary Education
Suite 300
140 North Eighth Street
P.O. Box 95005
Lincoln, NE 68509-5005
Phone: (402) 471-2847
Fax: (402) 471-2886
Web: *www.ccpe.state.ne.us/publicdoc/CCPE/default.asp*
Programs include: Nebraska State Grant, Midwestern Student Exchange
    Program, Western Governor's University.
    Nebraska College Savings Plan, Nebraska College Help
    (*www.necollegehelp.com*).

Nevada

Nevada Department of Education
700 East Fifth Street
Carson City, NV 89702
Phone: (775) 687-9200
Fax: (775) 687-9101
Web: *www.doe.nv.gov*
Associated link: *www.nevadamentor.org*
Programs include: Millennium Scholarship (open to all Nevada high school
    students who graduate with at least a 3.0 GPA), State Grants, Access Grant,
    Nevada Student Incentive Grant, Tribal Scholarships.

New Hampshire

New Hampshire Postsecondary Education Commission
Suite 300
3 Barrell Court
Concord, NH 03301-8543
Phone: (603) 271-2555
Fax: (603) 271-2696
Web: *www.state.nh.us/postsecondary*
Programs include: New Hampshire Incentive Program, Leveraged Incentive
    Grant Program, Scholarships for Orphans of Veterans, Workforce Incentive
    Program.

New Jersey

Commission on Higher Education (New Jersey)
20 West State Street
P.O. Box 542
Trenton, NJ 08625-0542
Phone: (609) 292-4310
Fax: (609) 292-7225

267

Web: *www.state.nj.us/highereducation*
Programs include: Educational Opportunity Fund, Special Needs Grant Program, English Language Minority Students Grant Program, College Bound Grant Program, High-Tech Workforce Excellence.

Higher Education Student Assistance Authority (New Jersey)
P.O. Box 540
Building 4
Quakerbridge Plaza
Trenton, NJ 08625-0540
Phone: (609) 588-3226, (800) 792-8670
Fax: (609) 588-7389
Web: *www.hesaa.org*
Programs include: Tuition Aid Grant, New Jersey Student Tuition Assistance Reward Scholarship (NJSTARS, offering tuition at county colleges to students graduating in top 20 percent of their class), Urban Scholars, Law Enforcement Officer Memorial Scholarship.

New Mexico

New Mexico Commission on Higher Education
1068 Cerrillos Road
Santa Fe, NM 87505
Phone: (505) 476-6500, (800) 279-9777
Fax: (505) 476-6511
Web: *http://hed.state.nm.us/index.asp*
Programs include: Allied Health Student Loan-for-Service, Competitive Scholarships, Lottery Success Scholarships, New Mexico Scholars, New Mexico Teacher Loan-for-Service, Student Choice Grants, Student Incentive Grants.
New Mexico Association of Student Financial Aid Administrators (*www. swasfaa.org/docs/NewMexico.html*).

New York

New York State Higher Education Services Corporation
99 Washington Avenue
Albany, NY 12255
Phone: (518) 473-1574, (888) 697-4372
Fax: (518) 474-2839
Web: *www.hesc.org*
Programs include: Tuition Assistance Program, AmeriCorps Education Award, Child of Veteran, Memorial Scholarship, Military Service Recognition Scholarship, New York State Scholarship for Academic Excellence, New York Lottery Leaders of Tomorrow Scholarship, NYS Volunteer Recruitment Service Scholarship, Regents Health Care Opportunity, Regents Professional Opportunity Scholarship, State Aid for Native Americans, Veterans Tuition Awards.

North Carolina

North Carolina State Education Assistance Authority
P.O. Box 13663
Research Triangle Park, NC 27709-3663
Phone: (919) 549-8614, (866) 866-2362 in North Carolina
Fax: (919) 549-8481
Web: *www.cfnc.org*
Programs include: Nurse Education Scholarship Loan Program, NC Student
    Loan Program for Health, Science, and Mathematics, Teacher Assistant
    Scholarship Fund, NC Teaching Fellows Scholarship Program, North Carolina
    Principal Fellows Program, Nurse Scholars Program, Prospective Teachers
    Scholarships/Loans.
    North Carolina's National College Savings Plan.

North Dakota

North Dakota University System
North Dakota Student Financial Assistance Program
Department 215
600 East Boulevard Avenue
Bismarck, ND 58505-0230
Phone: (701) 328-4114
Fax: (701) 328-2961
Web: *www.ndus.edu*
Programs include: North Dakota Scholars Program, Tuition Waivers, North Dakota
    Indian Scholarship Program, Technology Occupations Student Loan Program,
    Teacher Shortage Loan Forgiveness Program, ND State Student Incentive
    Grant Program, North Dakota/Minnesota Reciprocity.

Ohio

Ohio Board of Regents
State Grants and Scholarships Department
57 East Main Street
Fourth Floor
Columbus, OH 43215
Phone: (614) 466-7420, (888) 833-1133
Fax: (614) 752-5903
Web: *www.regents.state.oh.us/sgs*
Programs include: Ohio Instructional Grant, Ohio War Orphans Scholarship,
    Regents Graduate/Professional Fellowship Program, Ohio Safety Officers
    College Memorial Fund, Nurse Education Assistance Loan Program, Ohio
    Academic Scholarship, Ohio Student Choice Grant.

Oklahoma

Oklahoma State Regents for Higher Education
Suite 200
655 Research Parkway
Oklahoma City, OK 73104
Phone: (405) 225-9100, (800) 858-1840
Fax: (405) 225-9230
Web: *www.okhighered.org*
Programs include: Oklahoma Tuition Aid Grant Program, Oklahoma Tuition
    Equalization Grant Program, Academic Scholars Program, Oklahoma
    Higher Learning Access Program—Oklahoma's Promise, Regional
    University Baccalaureate Scholarship, Future Teachers Scholarship Program,
    Independent Living Act Foster Care Tuition Waiver, National Guard Tuition
    Waiver, Oklahoma Teacher Enhancement Program, Scholars for Excellence in
    Child Care, Teacher Shortage Employment Incentive Program.

Oregon

Oregon Student Assistance Commission
Suite 100
1500 Valley River Drive
Eugene, OR 97401
Phone: (541) 687-7400, (800) 452-8807
Fax: (541) 687-7419
Web: *www.osac.state.or.us* or *www.getcollegefunds.org*

Pennsylvania

Office of Postsecondary and Higher Education (Pennsylvania)
Department of Education
333 Market Street
Harrisburg, PA 17126
Phone: (717) 787-5041
Fax: (717) 772-3622
Web: *www.pdehighered.state.pa.us/higher/site*
New Economy Technology Scholarship
PA Tuition Account Program

Pennsylvania Higher Education Assistance Agency
Web: *www.pheaa.org*
Programs include: Pennsylvania State Grants, Aid for Veterans & National Guard
    Members, Partnership for Access to Higher Education, Pennsylvania Chafee
    Education and Training Grant Program, Pennsylvania Loan Forgiveness,
    PHEAA Academic Excellence Scholarship Award Program, Postsecondary
    Educational Gratuity, TANF Education Award Program, Tuition Account
    Program.

Rhode Island

Rhode Island Higher Education Assistance Authority
560 Jefferson Boulevard
Warwick, RI 02886
Phone: (401) 736-1100, (800) 922-9855
Fax: (401) 732-3541
Web: *www.riheaa.org*
Programs include: CollegeBoundfund Academic Promise Scholarship, Rhode
    Island State Grant Program.

Rhode Island Office of Higher Education

301 Promenade Street
Providence, RI 02908-5748
Phone: (401) 222-6560
Fax: (401) 222-6111
Web: *www.ribghe.org*

South Carolina

South Carolina Commission on Higher Education
Suite 200
1333 Main Street
Columbia, SC 29201
Phone: (803) 737-2260, (877) 349-7183
Fax: (803) 737-2297
Web: *www.che400.state.sc.us*
Programs include: South Carolina Tuition Grants, South Carolina Student Loan
    Corporation, South Carolina Income Tax Credit for College Tuition, South
    Carolina Tuition Prepayment Program.

South Dakota

South Dakota Board of Regents
Suite 200
306 East Capitol Avenue
Pierre, SD 57501
Phone: (605) 773-3455
Fax: (605) 773-5320
Web: *www.ris.sdbor.edu*
Programs include: South Dakota Opportunity Scholarship

Tennessee

Tennessee Higher Education Commission
Parkway Towers
Suite 1900
404 James Robertson Parkway
Nashville, TN 37243-0830

Phone: (615) 741-3605
Fax: (615) 741-6230
Web: *www.state.tn.us/thec*
Tennessee Scholar Dollars

Texas

Texas Higher Education Coordinating Board
P.O. Box 12788
Austin, TX 78711
Phone: (512) 427-6101, (800) 242-3062
Fax: (512) 427-6127
Web: *www.thecb.state.tx.us* or *www.collegefortexans.com*
Programs include: TEXAS Grant, Military Child Education Coalition, Tuition
    Exemption for Texas Veterans, Tuition Equalization Grant Program,
    Outstanding Rural Scholar Program.

Utah

Utah State Board of Regents
Gateway Center
60 South 400 West
Salt Lake City, UT 84101-1284
Phone: (801) 321-7103
Fax: (801) 321-7199
Web: *www.utahsbr.edu*

Utah Higher Education Assistance Authority
Web: *www.uheaa.org* or *www.UtahMentor.org*
Programs include: Utah Centennial Opportunity Program for Education, New
    Century Scholarship Program, Terrel H. Bell Teaching Incentive Loan.

Vermont

Vermont Student Assistance Corporation
Champlain Mill
1 Main Street, Third Floor
P.O. Box 2000
Winooski, VT 05404-2601
Phone: (802) 655-9602, (800) 642-3177
Fax: (802) 654-3765
Web: *http://services.vsac.org/ilwwcm/connect/VSAC*
Programs include: Vermont Incentive Grants, Vermont Non-Degree Grants, VSAC
    Scholarships, Vermont Opportunity Scholarship.

Virginia

State Council of Higher Education for Virginia
James Monroe Building

Ninth Floor
101 North 14th Street
Richmond, VA 23219
Phone: (804) 225-2600
Fax: (804) 225-2604
Web: *www.schev.edu*
Programs include: Commonwealth Award, Virginia Guaranteed Assistance
    Program, Tuition Assistant Grant Program, College Scholarship Assistance
    Program.

Washington

Washington State Higher Education Coordinating Board
P.O. Box 43430
917 Lakeridge Way
Olympia, WA 98504-3430
Phone: (360) 753-7800
Fax: (360) 753-7808
Web: *www.hecb.wa.gov/*
Programs include: State Need Grant, Educational Opportunity Grant, Washington
    Scholars, Washington Award for Vocational Excellence, Health Professional
    Loan Repayment and Scholarship, Future Teachers Conditional Scholarship
    and Loan Repayment, American Indian Endowed Scholarship.

West Virginia

West Virginia Higher Education Policy Commission
1018 Kanawha Boulevard, East
Charleston, WV 25301
Phone: (304) 558-2101
Fax: (304) 558-5719
Web: *www.hepc.wvnet.edu*

Wisconsin

Wisconsin Higher Educational Aids Board
Suite 902
131 West Wilson Street
Madison, WI 53703
Phone: (608) 267-2206
Fax: (608) 267-2808
Web: *http://heab.state.wi.us*
Programs include: Wisconsin Higher Education Grant, Wisconsin Tuition Grant,
    Talent Incentive Program Grant, Indian Student Assistance Grant, Minority
    Undergraduate Retention Grant.
    Academic Excellence Scholarship, Minority Teacher Loan, Nursing Student
    Loan, Minnesota-Wisconsin Tuition Reciprocity.

Wyoming

Wyoming Department of Education
2300 Capitol Avenue
Hathaway Building, Second Floor
Cheyenne, WY 82002
Phone: (307) 777-7690
Fax: (307) 777-6234
Web: *www.k12.wy.us*

Wyoming Community College Commission
Eighth Floor
2020 Carey Avenue
Cheyenne, WY 82002
Phone: (307) 777-7763
Fax: (307) 777-6567
Web: *www.commission.wcc.edu*

TERRITORIES

American Samoa

American Samoa Community College
Board of Higher Education
P.O. Box 2609
Pago Pago, AS 96799-2609
Phone: (684) 699-9155
Fax: (684) 699-2062
Web: *www.ascc.as*

Commonwealth of the Northern Mariana Islands

Northern Marianas College
Olympio T. Borja Memorial Library
As-Terlaje Campus
P.O. Box 501250
Saipan, MP 96950-1250
Phone: (670) 234-3690
Fax: (670) 234-0759
Web: *www.nmcnet.edu*

Puerto Rico

Puerto Rico Council on Higher Education
P.O. Box 19900
San Juan, PR 00910-1900

Phone: (787) 724-7100
Fax: (787) 725-1275
Web: *www.ces.gobierno.pr*

Republic of the Marshall Islands

Republic of the Marshall Islands
RMI Scholarship Grant and Loan Board
P.O. Box 1436
3 Lagoon Road
Majuro, MH 96960
Phone: (692) 625-3108
Fax: (692) 625-7325

Virgin Islands

Virgin Islands Board of Education
Charlotte Amalie
P.O. Box 11900
St. Thomas, VI 00801
Phone: (340) 774-4546
Fax: (340) 774-3384

Appendix B

SELECTED WEB SITES FOR STUDENTS AND PARENTS

GOVERNMENT WEB SITES

College Opportunities On-line
(COOL database)—*www.nces.ed.gov/ipeds/cool*

Search for colleges by region, type, and instructional program. Operated by the National Center for Education Statistics, the primary federal entity for collecting and analyzing education data.

FAFSA on the Web—*www.fafsa.ed.gov*

The official Web site for filing the Free Application for Federal Student Aid (FAFSA). You can begin by filling out a worksheet that will help you gather and organize necessary information. Note that there are some commercial Web sites that offer assistance—at a cost of as much as $100—with filling out the free form.

Federal Student Aid—*www.studentaid.ed.gov*

The Student Aid Web site provides an overview to available federal student aid loans, grants, and other programs. You can also jump from this page to the FAFSA on the Web, where students and parents can fill out the essential form for federal aid; the same form is also used for many state and institutional aid programs.

GovLoans.gov—*www.govloans.gov*

The official federal Web site for all sorts of government loans. You'll find details of PLUS Parent Loans, Perkins Student Loans, Stafford Loans, and Education Consolidation Loans, including necessary qualifications and loan terms.

Student Financial Assistance—
www.ed.gov/finaid.html

A U.S. Department of Education site with information on grants, loans, and work-study programs. There are pages for students, parents, teachers, and administrators.

Student Guide for Financial Aid—
www.studentaid.ed.gov/students/publications/student_guide/index.html

> The entryway to an online version (in English or Spanish) and downloadable PDF (printable) version of the official student guide to financial aid published by the U.S. Department of Education. It includes details on federal programs as well as a copy of the FAFSA and FAFSA worksheet.

Students.Gov—*www.students.gov*

> A broad spectrum of official information on government programs for students including loans, grants, and work-study financial aid; military service and college funding; and career development. There's also information about study-abroad programs.

ACADEMIC ORGANIZATIONS

College Board Online—*www.collegeboard.com*

> In addition to the entry portal for online registration for the SAT test, visitors can use the College MatchMaker to search for a college by name or type and read an introduction to financial aid strategies.

> The College Board is a not-for-profit association made up of more than 4,700 schools, colleges, universities, and other educational organizations. It offers the SAT, PSAT, and AP (Advanced Placement) tests.

CSS/Financial Aid PROFILE—
https://profileonline.collegeboard.com/index.jsp

> The online version of the supplemental financial aid application required by many private colleges. There is a charge for registering for the Profile and an additional fee for each college to which the results are sent.

College Is Possible—*www.collegeispossible.org*

> The American Council on Education's resource guide for parents and students, offering very general information about choosing a college and paying the bills.

National Association of Student Financial Aid Administrators—*www.nasfaa.org/subhomes/cash4college/index2.html*

> Information on financial aid from a site sponsored by college financial aid offices.

COMMERCIAL WEB SITES

Career Education—*www.career-education.us*

A searchable listing of specialized education including trade and vocational schools, adult education, online degrees, and more. The site is not fully inclusive—listings are sponsored—but there are easy links to request information and applications to more than 350 schools.

College Answer—*www.collegeanswer.com*

A database of information about preparation for college, selection of a school, the application process, and financing education. It is sponsored by SallieMae (also directly reachable at *www.salliemae.com*), one of the largest providers of education funding. SallieMae primarily provides federally guaranteed student loans.

CollegeNet—*www.collegenet.com*

A portal that includes an online college search, a scholarship matcher, and the ability to apply to many colleges around the nation.

Educaid—*www.educaid.com*

A Web site operated by Wachovia Education Finance, a private banking company. Information offered here is of value to its clients as well as others considering a federally guaranteed loan or other source of college funding.

FastWeb—*www.fastweb.monster.com*

A database claiming to hold more than 180,000 scholarships, grants, and loans searchable on the basis of a student's background and attributes. You'll have to wade through many advertisements and solicitations to get to the listings of possible scholarships, but it is worth the effort if you find one that's looking for someone exactly like you or your college-bound child. The site is owned by the online job search company Monster Worldwide, Inc.

FinAid! The SmartStudent Guide to Financial Aid— *www.finaid.org*

Another offering by Monster Worldwide, Inc., the site includes some valuable calculators for college costs, loan payments, and savings as well as information on various sources of financial aid including federal programs, military aid, and private grants.

Mapping Your Future—*www.mapping-your-future.org*

A portal to information about planning a career, selecting a school, and paying for higher education. The best parts of Mapping Your Future are the extensive links to specialized Web sites.

Scholarship Resource Network Express—*www.srnexpress.com*

Another commercially supported database of scholarships and student loan forgiveness programs.

Scholarships.com—*www.scholarships.com*

A Web-based search for college scholarships based on a student's personal profile.

StudentLoan.com—*www.studentloan.com*

Citibank's Web site for college loans. Even if you're not a Citibank client you'll find some valuable background about how to plan for college and how to apply, manage, and repay a student loan.

Upromise—*www.upromise.com*

A program that rewards users of particular credit cards and purchasers of certain products with rebates to a college education fund.

GLOSSARY

Financial Aid and Tax Terminology

Academic year

A one-year period that represents the beginning and end of a full cycle of classes; at most institutions the academic year runs from July 1 of one year through June 30 of the next.

Annual percentage rate (APR)

The cost of credit calculated on a yearly basis and expressed as a percentage. Not all types of loans use the same formula to compute APR.

Appeal

A formal request to a college's financial aid office for a review of a student's award letter. The applicant may be asking for consideration of changed circumstances or may be seeking to explain unusual elements of the family's finances. The review may be conducted on the basis of an exchange of letters with supporting documents, a telephone conference, or (least commonly) a person-to-person formal meeting.

Application fee

A charge levied by a lending institution, an agency, or a college to accept a submitted form for a loan or entrance.

Award letter

Formal notification from a college's financial aid office of the type of aid that will be made available to an incoming or returning student (including scholarships, grants, loans, and work-study) and a dollar amount for each.

Balloon payment

A lump-sum payment that may come due at the end of a loan.

Cancellation

The discharge or forgiveness of a loan by a government agency (or in some instances by a private lender) due to circumstances such as the borrower's death or disability.

Cap

A limit or ceiling on how high a variable interest rate can rise during the period of a loan agreement.

Capitalized interest

Under some loan programs, interest is not due when accrued but is instead added to the outstanding principal of the loan. Repayment of principal and interest in this sort of loan begins soon after a student graduates or withdraws from college.

Closing costs

Fees that may be assessed at a closing on an equity loan, including attorney's fees, title search, title insurance, and mortgage taxes.

Co-maker

A family member or other person who is a joint borrower on a loan and is equally liable for its repayment.

Consolidation

Combination of two or more outstanding debts into a new loan, usually at a lower rate of interest for the larger total.

Cost of attendance

(*see* Estimated cost of attendance)

Credit limit

The maximum amount, or maximum percentage of available equity, that is available to be borrowed under an equity loan.

Custodial parent

In analyzing financial information for a student whose parents are divorced or separated, colleges put the most weight on the information provided by the parent with whom the student lived the most during the preceding twelve months.

Debt-to-income ratio

A key indicator used by some lenders to determine a borrower's ability to repay a loan. It is calculated by comparing a would-be borrower's monthly net income to the total amount of all outstanding debts.

Default

Failure to meet any significant element of the terms of agreement of a promissory note, including late or missing payments. Under most federal loan programs, a borrower is in default when payments are 270 days or more delinquent.

Deferment

A period during which a borrower is not required to make payments. For example, borrowers in a Subsidized Stafford Loan or a Perkins Loan are generally not asked to make payments on the interest or principal of a loan while the student is still in school. In an unsubsidized loan, payments of the outstanding principal may be deferred but the borrower must keep current on the accrued interest.

Delinquency

Falling behind a due date for loan payment.

Dependency status

A student is considered dependent upon a parent or guardian for financial aid purposes unless he or she is an orphan or ward of the court, is at least twenty-four years of age, is married, in graduate or professional school, has a dependent child, or is a veteran of the U.S. Armed Forces. As a dependent, the student's financial aid award is based primarily on the parent's financial status.

Dependent

A student can claim to have a dependent if a child or other person lives with them and the students provides more than half of that person's support. In calculating financial aid, a spouse is not a dependent. And only one or the other spouse can claim the same child as a dependent.

Direct costs

College expenses billed directly to the student, such as tuition, room and board, and fees. An indirect cost would include personal expenses, supplies, and travel.

EFT (Electronic Funds Transfer)

Paperless transfer of funds from an individual's savings or checking account to a college or lender, or from a lender or agency to a college.

EIN (Employer Identification Number)

The federal tax ID assigned to employers, used in tracking exchanges of money.

Endorser

A person who signs (or cosigns) a promissory note along with the primary borrower, agreeing to repay the outstanding balance if the borrower defaults.

Entrance counseling, exit counseling

First-time Stafford Loan borrowers must graduate from a mini-college intended to assure that they fully understand the terms and conditions of the loan; most borrowers can go through the process online, although printed explanations are also offered. Close to the date of graduation or withdrawal from college, a second session, called exit counseling, is conducted. This session emphasizes both the standard repayment schedule and some alternative programs for satisfying the loan.

Equity

The portion of the value of your home that is above the amount that is mortgaged or otherwise owned by others or owed to others.

Estimated cost of attendance

The college's calculation of the total cost for a full year's tuition, fees, housing, meals, books, supplies, personal expenses, and travel to and from school. The only hard number in the estimate is tuition; most schools offer a range of plans for housing and meals, and the cost of books, supplies, and travel can vary.

Expected Family Contribution (EFC)

The EFC is the bottom-line result of the federal methodology for financial aid, and is based on the information provided in the FAFSA. The EFC is the amount of money the family is expected to contribute to the next year's cost of attendance. The EFC is intended to come from both the parents' and the child's income and resources.

When a college issues its award letter, it subtracts the EFC from the estimated cost of attendance; the result is the student's financial need. It is that gap that the financial aid office uses in determining need-based financial aid. Based on its available funds and its own calculations, a school may choose to meet the full financial need or just a portion of it. See also Institutional Methodology Expected Family Contribution.

Extended repayment

An option offered under some federal loan programs that permits borrowers with high balances to extend the repayment term from the standard of ten years to as much as twenty-five or thirty years. This reduces the monthly payment considerably but adds to the total amount of interest collected on the loan over time.

FAFSA

The Free Application for Federal Student Aid is the official application form, put forth by the U.S. Department of Education, for all federal financial aid programs; it is also used by many state programs and college grant committees as a base line to determine financial aid. Information about the form and an online filing system are offered at www.fafsa.ed.gov.

Federal methodology

The official calculation of the Expected Family Contribution as determined by the U.S. Department of Education; the methodology includes the number of family members in college, taxable and nontaxable income, and assets of the parents and the student. The federal calculation does not include the net value of the family's primary home; colleges can adjust the number based on their own formula, and they often do include the value of the home.

The federal methodology is usually adjusted each year to take into account the national economy, college costs, and available federal funds as set by Congress.

FFY

Federal Fiscal Year, which runs from October 1 through September 30 of the following calendar year. States often have fiscal years that cover a different span of months.

Financial need

The difference between the estimated cost of attendance at a college and the federally computed Expected Family Contribution. If a college were to meet the full needs of a student and family, this would be equal to the financial aid offer.

First-time student

An incoming student who has not previously attended any institution of higher education.

Fixed rate

An interest rate that is set at the time of the closing of a loan and does not vary during the term of the agreement.

Forbearance

Postponement of loan payments or reduction of the amount due (called rescheduling) granted by the lender because of extenuating circumstances, including some specified by federal regulations.

Free Application for Federal Student Aid

(*see* FAFSA)

Grace period

Under a federal Stafford Loan, a six-month period of time after a borrower graduates or leaves school, during which the borrower does not have to make principal payments.

Graduated repayment

A plan offered under some federal loan programs and by other agencies that adjusts the repayment schedule for education loans so that payments are lowest when the student first leaves school and rise over the term of the loan. The theory is to match the monthly payment to rising income over time. Another version of this is called income sensitive repayment, which adjusts monthly payments based on the borrower's current income.

Grant

Financial aid that does not have to be repaid, usually based on need.

Guarantee fee

A fee paid by the borrower (or deducted from the proceeds of the loan before it is received by the college) to a lender or guarantee agency. These funds are intended to insulate the lender or agency against default. The maximum guarantee fee under federal Stafford, PLUS, and Direct Student Loans is 1 percent; some state and private programs waive payment of the fee as a benefit to borrowers or as an incentive to gain loan customers. The guarantee fee is sometimes referred to as an insurance premium.

Guarantor

Also called guaranty agency. An agency or company that administers Federal Family Education Loans (FFEL) on behalf of the U.S. Department of Education and takes over collection of defaulted loans from the original issuer.

Index

The published rate used to calculate a variable interest rate for a loan. Examples of indexes include the prime rate (the rate banks charge their best customers), the federal funds rate (the rate banks charge each other for funds), and LIBOR (London InterBank Offered Rate, an overseas equivalent to the federal funds rate).

Indirect costs

Expenses related to college but not billed by the school. These include travel, personal expenses, and, for most attendees, books and supplies.

In-school status

The period during which a student receiving a federally guaranteed loan is enrolled at least half-time and is in good standing, and therefore eligible to borrow or defer payments of interest or interest and principal.

In-state student

A student who is enrolled in a college in the state where he or she has established residency. The various states have differing definitions and time periods required for residency purposes.

Individual Taxpayer Identification Number (ITIN)

An identification number, issued by the IRS, to track financial transactions with students who are not U.S. citizens or permanent residents.

Institutional Methodology Expected Family Contribution

A college or university's formula for computing the Expected Family Contribution for financial aid programs it administers. It may rework the information on the FAFSA using a different formula, or it may add in or subtract certain items based on additional information requested from the student and family.

IRA (Individual Retirement Account)

A personal savings account for retirement. Funds invested there are generally not included in calculating available assets for financial aid purposes.

Leave of absence

A student can request from the college a temporary withdrawal from enrollment; if the reason for the leave meets federal guidelines, the student will generally be able to avoid triggering the start of the repayment period for principal and interest.

Legal residence

A student's official state of residence as determined by state regulations and sometimes as also considered by college rules. Many state colleges have different tuition rates for residents and out-of-state students. In certain circumstances, the student's local address may also affect eligibility for certain types of state or regional aid.

Lender Identification Number (LID)

The Lender Identification Number is assigned by the federal government to institutions making loans under federal programs; it is usually preprinted on forms or prominently listed on application information. If you need to add this information to a form, call the lender or the college's financial aid office and request assistance.

Loan forgiveness

Cancellation of student loan debt for reasons including national service or filling an underserved job, including those in the teaching and medical professions.

Loan period

The span of academic years plus repayment time that is part of the promissory note.

Loan servicer

Once a loan has been made, most lenders or guarantee agencies transfer the management of the repayment (or the entire debt) to a servicing company. Borrowers make payments to that company.

Margin

An adjustment up (and sometimes down) from the index used by lenders in determining a variable interest rate.

Merit-based

Financial aid that is based on academic, artistic, athletic, or other skills and criteria.

Minimum payment

On a loan, the minimum amount that must be paid in each billing period (usually a month). Depending on the terms, the minimum payment may cover accrued interest only or a portion of the principal plus accrued interest.

Need-aware admissions

A policy by the admissions office of a college to take into account the financial needs of students as part of the review of applications. Compare to need-blind admissions.

Need-based

Financial aid that is based on the financial resources of the student and family.

Need-blind admissions

A policy by the admissions office of a college to admit students solely on the basis of their ability to do the work at the school without consideration of whether that student will require financial aid to afford to attend. Compare to need-aware admissions.

Origination fee

A fee paid by the borrower to the lender to open a loan account. The maximum origination fee for federal Stafford, PLUS, and Direct Student loans is 3 percent of the principal; some agencies and lenders reduce the fee as a benefit or incentive.

Payment plan

Some colleges and universities allow payment of each year's bill spread over a ten- or twelve-month period. There may be a fee imposed. At some schools, bills can be paid using a credit card; a service charge is added.

PIN (Personal Identification Number)

Used as an identifier or password for various programs including FAFSA filings and for online management of loans.

Points

Prepaid interest usually charged in addition to monthly interest; usually must be paid at closing. One point is equal to 1 percent of the credit line, or 1 percent of the amount borrowed in a loan.

Principal

The amount borrowed. In some plans, fees and insurance may be included in the principal (capitalized) but are subtracted from the amount disbursed to the college or university.

Professional judgment

College financial aid offices are allowed to make certain adjustments to the Expected Family Contribution or other elements of the financial aid methodology based on unusual circumstances including loss of employment, illness or death of a parent, or changes in dependency status. These adjustments are considered professional judgment.

Profile

The CSS/Profile is an additional disclosure form for financial aid required by many private colleges and universities; beyond the data collected for the FAFSA, the Profile also asks for information about the net value of the principal family residence and other investments and holdings. The Profile is administered by the College Board; there is a fee for filing the form and additional charges for each school to which data is sent. You can learn about the Profile and fill out the form online at the official Web site, www.collegeboard.com/profile/.

Promissory note

The legal document that spells out the terms and conditions of a loan, including the schedule for its repayment. A master promissory note can be used to cover multiple loans for the same student or the same dependent.

Scholarship

A financial aid award that does not have to be repaid. Scholarships are usually based on specific criteria such as academic performance, good citizenship, and special talents including artistic or sports abilities.

Separation date

The date a borrower graduates or withdraws from at least half-time attendance at a qualified institution; this marks the start of the grace period, which leads up to the beginning of repayment of the loan.

SSN (Social Security number)

Many federal programs use the SSN as an identifier for loans; most colleges have moved away from using the SSN for student IDs, instead generating their own number.

Standard repayment

A loan scheduled for monthly repayment at a level, unchanging amount over the agreed-upon term.

Student Aid Report (SAR)

This is the summary of the information contained on the FAFSA that is electronically transmitted to colleges for their use in calculating financial aid. If you fill out the FAFSA online, you will receive a SAR soon after completion and verification of the form; if you mail in a FAFSA form, you will receive a copy of the SAR by return mail after a delay of several weeks.

T-Bill (Treasury Bill)

A bond issued by the U.S. Treasury; it is one of several indexes used to set interest rates on student loans.

Title IV School Code

Every eligible college and university is assigned a Federal School Code; you must use this code in filling out the FAFSA and CSS/Profile to indicate where the information is to be sent. Codes are either six numbers beginning with a zero, or are five numbers preceded by a G, B, or E character. The codes that begin with characters indicate a professional or graduate school.

Variable rate

An interest rate that is adjusted up or down based on the performance of an index; the loan agreement specifies how often the rate can be adjusted and how sharply it can rise at any one time.

Verification

Financial aid offices may ask for verification of some or all of the information submitted on applications for financial aid. This may include copies of current state and federal tax forms, W2 and 1099 tax forms, and in some cases proof of citizenship and proof of registration with Selective Service for male applicants. In addition, the U.S. Department of Education randomly selects some applications for detailed verification.

If you see an asterisk next to the EFC (Expected Family Contribution) figure on the Student Aid Report, the information on the FAFSA has been selected for verification. Some schools automatically request documentation of certain elements of the FAFSA or CSS/Profile.

If errors or inconsistencies are found and cannot be cleared up, the federal government may change the expected family contribution, or the college may change its financial aid offer. Refusal to submit requested verification may result in the cancellation of financial aid offers.

Loan and Grant Programs

Basic Educational Opportunity Grant (BEOG)

Now the Federal Pell Grant Program— *www.ed.gov/programs/fpg.*

Federal Direct Student Loan Program (FDSLP)

If a college offers direct lending, a student can apply for a Stafford Loan with the financial aid office, and funds are paid to the school without the involvement of banks or other agencies.

Federal Family Education Loan Program (FFEL)

The federal education loan program operated by banks and other private lenders. Programs included under this umbrella include some subsidized and unsubsidized Stafford, PLUS loans, and consolidation loans.

Federal Pell Grant

A need-based financial aid program that in 2005 provided as much as $4,050 per year. The amount of aid is adjusted based on the family's FAFSA information as well as the cost of attendance.

Federal PLUS Loan

A federally guaranteed loan program administered by banks and other lending agencies. Loans are charged a variable interest rate.

Federal Stafford Loan

A federal plan that guarantees loans made by colleges, banks, and other agencies. Repayment of the principal can be deferred until after graduation. Need-based financial aid may include a subsidized Stafford loan; the federal government pays the interest during the time the student is in school. An unsubsidized Stafford loan, available without regard to financial need, allows deferral of payment of accrued interest, although that cost is capitalized, meaning it is added to the outstanding balance—*www.salliemae. com/apply/borrowing/stafford.html.*

Federal Supplemental Educational Opportunity Grant (FSEOG) Program

A federally funded grant program; colleges and universities must contribute 25 percent of the funding—*www.ed.gov/ programs/fseog.*

Federal Work-Study

A program that gives colleges money to be used to provide campus-based employment for financial aid recipients. Participants receive a paycheck from the college or university; funds are not deducted from tuition, room and board, and other billable expenses.

HPSL Program

Health Professions Student Loan Program—*www.bhpr.hrsa.gov/dsa/hpsl.htm.*

Leveraging Educational Assistance Partnership (LEAP)

A federal program that gives matching funds to states for the creation of need-based grants—*www.ed.gov/programs/leap/index.html.*

National Direct Student Loan Program (NDSL)

Now known as the Perkins Loan Program.

NSL

Federal Nursing Student Loan.

Parent Loans for Undergraduate Students (PLUS)

A guaranteed loan program available to parents through colleges or private lenders; it is not need-based.

Robert C. Byrd Honors Scholarship Program

A federal financial assistance program disbursed by states to students with outstanding academic achievement—*www. ed.gov/programs/iduesbyrd.*

Academic Terminology

A.A.

Associate of Arts degree.

A.A.S.

Associate of Applied Science degree.

Adjunct faculty

A faculty position for an instructor or professor with an occasional or temporary affiliation.

AP (Advanced Placement)

High school courses that, upon satisfactory completion and testing, can be used as college-level credits.

A.S.

Associate of Science degree.

Associate's degree

A degree granted upon completion of an educational program of less than baccalaureate level, generally requiring at least two but less than four academic years.

B.A.

Bachelor of Arts degree.

Bachelor's degree

Any earned academic degree at the bachelor's level generally representing satisfactory completion of the equivalent of four years of college work.

B.S.

Bachelor of Science degree.

Census date

The date in an academic term, after the deadline for adding or dropping a course, when a college or university makes an official count of enrolled students.

Ed.D.

Doctor of Education degree.

ESL

English as a Second Language; see TOEFL.

GED (General Equivalency Diploma; General Educational Development Certificate)

Official recognition of completion of a test that indicates completion of a high school equivalency exam.

GMAT

Graduate Management Admission Test. An assessment examination used by some colleges as part of the admission process for graduate management schools.

GPA

Grade point average. The scholastic record in high school or college, calculated on a scale on which an A is equal to four points and a D one point.

GRE

Graduate Record Examination. An assessment of college skills and knowledge for applicants to graduate school.

J.D.

Juris Doctorate degree from a law school.

287

Joint program enrollment

Students enrolled in a program that offers a single degree offered jointly by more than one institution.

Master's degree

A graduate degree that represents successful completion of at least one but not more than two years of academic work beyond the bachelor's degree level.

Open admission (also known as open enrollment)

A policy that declares that any student who meets specified minimum criteria will be accepted for enrollment.

Ph.D.

Doctor of Philosophy degree.

ROTC

Reserve Officers' Training Corps—*www. goarmy.com/rotc.*

SAT

Scholastic Aptitude Test. A commonly used assessment test given to high school juniors or seniors and used by admissions offices in making acceptance decisions—*www.collegeboard.com/.*

Student load

The number of programs and credits a student is enrolled in.

Student status

Eligibility of a student for a degree or certificate in a particular program.

TOEFL (Test of English as a Foreign Language)

A examination or certification of proficiency in the use of English for those who do not use English as their primary language.

Associations, Government Agencies, Programs, and Regulations

AACC

American Association of Community Colleges—*www.aacc.nche.edu.*

AASCU

American Association of State Colleges and Universities—*www.aascu.org.*

ACCSCT

Accrediting Commission of Career Schools and Colleges of Technology—*www.accsct.org.*

ACE

American Council on Education—*www. acenet.edu//AM/Template.cfm?Section=Home.*

ACICS

Accrediting Council for Independent Colleges and Schools—*www.acics.org.*

ACT, Inc.

American College Testing. The sponsors of an assessment test taken by some high school juniors and seniors and used by college admission offices as part of their decision-making process—*www.act.org.*

ADA

Americans with Disabilities Act—*www. usdoj.gov/crt/ada/adahom1.htm.*

AFDC

Aid to Families with Dependent Children—*www.acf.dhhs.gov/programs/afdc/afdc.txt.*

American College Testing *see* ACT

BIA

U.S. Bureau of Indian Affairs—*www.doi. gov/bureau-indian-affairs.*

CAA/CAP

Community Action Agency Program.

CSS

College Scholarship Service—
www.collegeboard.com.

**Department of Veterans Affairs
(DVA)**

Formerly the Veterans Administration—
www.va.gov.

DVA

Department of Veterans Affairs.

ETS

Educational Testing Service.

FDIC

Federal Deposit Insurance Company—
www.fdic.gov.

FRB

Federal Reserve Board—*www.federalreserve.gov.*

FSA

Federal Student Aid.

INS

U.S. Immigration and Naturalization
Service. Now the U.S. Citizenship and
Immigration Services—*www.uscis.gov.*

IRS

Internal Revenue Service—*www.irs.gov.*

NACCAS

National Accrediting Commission of
Cosmetology Arts & Sciences—*www.
naccas.org.*

NAICU

National Association of Independent
Colleges and Universities—*www.naicu.edu.*

NASSGAP

National Association of State Student
Grant and Aid Programs—*www.nassgap.org.*

NASULGC

National Association of State Universities
and Land Grant Colleges—*www.nasulgc.org.*

National Student Clearinghouse

Formerly the National Student Loan
Clearinghouse—*www.studentclearinghouse.org.*

**National Student Loan Data
System (NSLDS)**

A database of information from lenders,
schools, agencies, and the U.S. Department
of Education about Title IV student
financial assistance—*www.nslds.ed.gov.*

NCAA

National Collegiate Athletic
Association—*www2.ncaa.org.*

NCHELP

National Council of Higher Education
Loan Programs—*www.nchelp.org.*

NDSL

National Direct Student Loan Program.

NSLDS

National Student Loan Data System—
www.nslds.ed.gov.

Sallie Mae

See Student Loan Marketing Association.

SSA

Social Security Administration—*www.ssa.
gov.*

SSI

Supplemental Security Income.

**Student Loan Marketing
Association (SLMA)**

An organization that resells student loans
in the secondary market; it is commonly
referred to as Sallie Mae—*www.salliemae.com.*

USSA

United States Student Association—*www.
usstudents.org.*

Veterans Administration (VA)

Renamed the Department of Veterans
Affairs—*www.va.gov.*

INDEX

ABOUT THE AUTHOR

Corey Sandler has written more than 150 books on business, personal finance, travel, and sports topics. A former newsman for Gannett Newspapers and a correspondent for the Associated Press, he served as editor of two national business-oriented magazines before becoming a full-time author of books.

He has an undergraduate degree from Syracuse University and also attended graduate school there. He and his wife, Janice Keefe, also an author, have put two children through private colleges . . . and lived to tell the tale.

You can write to the author by e-mail at *csandler@econoguide.com* and visit his Web site at *www.econoguide.com*.